Mance

Alan Parkinson

the Institute
of Management

F O U N D A T I O N

BUTTERWORTH
HEINEMANN

To the Crowley extended family, here and now, past and future.

Butterworth-Heinemann
Linacre House, Jordan Hill, Oxford OX2 8DP
A division of Reed Educational and Professional Publishing Ltd

℞ A member of the Reed Elsevier plc group

OXFORD BOSTON JOHANNESBURG
MELBOURNE NEW DELHI SINGAPORE

First published 1997

British Library Cataloguing in Publication Data
A catalogue record for this book is available from the British Library

ISBN 0 7506 1826 4

Typeset by Avocet Typeset, Brill, Aylesbury, Bucks
Printed and bound in Great Britain by Biddles Ltd,
Guildford and Kings Lynn

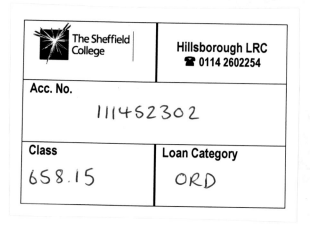

Contents

Series adviser's preface

This book is one of a series designed for people wanting to develop their capabilities as managers. You might think that there isn't anything very new in that. In one way you would be right. The fact that very many people want to learn to become better managers is not new, and for many years a wide range of approaches to such learning and development has been available. These have included courses leading to formal qualifications, organizationally based management development programmes and a whole variety of self-study materials. A copious literature, extending from academic textbooks to sometimes idiosyncratic prescriptions from successful managers and consultants, has existed to aid – or perhaps confuse – the potential seeker after managerial truth and enlightenment.

So what is new about this series? In fact, a great deal – marking in some ways a revolution in our thinking both about the art of managing and also the process of developing managers.

Where did it all begin? Like most revolutions, although there may be a single, identifiable act that precipitated the uprising, the roots of discontent are many and long established. The debate about the performance of British managers, the way managers are educated and trained, and the extent to which shortcomings in both these areas have contributed to our economic decline, has been running for several decades.

Until recently, this debate had been marked by periods of frenetic activity–stimulated by some report or enquiry and perhaps ending in some new initiatives or policy changes – followed by relatively long periods of comparative calm. But the underlying causes for concern persisted. Basically, the majority of managers in the UK appeared to have little or no training for their role, certainly far less than their counterparts in our major competitor nations. And there was concern about the nature, style and appropriateness of the management education and training that were available.

The catalyst for this latest revolution came in late 1986 and early 1987, when three major reports reopened the whole issue. The 1987 reports were *The Making of British Managers* by John Constable and Roger McCormick, carried out for the British Institute of Management and the CBI, and *The Making of Managers* by Charles Handy, carried out for the (then) Manpower Services Commission, National Economic Development Office and British Institute of Management. The 1986 report, which often receives less recognition than it deserves as a key contribution to the recent changes, was *Management Training: context and process* by Iain Mangham and Mick Silver, carried out for the Economic and Social Research Council and the Department of Trade and Industry.

It is not the place to review in detail what the reports said. Indeed, they and their consequences are discussed in several places in this series of books. But essentially they confirmed that:

- British managers were undertrained by comparison with their counterparts internationally.
- The majority of employers invested far too little in training and developing their managers.
- Many employers found it difficult to specify with any degree of detail just what it was that they required successful managers to be able to do.

The Constable/McCormick and Handy reports advanced various recommendations for addressing these problems, involving an expansion of management education and development, a reformed structure of qualifications and a commitment from employers to a code of practice for management development. While this analysis was not new, and had echoes of much that had been said in earlier debates, this time a few leading individuals determined that the response should be both radical and permanent. The response was coordinated by the newly established Council for Management Education and Development (now the National Forum for Management Education and Development (NFMED)) under the energetic and visionary leadership of Bob (now Sir Bob) Reid, then of Shell UK and subsequently chairman of the British Railways Board.

Under the umbrella of NFMED a series of employer-led working parties tackled the problem of defining what it was that managers should be able to do, and how this differed for people at different levels in their organizations; how this satisfactory ability to perform might be verified; and how an appropriate structure of management qualifications could be put in place. This work drew upon the methods used to specify vocational standards in industry and commerce, and led to the development and introduction of competence-based management standards and qualifications. In this context, competence is defined as the ability to perform the activities within an occupation or function to the standards expected in employment.

It is this competence-based approach that is new in our thinking about the manager's capabilities. It is also what is new about this series of books, in that they are designed to support both this new structure of management standards, and of development activities based on it. The series was originally commissioned to support the Institute of Management's Certificate and Diploma qualifications, which were one of the first to be based on the new standards.

However, these books are equally appropriate to any university, college or indeed company course leading to a certificate in management or diploma in management studies.

The standards were specified through an extensive process of consultation with a large number of managers in organizations of many different types and sizes. They are therefore employment based and employer supported. And they fill the gap that Mangham and Silver identified – now we do have a language to describe what it is employers want their managers to be able to do – at least in part.

If you are engaged in any form of management development leading to a certificate or diploma qualification conforming to the national management standards, then you are probably already familiar with most of the key ideas on which the standards are based. To achieve their key purpose, which is defined as achieving the organization's objectives and continuously improving its performance, managers need to perform four key roles: managing operations, managing finance, managing people and managing information. Each of these key roles has a sub-structure of units and elements, each with associated performance and assessment criteria.

The reason for the qualification 'in part' is that organizations are different, and jobs within them are different. Thus the generic management standards probably do not cover all the management competences that you may need to possess in your job. There are almost certainly additional things, specific to your own situation in your own organization, that you need to be able to do. The standards are necessary, but almost certainly not sufficient. Only you, in discussion with your boss, will be able to decide what other capabilities you need to possess. But the standards are a place to start, a basis on which to build. Once you have demonstrated your proficiency against the standards, it will stand you in good stead as you progress through your organization, or change jobs.

So how do the new standards change the process by which you develop yourself as a manager? They change the process of development, or of gaining a management qualification, quite a lot. It is no longer a question of acquiring information and facts, perhaps by being 'taught' in some classroom environment, and then being tested to see what you can recall. It involves demonstrating, in a quite specific way, that you can do certain things to a particular standard of performance. And because of this, it puts a much greater onus on you to manage your own development, to decide how you can demonstrate any particular competence, what evidence you need to present, and how you can collect it. Of course, there will always be people to advise and guide you in this, if you need help.

But there is another dimension, and it is to this that this series of books is addressed. While the standards stress ability to perform, they do not ignore the traditional knowledge base that has been associated with 'management studies'. Rather, they set this in a different context.

The standards are supported by 'underpinning knowledge and understanding' which has three components:

- Purpose and context, which is knowledge and understanding of the manager's objectives, and of the relevant organizational and environmental influences, opportunities and values.
- Principles and methods, which is knowledge and understanding of the theories, models, principles, methods and techniques that provide the basis of competent managerial performance.
- Data, which is knowledge and understanding of specific facts likely to be important to meeting the standards.

Possession of the relevant knowledge and understanding underpinning the standards is needed to support competent managerial performance as specified in the standards. It also has an important role in supporting the transferability of management capabilities. It helps to ensure that you have done more than learned 'the way we do things around here' in your own organization. It indicates a recognition of the wider things which underpin competence, and that you will be able to change jobs or organizations and still be able to perform effectively.

These books cover the knowledge and understanding underpinning the management standards, most specifically in the category of principles and methods. But their coverage is not limited to the minimum required by the standards, and extends in both depth and breadth in many areas. The authors have tried to approach these underlying principles and methods in a practical way. They use many short cases and examples which we hope will demonstrate how, in practice, the principles and methods, and knowledge of purpose and context plus data, support the ability to perform as required by the management standards. In particular we hope that this type of presentation will enable you to identify and learn from similar examples in your own managerial work.

You will already have noticed that one consequence of this new focus on the standards is that the traditional 'functional' packages of knowledge and theory do not appear. The standard textbook titles such as 'quantitative methods', 'production management', 'organizational behaviour', etc. disappear. Instead, principles and methods have been collected together in clusters that more closely match the key roles within the standards. You will also find a small degree of overlap in some of the volumes, because some principles and methods support several of the individual units within the standards. We hope you will find this useful reinforcement.

Having described the positive aspects of standards-based management development, it would be wrong to finish without a few cautionary remarks. The developments described above may seem simple, logical and uncontroversial. It did not always seem that way in the years of work which led up to the introduction of the standards. To revert to the revolution analogy, the process has been marked by ideological conflict and battles over sovereignty and territory. It has sometimes been unclear which side various parties are on – and indeed how many sides there are! The revolution, if well advanced, is not at an end. Guerrilla warfare continues in parts of the territory.

Perhaps the best way of describing this is to say that, while competence-based standards are widely recognized as at least a major part of the answer to improving managerial performance, they are not the whole answer. There is still some debate about the way competences are defined, and whether those in the standards are the most appropriate on which to base assessment of managerial performance. There are other models of management competences than those in the standards.

There is also a danger in separating management performance into a set of discrete components. The whole is, and needs to be, more than the sum of the parts. Just like bowling an off-break in cricket, practising a golf swing or forehand drive in tennis, you have to combine all the separate movements into a smooth, flowing action. How you combine the competences, and build on them, will mark your own individual style as a manager.

We should also be careful not to see the standards as set in stone. They determine what today's managers need to be able to do. As the arena in which managers operate changes, then so will the standards. The lesson for all of us as managers is that we need to go on learning and developing, acquiring new skills or refining existing ones. Obtaining your certificate or diploma is like passing a mile post, not crossing the finishing line.

All the changes and developments of recent years have brought management qualifications, and the processes by which they are gained, much closer to your job as a manager. We hope these books support this process by providing bridges between your own experience and the underlying principles and methods which will help you to demonstrate your competence. Already, there is a lot of evidence that managers enjoy the challenge of demonstrating competence, and find immediate benefits in their jobs from the programmes based on these new-style qualifications. We hope you do too. Good luck in your career development.

Paul Jervis

Introduction

The pressures on managers in organizations of all types, shapes and sizes appear to be increasing continuously. As a consequence, the concept of the specialist or functionalist manager is disappearing, with managers being expected to acquire and use additional knowledge and competences. This most certainly applies to financial matters, with expectations that individuals and groups of managers are able not only to manage routine budgetary information, but also to manage financial information in a wider sense. This necessarily involves understanding the world of the financial community, its customs and practices, and, not least, its jargon. Not surprisingly, for many managers this presents challenges. And faced with such challenges, managers can feel at best concerned and at worst isolated and threatened.

This book is designed to help you, as an existing or prospective manager, to respond to the challenges faced. It does so by imparting the knowledge and understanding you need to be able to live in an increasingly financially oriented management world. You are provided with insights into the financial decision making frameworks commonly used in organizations. Much of this is concerned with the management of what can be termed the flow of finance. This flow reflects the financing and investment decisions common to all organizations, and the ongoing day-to-day decisions necessary to ensure that the flow of finance, being dynamic, is continuously managed appropriately.

You discover what is meant by financing and investment decisions, look at generic frameworks for associated decisions, and explore in depth the applications of financial frameworks to assist in both long- and short-term decision-making. In so doing you encounter the ideas of external financial statements such as balance sheets and profit and cash flow statements, capital structures and their gearing, cost structures, capital investment appraisal methods, ad hoc decision-making, working capital management, business valuation, budgetary control and financial performance measurement.

You may have a fear that this book sets out to teach you to become an accountant, accompanied by all that such might entail. Be reassured, however. This book intends, rather, to equip you with the knowledge and skills to work with and through financial advisers, allowing them to undertake the complex calculations required but with you in a position to understand the rationale of advice given and the consequences of implementing such a decision. A bonus is that the content of this book aligns with the NVQ or SQV Diploma in

Management and should thus help not only in practical management terms but in study for qualifications too.

As a footnote, you should be aware of the Butterworth-Heinemann text *Managing Financial Resources* which covers the NVQ or SQV Certificate in Management. While this book stands alone in its own right, it builds upon the foundations set at Certificate level.

Acknowledgements

- Thank you Pam Cook for fast fingers and a bright brain.

- Thank you Malcom Bingham, Chris Dickin and Bob Ryan for the lessons from P781.

- Thanks to the Butterworth-Heinemann staff for forbearance and professionalism

Part I The Flow of Finance

1 Understanding and managing the flow of finance

Introduction

In this chapter you will meet the idea of the *flow of finance* within organizations, its significance and the challenges faced by management teams in managing it. You will discover the reality of the organizational *pyramid of purpose,* and its reflection of the need for it be accompanied by managerial decisions relating to *financing* and *investment* matters. You will consider some of the reasons why organizations exist and the influence, particularly in commercial concerns, of their specified objectives. As you work through the chapter you will draw analogies with your own personal life. This will help you in getting a grip on the nature of the flow and the complexities of managing it.

By the end of this chapter you will:

- understand the nature and significance of the pyramid of purpose
- understand the nature and significance of the flow of finance
- have gained insights into the complexities of managing the flow of finance
- have recognized the relevance of the flow of finance for later and further considerations within this book.

What organizations do

All organizations, large or small, private or public or voluntary sector, have a commonality in that they all are faced with finding finance and deciding how best to spend it, in light of their objectives. It may be that an organization's management team (comprising one person or many) wishes to maximize the wealth of the owners, or provide value for money services to the community, or help the disadvantaged. Whatever, the financial challenges facing management teams require on their part appropriate knowledge, understanding and competences to be able to respond appropriately. Initially, any response necessitates understanding what an organization sets out to do. This is vital as it determines what financing is required and what happens to it when spent.

The pyramid of purpose

All organizations have purposes, reasons for their existence. For many there exists an ultimate vision of what an individual organization might achieve. This vision is then translated into a mission statement which defines in broad terms how the organization sets about achieving its vision and the necessary accompanying values. If the mission statement, and thus the vision, is to become a reality, more measurable and tangible aims need to be identified. Such aims are then translated into very specific objectives, often on an annual basis, which determine the day-to-day targets and required activities of staff at operational as opposed to senior management level.

This is encapsulated within Figure 1.1 and is depicted as a pyramid of purpose. The vision and mission at the top capture why the organization exists and where it is going – the resulting demands can then be translated and passed down from senior management to others to 'do the doing'. The arrow on the right-hand side illustrates the tasks of managers at differing levels and reflects the associated time horizons of their work. Senior managers think and plan for the long term, concerning themselves with strategic matters. Further down the pyramid, more immediate challenges and demands face operational managers, the timescale being much shorter. It is important for all managers, not just accountants, to understand the organization's vision, mission and values. If they do not, they cannot be sure that they are pursuing the right targets and carrying out the right activities.

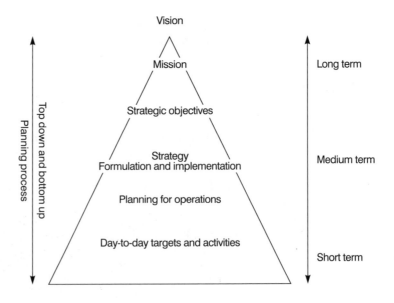

Figure 1.1 The pyramid of purpose

In many organizations the pyramid becomes a reality through the operation of an effective budgetary planning and control system, with an emphasis on resource allocation and periodic feedback. You will concentrate on this in greater detail later in this book. For the present, it is important to focus on resource allocation only, and in broad terms.

The pyramid of purpose and resources

The carrying out of necessary activities to achieve day-to-day targets requires managers to be allocated resources. At the operational level this is effected by the budgetary process referred to above. At the more senior management, and thus more strategic, level broad decisions about where the resources are to be funded from and how the funding is to be divided up are necessary. This involves management teams making what might be termed *financing* and *investment decisions* to enable the pyramid of purpose to become a reality. This is depicted in Figure 1.2, which shows the pyramid of purpose encircled by a stream of finance to fund the resources and activities necessary to carry out what needs to be done.

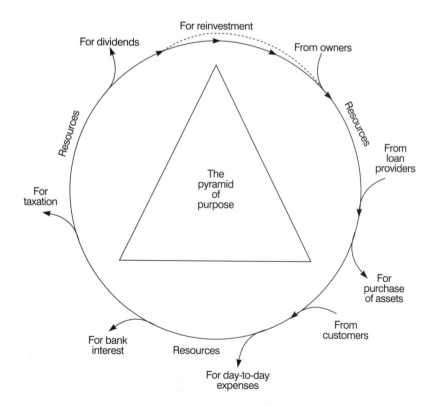

Figure 1.2 The financial dimension of the pyramid

It is this stream of finance surrounding, and thus enabling, the pyramid of purpose which gives rise to the term *flow of finance*, as you see next.

Meeting and analysing the flow of finance

The stream of finance in Figure 1.2 is shown externally, encircling the pyramid of purpose. This is very appropriate, as the financial decisions required to translate the vision of the organization into reality may be viewed as reflecting decisions required to support a circular flow of finance within the pyramid of purpose. This flow is illustrated in Figure 1.3, which shows the flow associated with:

Stage 1 – The raising of finance.
Stage 2 – The investment of finance in operating assets (i.e. assets to be used).
Stage 3 – The use of operating assets to produce or provide goods or services for sale to customers or to other clients.
Stage 4 – The control of day-to-day operating costs to ensure an operating profit (sales less day-to-day costs) or, where surpluses are not allowed and deficits must be avoided, break even .
Stage 5 – In commercial concerns, the distribution of the operating profit to:
    (a) reward providers of loan capital financing, such as banks, receiving interest, leaving net profit
    (b) provide for corporation tax due on profit
    (c) reward providers of share capital financing, the owners, through a return of some of the profits owned by them
    (d) refinance the organization through profits retained.

At each stage, managers must be prepared to make appropriate decisions. At Stage 1, the balance between differing types of capital must be assessed, usually referred to as the *gearing* decision. Stage 2 requires a decision which provides for an appropriate balance between *investment in fixed assets* – buildings, equipment, vehicles – and *working capital*. Stage 3 demands decisions on how to market goods and services to clients and to attract sales from customers. At Stage 4, managers will need to ensure that *operating costs* are controlled. This is necessary to provide an *operating profit* at Stage 4 for its subsequent distribution, or in public and voluntary sector concerns, to ensure at least a break-even situation. This operating profit is then used to provide for payment of loan interest, any taxation, dividends to shareholders and the reinvestment of any retained profits.

Of course, there are complexities in managing such a flow. Managers in organizations will need to:

- take account of where to obtain financing, the mix of differing funding sources, and the relative cost of each source
- be prepared to prioritize between differing and competing projects and activities on which financing obtained may be spent
- assess the risk/return profile of projects and activities
- devise systems to account for financing and investment decisions and thus to provide feedback on what has happened.

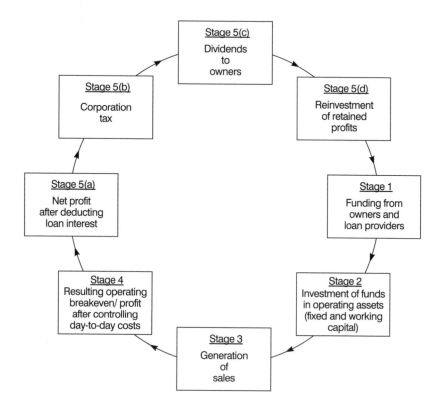

Figure 1.3 The flow of finance

It is such complexities which can present even greater challenges. After all, the financial dimension worries many managers even in uncomplicated situations. Perhaps, like you, they are not all financial specialists. With both the financial dimension and complexities in mind, it is appropriate to demonstrate to you that managing the financing and investment decisional resources within an organization is basically no different to managing finances on a day-to-day basis in your own life.

The flow of finance on a personal level

Here you examine more closely what occurs in day-to-day life in trying to manage personal financial resources – managing the inflows and outflows, the flow of finance. As we all know, we have to balance expenditure against income. Mr Micawber summed it up in Charles Dickens' *David Copperfield* when he said:

Annual income twenty pounds, annual expenditure nineteen nineteen six, result happiness. Annual income twenty pounds, annual expenditure twenty pounds ought and six, result misery.

Financial inflows

Life can be difficult enough even when there is a regular weekly or monthly income. There will usually be all sorts of competing demands for the scarce resource or limited pool of available money:

- buying or renting a house
- maintaining that property
- paying for household bills
- acquiring and running a car
- buying clothes.

The list is endless. This balancing of income against expenditure is really individuals having to manage the personal flow of finance, money in against money out. In principle, this is no different to the balancing process that management teams within organizations have to achieve.

Financial outflows

It may be, of course, that you recognize that your regular income is not enough to pay for all you want. You might decide that you want to go on holiday but do not have enough income to pay. Similarly, another car might be on the agenda, or another house. What can you do? It is likely that you will look at a number of alternatives. These alternatives could include:

- identify how much you can save regularly from your income
- take on another job
- borrow the money from somewhere
- make economies.

There are, of course, others. Indeed, you may choose just one of the foregoing or a combination.

The realities of finding and spending money

Stop for a moment and think about the factors you would consider in arriving at decisions about finding and spending money.

In deciding how to finance your desires you might find that the holiday could be funded out of relatively short-term policies – economies or an overdraft loan. A car or house would probably need a longer term strategy, perhaps a long-term loan of some sort. It is likely that there will be choices of long-term loan sources, each with differing terms, conditions and costs. It may be that your income is such that you have to make choices about which desire takes priority, go for two and forgo one, or indeed, forgo two. In making your decision you would have to rank the alternatives in relation to your perceptions of the return you would gain (in these examples including returns in the form of satisfaction gained) . You would also have to feel sure that the perceived returns outweigh the costs of any loans, and additionally take account of any risks associated with what you do. The process is complex and challenging and is so for managers in organizations for similar reasons.

Factors influencing the flow of finance

Illustrated above is a financial fact of life: everything costs and we (you, me and managers) consequently cannot always have what we want. We need to manage our financial resources, taking account of factors like:

- length of loan
- length of investment
- cost and terms of competing finance sources
- competing investment alternatives
- perceived returns against costs of funding.

An additional factor arises where there are surpluses. Even if money were pumped into a variety of investments, we would need to ensure that we were gaining more than we would get just by leaving it in the bank. It may even be that we still have money left over and would have to worry about looking after our surplus funds. We could thus add to the list of factors:

- the management of surplus funds.

In weighing up the pros and cons we would need relevant information to enable us to make a decision. Post investment we would need to have some form of feedback, either factual or in our minds, about our perceived value for money. We could thus add:

- feedback and information.

The ever increasingly complex scenario is shown in Figure 1.4.

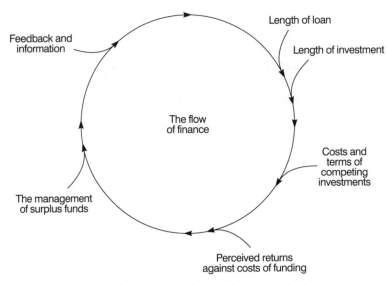

Figure 1.4 The flow of finance and the influencing factors

The interrelationships between the factors

These factors are not just theoretical ones which have been made up. They really do exist and are important practicalities which must be taken account of in the balancing act of managing personal and organizational financial resources. The theoretical aspect is that the factors are as relevant to organizational life as personal life. What faces managers is putting theory into practice. As with most aspects of life, this is easier said than done. In this case it is not sufficient just to recognize that the factors identified will affect the flow of finance – the degree of influence of each factor will vary. There are two reasons for this variation in influence. They are:

- within any one decision, one (or several) factor(s) may be more (or less) important than another or others
- the factors have an inherent relationship with each other and thus influence each other.

Each of these factors will have a variable degree of influence upon a decision. This can cause problems enough in the management of the personal flow of finance, but the complications really start when related to an organizational rather than personal scenario, with all the detail managers must attend to.

The complexity of the flow of finance

There is a great deal of managing to do when faced with the flow of finance depicted earlier in Figure 1.3. In some respects, managers in organizations may be seen as managing a plant for processing money, a plant with a deal of detail to be attended to.

As a plant for processing money, the organization:

- gathers in money from a variety of sources
- translates this money into a package of operating assets (e.g. premises, equipment, vehicles and stocks) bought from suppliers
- uses its assets to produce products and services for sale to customers and to provide services to clients
- the sales made and activities undertaken generate a surplus or break even, if costs are controlled
- the surplus is used to reward the providers of capital, to pay taxes and residually, to refinance the organization itself.

This process for making money requires management teams to do just that – manage – making decisions as appropriate. Thus mapping onto the flow of finance in Figure 1.3 and taking account of the influencing factors in Figure 1.4, decisional challenges to managers arise. These are reflected in Figure 1.5 with an accompanying explanation below.

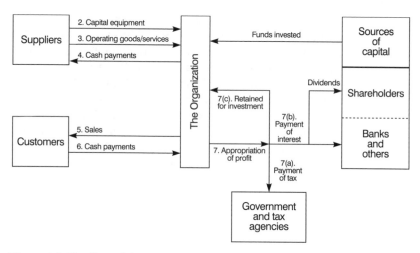

Figure 1.5 The financial context of management decisions

Funds are raised by the organization from a variety of sources: shareholders, banks, reinvested profits. *Ongoing* decisions will have to be made concerning the optimum mixture of finance types; this is the **financing decision.** An appropriate package of capital will be one which has a good degree of *matching* between the type of capital and the use to which it is put. So buildings, for example, may appropriately be financed by long-term loan capital; machinery by medium-term capital, and so on.

All the time, the mixing of capital types must seek to minimize the overall cost of the mixture and minimize the level of **financial risk** inherent in the selected structure. The financing decision is a vital ongoing aspect of financial management, particularly because of its dynamic, changing nature.

Capital equipment is obtained from suppliers. This is a *choosing* situation, requiring careful evaluation. 'Shall we have this machine or that machine?' 'This vehicle or that vehicle?' 'Shall we buy it or lease it?'

Operating goods and services are obtained from suppliers – raw materials, electric power, insurance, etc. Note that, in the context of Figure 1.5, labour could be seen as one of the services 'obtained'. Lines 2 and 3 together represent the firm's **investment decisions.**

Suppliers, who become **creditors** until they are paid, eventually receive cash – part of the funds raised are committed to suppliers in return for capital and operating goods and services.

Within the organization operations produce goods and services which are sold to customers/consumers (line 5) who become **debtors.** At line 6 the debtors settle their debts and cash is received by the organization. Assuming that a surplus or profit has resulted, the organization can make certain appropriations of profit (line 7).

Line 7(a) represents payment of taxation, and line 7(b) covers payment of interest to loan capital providers and payments of dividends to share capital investors. To the extent that the surplus or profit generated is not used to make payments to the various stakeholders mentioned, there will be a surplus which can be retained within the organization (line 7(c)). This represents an **organic** source of finance, in that the residual or undistributed surplus is retained. We sometimes refer to this retaining of surplus as 'ploughing back' profits. Retentions of undistributed profits contribute by far the largest source of finance utilized by limited companies in the UK. This is a *flow* process, with finance coming into the organization and circulating via production and marketing, to reward finance providers and perhaps eventually return to them.

The significance

Getting to grips with the flow of finance is a challenge to accountants and other managers alike. In light of the complexity revealed in Figure 1.5, it is not unreasonable to wonder why organizations bother with the flow of finance and its accompanying demands on managers. The answer lies in a vital influencing factor upon the pyramid of purpose – the objectives of the organization.

The objectives of the organization

Given the significance of the pyramid of purpose, the vision and mission will be all important. It is therefore essential, being at the apex of the pyramid and with all else flowing from it, that the driving force behind the vision and mission is clearly defined. In many public and voluntary sector concerns there is little dispute over the *raison d'être*. With larger commercial concerns the situation can produce tensions, given that such concerns exist in the main to maximize shareholders' wealth.

A sole-trader, utilizing skills and capital in a profit-seeking, free-market economy, would run the business in a way they wanted to. The manner in which capital was raised, was invested and how much of any surplus was drawn out of or left in the business, would be entirely at the owner's discretion. The business would be operated to suit the owner and whatever any associated aspirations and objectives may be.

However, problems arise when the business grows and other people or groups of people have an interest in its activities in addition to the owner. Their motives, their aspirations and attitudes inevitably influence the operation and hence the objectives of the firm.

Benefiting the owners: shareholders' wealth

Theoretically, the overall objective of a commercial business is to benefit its owners – the shareholders. This is particularly so with the larger and publicly quoted limited liability companies. Many studies assert that the dominant objective of the firm is to *maximize the wealth* of its shareholders in the medium/long term, where wealth is expressed in terms of dividend income plus gains in the share price of the business. Where this is a major influence upon managers, theoretically managers should take decisions which overtly may be seen to benefit shareholders. However, it may be that managers have other interests that they may be keen on pursuing .

Managerial objectives

In commercial concerns, shareholders own the business, and in principle they control the composition of the management team. Managers for their part are supposed to operate in the best interests of the shareholders. However, in practice shareholders find it difficult to change managers and managers may prefer to act in their own best interest. There may therefore arise a set of managerial objectives which clash with the shareholders' objective of maximizing wealth. It is sometimes argued that managers do just enough to provide shareholders with a *reasonable* level of return and devote the balance of their efforts to their own interests. The claim is that managers are not particularly *shareholder conscious* in their day-to-day working. Certainly, the temptation for a manager to 'play safe' is understandable. Shareholders are usually well diversified in their investments, whereas the manager's entire future livelihood may well be invested in the firm, the failure of which would be crucial to the manager but less so to the shareholder.

It is interesting to note that managers with reward packages linked to annual performance may be tempted to take decisions which look good now (and thus harvest immediate performance-related rewards) but may over the longer period not be in the best interests of the shareholders.

Social objectives

The 1980s and 1990s have seen parties other than shareholders jockeying for position, particularly with regard to the organization's social responsibility stance (or lack of as the case may be). As a result, conflicts have arisen between a business operating solely in the best interests of its shareholders and its responsibility for employees, customers and local and national communities.

In a competitive situation, the increased costs arising from the operation of a social responsibility policy might be deemed acceptable by one business if another competing business followed suit to approximately the same extent.

Even highly profitable businesses, unless owned by relatively few shareholders, are often constrained against spending on social actions. This is not to say that firms are not socially responsible, but it is noticeable that in many competitive economies social measures have to be placed on a mandatory rather than a voluntary basis.

Profit maximization

Advocates of shareholders' wealth maximization claim that the process of increasing share prices in the Stock Market requires firms to market their goods and services as cost efficiently as possible – seeking always the market needs, the latest technology and the highest quality of customer service. They also claim that all of these activities, in seeking to improve the perception of the share-price markets, also simultaneously improve and benefit society at large. At issue then becomes how the objective of share price maximization in order to maximize shareholder's wealth can be translated into management actions.

For example, if management attempts to maximize profits, is this equivalent to trying to maximize shareholders' wealth? The answer to this question is, perhaps surprisingly you might think, certainly not! It is perfectly possible for managers to take actions which will increase profit, particularly in the short term, but which will not enhance shareholder wealth. This reinforces the point made earlier about performance-related pay.

Say, for example, a manager curtails all expenditure on such activities as maintenance, advertising, research and training. Certainly short-term profit will improve but the longer-term viability of the firm will sooner or later result in falling share prices as investors learn of the actions. Claims that a predator company in an unwelcome takeover bid will indeed curtail necessary expenditure have been used as a defence by victim companies in recent times.

In perspective

The financial manager, in carrying out financing and investment decisions, will need to have a constant view of the operating implications described above in seeking to achieve the firm's overall objective, whatever it may be, but particularly so in commercial concerns with regard to shareholder wealth maximization in the medium/long term. Such a course may not be the perfect answer to the determination of an organization's dominant objective, but it does provide an acceptable working basis for the financial decision-making process. One point that cannot be denied is that many organizations which have regularly ignored the shareholder wealth aspect have in the past gone out of business.

And, of course, the flow of finance is key to survival of the organization. If managers fail to manage it properly, then both shareholders' expectations and performance-related pay matter for nothing. The wrong financing package, inappropriate investment decisions, poor control of costs and so on, will lead to poor performance and possibly ruin.

Summary

Having completed this chapter you should now be able to:

- understand the nature and significance of the pyramid of purpose
- understand the nature and significance of the flow of finance
- have gained insights into the complexities of managing the flow of finance.

In light of this, the rest of this book from Part II onwards considers how to manage the flow of finance more effectively, harnessing skills and techniques which can help to achieve just that. Before that, however, following a self-assessment question, Chapter 2 looks at how organizations account for the flow of finance.

Self-assessment question

SAQ 1. 1

Think about an organization you are familiar with, perhaps your own if you are in employment. Have you a clear idea of its objectives, particularly the financially based ones? Are objectives defined and discussed formally? Do they appear as a policy statement in some organizational publication, the published financial statements perhaps? If such statements do not appear, do you have a view concerning the desirability of their publication and discussion? Do you consider that a focusing of management attention is likely to result, or will they be overpowered by more urgent day-to-day considerations of operational significance?

Further reading

Pike, R.H. and Ooi, T.S., 1988. The impact of corporate investment objectives and constraints on capital budgeting practice, *British Accounting Review* (August)

Grinyer, J.R., 1986. Alternatives to maximisation of shareholders wealth, *Accounting and Business Research* (Autumn)

Findley, C.M. and Whitmore, G.A., 1974. Beyond shareholder wealth maximisation, *Financial Management* (Winter)

Phillips, G. and Ross, J., 1966. The future structure of the function parts 1 and 2, *Management Accounting* (Part 1: February, Part 2: September)

2 Accounting for the flow of finance

Introduction

In this chapter you will look at how the flow of finance you met in Chapter 1 is usually accounted for by and within organizations. It is important to point out that the purpose of doing so is contextual; it is not the purpose to establish how a variety of financial statements are constructed. Rather you are concerned here with the nature and utility of the range of statements prepared and used by managers. (As stated in the introduction to this book, for an in-depth consideration of the preparation of financial statements you should refer to another excellent Butterworth-Heinemann text *Managing Financial Resources*, by Broadbent and Cullen.)

In this chapter you will identify key financial statements, their nature and their utility. Understandably their relationships to the flow of finance are highlighted. As such, reference is made back to three key figures from Chapter 1 and you may wish to prepare yourself by finding these figures now. They are:

- Figure 1.2 The financial dimension of the pyramid of purpose
- Figure 1.3 The flow of finance
- Figure 1.5 The financial context of management decisions

By the end of this chapter you will:

- understand the nature of profit and income and expenditure statements, balance sheets, cash flow statements and budgets
- recognize the utility of those statements in managing the flow of finance
- appreciate the limitations of those statements.

Accounting externally

The flow of finance detailed in Chapter 1 is of significance both to management teams and owners and funders of organizations. Viewed from the owners' perspective, the flow needs to be managed appropriately before there can be a chance of there arising earnings for them (termed in accounting jargon earnings attributable to ordinary shareholders – EATOS), with the subsequent payment of a dividend and the reinvestment of profits (the organic funding referred to in Chapter 1) in the future of the organization. Other funders too, such as banks, will be interested in how the flow has been managed. After all, if not enough operating profit is made, there will not be enough profit left to cover any bank loan interest due, nor to provide for dividend appropriations by owners and subsequent reinvestment of profits.

Another aspect of the flow is the need to generate cash as well as profits. As you will discover shortly, profit and cash, for sound and understandable reasons, are not the same. If cash flow is not managed, even though profits may be high enough on paper to satisfy all interested parties, there may not be enough cash to actually pay for bank interest and loans, or dividends. Neither, of course, will there be enough to pay more immediate and urgent bills. For all interested parties to be satisfied, it is essential that managers manage – and do so within the context of the flow of finance.

All the stages of the flow, as depicted in Figure 1.3, demand of managers skills and expertise which must be applied to ensure an acceptable output from the flow of finance. This acceptable output will vary from period to period, but more often than not will include the achievement of a certain operating profit level (usually in relation to capital sums invested by owners and other funders), target EATOS and specified reinvestments of profits. The financial quantification of the flow, at least at the corporate level and in a global sense, is normally reflected in a balance sheet. This in turn is normally accompanied by two further statements, the profit statement (sometimes termed profit and loss account or, in non-profit making organizations, income and expenditure account) and the cash flow statement. These are considered individually next.

The balance sheet

Figure 1.3 from Chapter 1 may be reproduced as shown in Figure 2.1. Notice how on the right-hand side the words *balance sheet* have been entered. They have been placed adjacent to the *funding obtained* and *investment in assets* stages of the circular flow. It is not unreasonable for funders, particularly owners such as shareholders, to wish for information from management teams about what sources of funding there were and what has happened to that funding, at least in terms of the assets it has been invested in.

> Assume that the initial funding in a new business amounted to, say £100,000, comprising £80,000 from shareholders and £20,000 as a bank loan. If this were invested thus, £10,000 in office equipment £50,000 on a 5-year office lease, £30,000 in stocks of goods

for resale, with the remaining £10,000 held in cash, a simplified balance sheet would look like this:

Sources of funding	£	*Investment in assets*	£
Owners' share capital	80,000	Office lease	50,000
Bank loan	20,000	Equipment	10,000
		Stocks of goods for resale	30,000
		Cash/bank balances	10,000
	100,000		100,000

This is a reasonable statement to provide interested parties with. It shows what has happened in terms of the major financing and investment decisions and that is essentially one of the main purposes of the balance sheet. The owners can see clearly that if the values of the assets were realized (£100,000), and the bank loan of £20,000 repaid that the net worth of the business – £80,000 – would available, representing the amount owed to them in light of their investment. (Of course, the assets might not realize the values shown, in which case the net worth to the owners would be correspondingly higher or lower.)

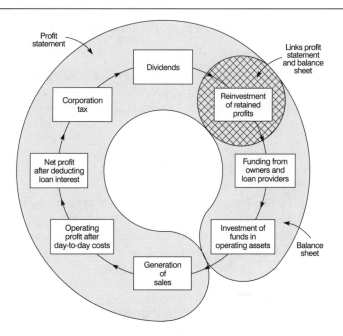

Figure 2.1 Mapping the balance sheet and profit statement onto the flow of finance

A feature not revealed by the particular balance sheet in the box above is the result of the management team's activities in managing the rest of the flow of finance. As you will see shortly, this is reflected within the profit statement. At the bottom of the profit statement would be a figure relating to the amount of profit retained and reinvested within the organization. In such a case and assuming such a figure to be, say, £10,000, an additional source of funding would need to be shown. This is shown on the simplified balance sheet in the next box, and assuming the other values having changed in light of activities and transactions leading to the profit generation.

Sources of funding	£	Investment in assets	£
Owners' share capital	80,000	Office lease	40,000
Retained profits or Reserves	10,000	Equipment	8,000
Bank loan	20,000	Stocks of goods for resale	20,000
		Cash/bank balances	42,000
	110,000		110,000

The retained profits – often referred to as *Reserves* – has the effect of increasing the net worth of the organization – the book value of the owners' investment from £80,000 as it was to £90,000 by way, of course, of the additional profit made and retained.

The balance sheet now shows all the sources and investments and becomes of use to appropriately interested parties, not least in summarizing a financial quantification of the state of play, at the date the balance sheet is drawn up, of the flow of finance.

Features of the balance sheet

The balance sheet has a number of features it is important to note. These are detailed below and should be borne in mind when reading or using any balance sheet for any organization.

Values

The values shown on the balance sheet are book values only. They show only the values as recorded in the books of account, whether computerized or maintained manually. The economic value of any one item may be higher or lower than that stated in the books of account.

After all, an item (or indeed a business) is only worth whatever the buyer wishes to offer and the seller to accept.

Omissions

The balance sheet lists only those items which have resulted or will result in cash flows into or out of the organization. Given this, it is not normal to see people valued and placed on the balance sheet. You might think this strange, since for many organizations people are the most important and valuable asset. Similarly it is still not common practice to show intangible assets such as customer goodwill, or the value of excellent information systems or administration procedures. The reason is that the values are to a degree subjective and thus unreliable.

Layout

You may already be familiar with balance sheets to a lesser or greater degree. If so, you will be aware that they are not normally presented in the manner shown in the two preceding boxes. The simplified balance sheets are shown horizontally and detail straight listings of items. Most balance sheets are presented in a more formal manner, with the items being categorized into groups.

It is standard to group items thus:

- *Fixed or long-lived assets* being those items which, when purchased, are likely to be used for longer than 1 year. Examples include land and buildings, plant and machinery, equipment, and vehicles.
- *Current assets* are those assets which will be used within a year. The item name may be an eternal constant on the balance sheet, but the value will be constantly changing during the year. Examples include stocks of goods for resale, stocks of consumables, debtors (those, particularly customers, who owe the organization money), and cash and bank balances.
- *Current liabilities* are formally referred to as *Creditors – amounts falling due within 1 year* and represent the more immediate bills of the organization. Examples include bills from creditors for stocks purchased (often payable within 30 days) and bills for use of utilities such as electricity and water.
- *Long-term liabilities* are often termed *Creditors – amounts falling due after more than 1 year.* They represent any long-term debts. Typically, bank loans would be included in this category. (Note, however, that the loan would become a current liability in the year in which it is due for repayment.)

The formal layout is usually presented vertically, starting with fixed assets at the top and progressing downwards to the net worth of the organization, detailing the book value of the owners' investment. This is shown in the next box.

A practical illustration of a balance sheet
A good, practical illustration of a balance sheet is shown in Figure 11.1 (see p. 169) and there, the balance sheets relating to British Airways Plc as at the end of financial years 1985–94 inclusive are shown. Looking at the statements you can see the categories of assets, the net worth as shown (particularly for 1994) by the Shareholders' equity and the terms referred to earlier, including Reserves.

An interesting point to note is that the net worth (1994) is shown as £1,827 million. This is the book value of the business. At the close of business on the last day of the 1994 financial year the market value according to the UK *Financial Times* was twice that value. This places an economic value on British Airways which is some distance from the book value as depicted in the net worth figure.

Of course, for both our earlier example and British Airways it is not unreasonable for interested parties to want to know how the extra source of funding – the Reserves (retained profits) – arose. This is answered by an examination of the profit statement.

The profit statement

As stated earlier, Figure 1.3 has been reproduced as Figure 2.1. Notice that, in addition to the words balance sheet, the words *profit statement* have been inserted on the left-hand side of the flow. The profit statement summarizes the costs and sales arising from the management team's efforts in using the assets financed by funding to generate profits. The profit statement attempts to measure, within the parameters of a particular financial framework, what might be deemed a true and fair assessment of the profits or losses arising as a result of the transactions and activities in a particular accounting period (be that 1 month, a quarter or a year). A key phrase here is *true and fair*. In measuring the profit (hopefully!), it may be that there is more than one way of measurement, as you see in the following box. In addition, the profit statement is constructed applying what is known in accounting jargon as the *matching principle*. An illustration appears in the box on page 23.

Building the profit statement
Assume that a new business starts with £100,000 capital, comprising £80,000 owners' share capital and £20,000 10% bank loan repayable in 5 years. This capital is spent on the assets detailed in the earlier box referring to the balance sheet on page 19. Thus before any sales are made the situation is:

	£		£
Owners' share capital	80,000	Office lease	50,000
Bank loan	20,000	Equipment	10,000
		Stocks of goods for resale	30,000
		Cash/bank balances	10,000

During the first year the following occurred:

- stock costing £10,000 was sold for £60,000 cash
- the office lease was depreciated (amortized is a jargon term often used) by £10,000
- the equipment was depreciated by £2,000
- wages/salaries and other expenses totalling £20,000 were paid in cash
- the owners withdrew £2,000 in cash by way of dividends.

Applying the matching principle, the profit statement starts by identifying the sales made in a period and then matching the costs incurred during that period in generating those sales. This has significant implications. Thus, although the business has spent £30,000 in acquiring stocks for resale, only £10,000 should appear on the profit statement as this is the cost of the stock now sold. The balance of £20,000 remains on the balance sheet until sold at some point in the future. Similarly with the lease and equipment. If these are to last 5 years, it is patently unfair to charge Year I's profit statement with all of the cost of the lease and equipment. Much better is to charge one-fifth of the total cost only to Year 1. The wages/salaries and other costs appear to relate only to Year 1 and thus should appear as a charge to Year 1's profit statement. In addition, the bank loan interest should be taken account of, this being £2,000 (10% of £20,000). Even if it has not been paid, under the matching principle it would still need to be shown as a charge in order to ascertain an appropriate profit for the year. Finally, assume tax at 25% of net profit is paid in cash.

Applying this we obtain:

Profit Statement for Year 1	£	£
Sales (all cash)		60,000
less Cost of goods sold		10,000
Gross profit		50,000
less Wages/salaries/other costs	20,000	
Amortization of lease	10,000	
Depreciation of equipment	2,000	32,000
Operating profit		18,000
less Bank interest		2,000
Net profit		16,000
less Taxation at, say, 25 %		4,000
Net profit after tax (EATOS)		12,000
less Dividends withdrawn		2,000
Balance profits retained in the business, to Reserves		10,000

Features of the profit statement

The profit statement has a number of features which are important for you to grasp. These and the relevant significances are detailed below.

Profit and cash differences

The profit statement is constructed without regard to whether or not the source transactions and activities it is derived from have already involved or have yet to involve cash flows. In adopting and implementing the matching principle the focus is on an assessment of the profit or loss arising and not cash flows. (Of course, cash flow is important and you will look at this aspect shortly.)

The amortization and depreciation charges in the box above relate to assets which have already been purchased for cash, but the charges themselves are only one-fifth each of the actual cash expenditure. Further charges will take place over the subsequent 4 years and again in each of those years there will be no corresponding cash flow in any of the years. The same principle applies to the cost of the stock bought and now resold. Although £30,000 was spent in cash, only £10,000 is charged to the profit statement. Next year all the stock might be resold and the cost thus charged to the relevant profit statement. There will, however, be no corresponding cash flow in that year. Of course, this difference in treatment has already been explicitly exposed in the box above with the charging of the bank loan interest, even though the cash has not yet been paid. The interest will presumably be paid next year. In next year's accounts the cash figure will be then adjusted downwards, but there will no further entry relating to this year's bank interest in next year's profit statement as it has already been accounted for in this year's.

True and fair

Traditionally, within particularly the financial frameworks adopted by the financial communities of the UK and USA, it has been acknowledged that in measuring profit there may be more than one way of assessing the financial value of a transaction or cost. An example occurs with depreciation.

In the box above, both the lease and equipment are being amortized and depreciated, respectively, over a 5-year period – hence the respective charges of £10,000 (one-fifth of £50,000) and £2,000 (one-fifth of £10,000). This approach is charging via what is termed the *straight line* approach. An acceptable alternative might be the *reducing* or *declining* balance approach which is calculated on a different basis. The whole of the cost of the asset will still be charged to five successive profit statements but in different size portions, specifically higher amounts in the early years, scaling down to lower amounts in later years. Scope for judgement might also arise where stock costs change and values could be worked out using a *first in, first out (FIFO)* or *average cost (AVCO)* basis.

The cash flow statement

It has been established that profit and cash differ. Given that the profit statement measures the profit or loss arising in a particular period, it is understandable that management teams and other interested parties should want to see a statement which shows what has happened to the cash situation over that same period. After all, to report a profit might seem on the surface to be particularly positive but if, for example, sales on account were not converted into cash, the organization might go under.

In 1992 the Polly Peck Group of companies reported impressive profits, as indeed it had from the mid-1980s. Unfortunately, for all sorts of reasons it had no cash. And yet it had been consistently tipped by investment analysts as one of the companies to invest in.

In 1995 it was confirmed that South Thames Training & Enterprise Council (TEC) had mismanaged its working capital situation and had run out of cash. With no money to pay its bills the TEC, funded primarily by the UK government but nevertheless a limited liability company, was allowed to go under.

Managing cash flow is an essential part of effective working capital management which is covered later in this book. For the moment it is sufficient to recognize the significance of keeping an eye on cash. If you return to Figure 1.5, you are reminded of the complexity of the finance flows within and into and out of a typical organization. Some represent day-to-day flows, others are longer term; whichever, the cash implications are significant. This is why organizations need management teams to plan for and manage cash effectively internally and why funders and other interested parties are interested in the cash flow statement accompanying the published profit statement and balance sheet. Such a statement will normally show the cash flows in broad terms, divided into operating (day-to-day) flows and more major and longer term items.

A practical illustration of a cash flow statement
Figure 11.3 on page 178 shows the cash flow statements for the British Airways group of companies for the financial years 1990–94. The statements each start with the net cash flow arising from operating activities. Thereafter, detail is devoted to:

- interest and dividends paid and received, termed **returns on investments and servicing of finance**
- taxation paid
- investments in and proceeds from the sale of fixed assets and investments
- net flows arising from changes in bank loans, share capital in issue and bonds (a form of long-term loan).

The statements are completed with the net change, increase or decrease, in cash over the year.

The cash flow statement is thus useful not least as it compensates for the true and fair approach reflected within profit statements. In this respect it may be said to be true and accurate. Having said that, it should be remembered that companies which have produced and published cash flow statements and received auditors' approval of their records have still had solvency problems (not least Polly Peck).

Accounting internally

The pyramid of purpose and accompanying flow of finance given in Figure 1.2 translates the pyramid of purpose into reality. Such a translation demands of management teams a series of decisions, not least financial, reflecting an adeptness of management skills. These skills will include the design of a structured and systematic model to implement the pyramid of purpose – to make it happen if you like. In addition, however, it is equally important for the accompanying resources to be managed properly. The most impressive-looking illustrations on paper mean nothing unless the models being depicted are designed, implemented and managed properly.

Planning for the pyramid of purpose

As was established in Chapter 1, the starting point for the pyramid of purpose is the vision of the organization and the subsequent determination of the mission. This is invariably achieved by the senior management, although usually involving consultation with, certainly, other employees, and perhaps clients, customers and suppliers, and, where appropriate, shareholders.

The establishment of goals and their translation into day-to-day targets and activities at the operational level also involves more than just the senior team. The planning process demands consultation with operational managers. Rather than edicts from on high – a *top down* approach – *bottom up* views are sought from the day-to-day areas. In reality, a combination of top down and bottom up is applied at this planning stage. And within the planning, it is important to plan ahead for when the model is in operation, allowing particularly for feedback mechanisms, again both top down and bottom up based. The planning, implementation and operation of the pyramid of purpose require a structured approach from management teams to ensure that an appropriate framework for budgeting is established.

Establishing a framework for budgeting
- Set a broad statement of what needs to happen to realize the vision – a mission statement capturing where the organization is going.
- State the values of the organization within which the mission statement will apply.
- Define goals – staging posts if you like – which must be achieved if the mission statement is to become a reality.
- Analyse (usually through PEST, SWOT and other analyses) where the organization is and the starting point for the journey ahead
- Define a range of relevant strategies.
- Select the most appropriate strategy.
- Implement the strategy by:
  (a) ensuring that the right mix of staff, skills, structures and systems are available
  (b) ensuring that staff are aware of the day-to-day targets they

should achieve and the activities necessary to achieve them
(c) ensuring that resources are available to help staff to work effectively and efficiently.
- Obtain feedback on how well:
 (a) targets are being achieved
 (b) resources are being used.

Thus the points below become genuine points of significance in that:

- the pyramid of purpose becomes for managers an agenda for action
- resources, particularly financial, are inextricably linked to goals, targets and activities
- making the pyramid of purpose work is a management challenge not just a financial one.

The bottom section of the pyramid assumes a great significance for operational managers, with the budgeting system becoming the internal accounting mechanism for resources consumption, expenditure and the charting of progress forwards.

Accounting for working capital and fixed assets

The implementation and operation of a budgetary system is the role focus for operational managers. The results of their decisions and actions are quantified in a conventional manner within the profit statement and balance sheet. In addition, however, other managers are charged respectively with caring for cash, purchasing and controlling stocks, debtor and creditor control, accounting for fixed assets and investment appraisals.

Internally, as part of the implementation duties within the pyramid of purpose, the senior management team must ensure that systems are in place which will enable those managers charged with the above duties to carry them out effectively. Later in this book you will examine a number of the related and significant aspects of this requirement.

Organizing for financial management

Every organization needs a basic structure to build its operational, including accounting and decision-making, activities around. Such a structure usually groups activities with a common theme together under specific headings, and this is particularly the case as far as financial activities are concerned. Although a basic organizational structure is desirable, different concerns will demand variations on it. The size of an organization, the stage of its development, its management style and custom, the nature of its ownership – private or public sector, group or independent – will all have an impact upon the final appearance of any structure. This applies equally to an organization's financial management activities as to its others.

Figure 2.2 sets out in chart form fairly typical divisions between broad areas within an organization's accounting and financial activities. The financial resources process is clearly detailed. A senior manager in overall control – normally the Finance Director or equivalent – will be charged with the daunting responsibility of advising managers with regard to the acquisition and investment of resources and subsequently helping to account for them. In addition, the financial system will generate information which will help to measure the effectiveness of past decisions relating to financial resources, and to make decisions concerned with future management. Having said this, it is important to recognize that Figure 2.2 is not meant to convey that accountants are the only ones to deal with these activities; all managers have a part to play in them. In many respects, the accountants may be seen not as the king pin or queen bee but, rather, the providers of linchpin information around which managerial activities revolve.

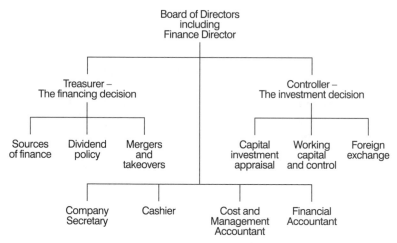

Figure 2.2 Broad areas of financial activities

In some organizations – usually smaller ones – the Finance Director or equivalent will also be the Accountant, the Secretary, the Cashier, and so on, all rolled into one. In other organizations, large departments, each with management hierarchies, will control just one of these functions. Whichever, some form of grouping is required as a prerequisite to efficiency and effectiveness of the financial system which will produce information to enable managers to do their jobs better.

Managing the finance function

No matter how the individual financial activities are divided up, there are dimensions to the role of the person with overall charge which are relevant to and prevail within just about any organization. The structure, or body, can exist but there needs to be direction and vision to optimize efficiency and effectiveness; a brain for the body if you like. These dimensions are depicted in a matrix form in Figure 2.3.

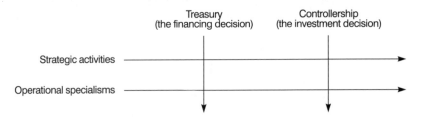

Figure 2.3 The dimensions of financial activities

What is important – and difficult! – is that the right blend of the ingredients shown in the matrix in Figure 2.3 is obtained. As ever, this is easier said than done. There might exist a wonderfully efficient system of credit control. If, however, the wrong or inappropriate decisions are made at a strategic level in relation to direction and policy, credit control and other activities can be efficient as systems but the organization will not really prosper. Likewise, sound strategy accompanied by poor operational performance could be just as bad, or even worse!

The illustration in Figure 2.2 illustrates a typical grouping of organizational financial activities, with the strategic dimensions depicted in the matrix in Figure 2.3 which are also present. As you can see, the financial activities are categorized into two groups:

- those requiring what is usually termed *Treasury* management, and
- others concerned with *Controllership* management.

Both these areas require a strategic management presence. Those activities falling within the broad category of the *financing decision* are linked to Treasury management; those to *investment decisions* to Controllership management.

The typical activities within each group are considered under various headings below.

Mergers and takeovers

The competitive state of the current world has brought about a situation where many organizations are constantly involved in a hunter and hunted scenario. Organizations need to be aware of possible predators preparing to make unwelcome bids. Equally, management teams may recommend bids to be made for other organizations, requiring a need to understand the principles of business valuation. (Of course this has clear links with both the financing and investment decisions – nothing ever exists in isolation.)

In this book you do not consider mergers and takeovers, in light of their complexity. You do, however, gain insights into the ideas of business valuation in Chapter 11. If you are interested in taking matters further in this area, references are detailed at the end of this chapter under 'Further reading'.

Capital investment appraisal

This is a vitally important activity which is the key in supporting the investment decision. Any investment proposal requires careful appraisal. By their very nature, many fixed asset acquisitions involving large amounts of finance are not easily and cheaply aborted or reversed. In addition, they often require significant accompanying investments in supporting working capital. We spoke about pressures identified earlier, producing a further pressure to make sure that the investment decision taken is the correct one.

You are exposed to techniques for investment decisions and associated managerial considerations in Part III.

Working capital management

Working capital, as you will discover later, is a vital component of organizational life, around which the operational aspects of the flow of finance often revolve. Working capital comprises:

- any stocks, be they raw materials, work in progress, finished goods, consumables, etc.

- debtor and creditor balances
- cash.

These are the items that work in conjunction with an organization's fixed assets in order to produce products and provide services. The level of working capital balances, both individually and as a composite can vary from day to day. For this reason alone, working capital would need managing. When you realize, as you will later in Part IV, that poor working capital management can mean disaster, the need is only enhanced.

Within this area lies, understandably, the important aspect of cash management. This involves a relationship with banks and other financial institutions. Holding excessive cash means forgoing investment opportunities that might exist. This is as undesirable as being without sufficient cash to meet operational needs. Of course, the nature of the organization will need to be considered here. Retail concerns such as supermarkets handling large volumes of cash takings will need highly organized bank deposit arrangements, and here the Cashier will be in high profile. Conversely, a manufacturing concern is unlikely to have the same cash handling requirements.

Part IV includes a much closer look at effective working capital management.

Foreign exchange

Each country throughout the world has its own currency. Each has a value which, from an international if not domestic viewpoint, fluctuates according to circumstances at any one point in time. A number of major currencies, known as *hard* currencies, are actively traded and speculated upon.

The early 1970s saw an almost universal acceptance of the floating of many exchange rates. Since then a significant feature of the financial management of exchange rates has been their increased *volatility*. This volatility results in an *exchange rate risk* or *exposure*, whereby a profitable sale or economic purchase across national boundaries can be adversely affected by exchange rate fluctuations between the time at which the deal is agreed and the time at which the foreign currency is collected.

Most organizations will, understandably, develop strategies to minimize foreign exchange losses. Indeed, many organizations will develop strategies to minimize gain because it is much better to start off from a position of certainty than uncertainty. These strategies are usually referred to as *hedging* strategies. Hedging is simply a means of locking into a future exchange rate by agreeing now to buy or sell a currency at a fixed time in the future at a predetermined rate. This is important even where countries operate contractual arrangements such as the European Union's Exchange Rate Mechanism – ERM.

It is not the purpose of this book to expose you to the intricacies of foreign exchange management. You should bear in mind, however, the implications for management decisions. The list of Further reading at the end of the chapter gives more information for those interested.

Cost and management accounting

The function of this activity is to provide regular internal management accounts for control purposes and cost data for decision-making, particularly in relation to evaluating possible future courses of action. All managers require information about the consequences of both their past and proposed actions; it is here that the management information systems come into their own.

Financial accounting

Here, financial records of past events are maintained and from these records profit and loss accounts and balance sheets and fund flow statements are produced.

Offshoots of this specialist area include *internal auditing* and *taxation management*. The first involves the carrying out of internal checks as a safeguard against significant error and possible malpractice; the second is concerned with minimizing an organization's tax liability through all legal means.

The areas detailed above represent the major activities undertaken by the finance function. They do not exist just because somebody somewhere fancied setting up such activities. They exist because they form a logical design for a structural body. They are, if you like, the arms and legs and other parts of the body which enable what needs to be done, to get done. Of course, in an organization this means providing financial information and advice to managers. A problem arises, however, in that different interested parties have differing views on how financial affairs and decisions should be handled, as you see next.

Complicating variables within the flow of finance

The financial information system of an organization will need to take account of a number of factors, none of which will necessarily be treated identically in all concerns. These can be seen as additional variables which complicate the management of an organization's financial resources. The more typical of these were highlighted in Chapter 1 and include not least:

- the demands by shareholders for maximization of their wealth
- the objectives of the management team
- social objectives.

Quantifying the variables

As you will appreciate it is difficult for managers, not least in the financial community, to decide on how to balance the implications of these and other variables when managing the flow of finance. One often-used approach is through quantifying the consequences of courses of action.

Take, for example, a limited liability organization with the following extracts from its financial statements:

Ordinary share capital of 4 million shares with a £1 nominal/par value per share:

Pre-tax reported profit	£2 million
After tax profits	£1 million (assume tax at 50%)
(EATOS – earnings attributable to shareholders)	

$$\text{Earnings per share (EPS)} = \frac{£1 \text{ million}}{4 \text{ million}} = £0.25 \text{ per share}$$

If the management wish to expand they may decide to opt for raising additional funds by asking the shareholders to buy an additional issue of 1 million shares. Having obtained the funds, the organization generates additional profits, say £200,000 after tax. The figures now might be:

Ordinary share capital	5 million shares
Pre-tax reported profit	£2.4 million
After tax profits (EATOS)	£1.2 million

$$\text{Earnings per share (EPS)} = \frac{£1.2 \text{ million}}{5 \text{ million}} = £0.24 \text{ per share}$$

Despite the increased profits, this policy has driven down the shareholders' EPS and they may well be none too pleased.

Of course, the management might have raised the extra finance from a bank, thus acquiring *loan or debt capital* The financial statement extracts would now be:

Capital:	
Ordinary shares	£4 million
Bank loan	£1 million

The original after tax profits were, of course, £1 million. In this case they would not, however increase to £2.4 million. This is because the interest on the bank loan would be treated as a business expense, thus reducing the amount of reported profit. The figures will show:

Pre-tax profits: £2,000,000 + £400,000 =	£2,400,000
Less chargeable interest –10% of loan	£100,000
Pre-tax reported profit	£2,300,000
Less tax at 50%	£1,150,000
Profit attributable to shareholders	£1,150,000
Number of shares	4 million
EPS (£1,150,000 ÷ 4 million)	£0.2875 per share

Here the shareholders might be happier, given that EPS has increased. They will have to decide, however, if this is adequate compensation for their organization taking on board additional liabilities. Remember, the loan will have to be repaid at some time and each year £100,000 interest will have to be paid before the shareholders see any profits.

A further quantification

We can see that many managers and accountants will thus worry about making decisions that affect EPS. Some managers worry so much that they are actually driven to making acquisitions of other organizations in situations where short-term gains are made, but at the expense of long-term loss. Look at the figures shown in Table 2.1.

Table 2.1 Details for takeover analysis example

Detail	Organization		
	A	B	A+B
	£	£	£
After-tax profits	10m	2m	12m
Market value	100m	8m	108m
No. of shares	10m	4m	10.8m
EPS	1.00	0.50	1.11
Market price of shares	10	2	10
PE ratio	10	4	9

Organization A has shares valued by investors at £100 million and a price/earnings (P/E) ratio of 10 (market price of £10 divided by EPS of £1). Organization B has shares valued at £8 million with a P/E ratio of 4 (£2 divided by £0.50). When A buys B, paying with 800,000 shares valued at £10 each, it manages to increase EPS – good news for its shareholders. The bad news is that its P/E ratio drops from 10 to 9 (£10 divided by £1.11), indicating lower growth in the future; jam today instead of jam tomorrow!

This 'jam' strategy can fool investors who appear to prefer immediate benefits without realizing that lower growth in the future will be a very real cost. It can also apply to dividend policy, where some shareholders may prefer dividends now rather than capital gains when selling shares in the future, a sort of 'bird in the hand' argument. Others who are taxed more heavily on dividends than on capital gains may prefer the reverse. Management teams are thus faced with taking strategic and operational decisions which must reconcile conflicting demands from a diverse shareholder clientele.

There is little doubt that the maximization of shareholder wealth is seen by the majority of managers in limited liability companies as being their major objective. This tends to override profit maximization and, unless relatively current sales are affected, social objectives and business ethics are viewed as being desirable objectives with potential benefits, but with such benefits not accruing immediately.

For the average manager (if there is such a beast), the financial dimension of managing the flow of finance is strewn with dilemmas and pitfalls. As a consequence it is essential that you and all managers should:

- appreciate the need to understand techniques to help with financing and investment decisions
- be able to manage costs
- recognize the role played by information in helping to plan ahead and to monitor the consequences of decisions.

Summary

Having completed this chapter you should now be able to:

- recognize further the significance of the flow of the finance within organizations
- understand the nature and purpose of profit statements, balance sheets, cash flow statements and budgets
- recognize the role played by the finance function in supporting managerial decisions
- appreciate some of the dilemmas that can face managers in making financial decisions
- place the rest of this book in the context of the flow of finance.

Before you move to those later parts of the book, attempt the following self-assessment questions.

Self-assessment questions

SAQ 2.1

Detail the nature and purpose of and distinguish between the profit statement, the cash statement and the balance sheet.

SAQ 2.2

Comment on the statement 'The balance sheet is an appropriate representation of the worth of an organization'.

SAQ 2.3

A business is currently generating an operating profit of £100,000 on capital employed of £1,000,000 (comprising £750,000 share capital and £250,000 reserves). It is seeking to raise an additional £500,000 and has the option of raising it all from shareholders, all via a 10% long-term bank loan, £250,000 from each source. It is anticipated that an additional profit of £50,000 will arise after the injection of funds. What would your advice be to the management team? Shares have a nominal value of £1 each. Any new shares will be issued at £1.

Further reading

Broadbent, M. and Cullen, J., 1994. *Managing Financial Resources*, Butterworth-Heinemann

Murphy, M.J., 1966. Accruals accounting in government: the Irish experience, *Management Accounting* (October)

Part II The Financing Decision

3 Finding finance

Introduction

Part I established that the management of financial resources has a strategic dimension in addition to the day-to-day operational perspective. This strategic dimension requires managers and their specialist financial advisers to have an appropriate strategy to ensure that:

- a suitable value of funds is available to and within the organization
- as and when required
- at the minimum cost possible.

This in itself is a challenge – a challenge which is compounded by the very real fact that at any one time there is available more than one single source of finance. Indeed there are many sources, each with different features and, importantly, different costs. Cost minimization too will play a major role within the challenge, and complicate matters, thus presenting an even greater challenge.

This challenges managers within the organization with the task of selecting not just one source but possibly of blending together a mixture of the various available finance types, with a view to achieving an optimum package of finance. This challenge is made even stiffer by the fact that trying to achieve an optimum package is a dynamic process. It is dynamic in the sense that it is constantly under review as:

- new demands for additional and/or replacement funding appear
- new types of funding sources become available
- changes occur within the organization's operating practices.

It is essential that every opportunity is taken to ensure that the mix of financing is the most appropriate in light of this dynamic process. In this chapter you will examine the characteristics of differing types of finance sources and the significance of each type within the financing decision. By the end of this chapter you will:

- be able to identify the major types of finance sources available to organizations
- be able to attribute characteristics to each type
- recognize the general considerations managers should take account of in opting for one or a blend of particular type(s) of finance.

Financial jargon

Before moving on to discover how this challenge is responded to, it would be as well to establish and interpret some of the financial jargon that lies ahead. This specialist technical jargon relates to ideas you have already met, as with most matters financial for the non-specialist. For example, external funding sources *(finance raised from outside the organization)* are often saddled with the term **capital instruments.** The mix of finance, usually a package of internally generated and externally raised funding, is commonly referred to as the organization's **capital structure.** Any one capital structure may comprise a combination of different sources of finance. Consequently the manner in which the structure is arranged – the relationship between the sources – is called the structure's **gearing** or **leverage.** The funding for a capital structure in a commercial concern will originate from either external loans, **loan capital** or **debt finance,** and/or shareholder funding, **share capital** or **equity finance** (including, where appropriate, retained earnings). Any provider of funds is usually called the **investor,** be the funds from a lending bank or a shareholder. Profits after deduction of interest and tax belong to shareholders and any portion taken back is referred to as dividends. The **share price,** as quoted on the Stock Exchange, is termed **ex-div** or **cum-div,** reflecting respectively whether or not the declared dividend has been paid or not. Finally, given that raising finance sometimes involves having to pay interest, it is worth noting that the term **coupon** is often used as an official substitute for interest.

Of course the financing challenge needs a response. This response starts with a consideration of the general characteristics of finance sources and their implications for capital structure.

The characteristics of finance sources

Anybody making finance available to an organization will do so in order to receive, at some stage in the future, a return. Banks will lend money in return for interest (in addition, of course, to receiving the original loan amount back). Shareholders will invest in return for regular dividends and an increase in the marketable price of their shares. Of course, what they expect in return will vary according to the nature and status of their investment in an organization. Coupled with the challenge to managers in organizations of creating the most appropriate mix of finance, it is important for both providers and users of finance to understand the nature and implications of the characteristics of finance sources. Remember, just as anybody funding an organization is an investor, so is the manager deciding what to do with money. In such circumstances, an understanding of the characteristics of potential sources of financing is desirable.

Typical characteristics

The more typical characteristics include:

- the degrees of permanence and/or redeemability
- the types and rates of return and reward
- the degree of security
- the length of the financing period.

These characteristics are depicted in Figure 3.1, each being considered in turn below. As each is addressed, examples are given. Do not worry if you are unfamiliar with the precise nature of the examples given – they will be explained comprehensively later (for example, the terms *debentures* and *bonds* might fall into this category).

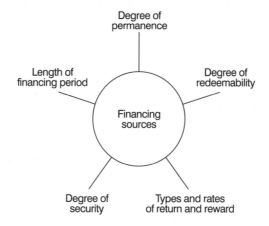

Figure 3.1 The characteristics of finance

Permanent and redeemable capital

The term **permanent** means that once a financing sum has been invested in or loaned to an organization it is *not refundable* unless the organization is wound up. Ordinary share capital from shareholders is a good example of permanent capital. Shareholders usually invest long term. If they wish to realize the investment during the life of the organization, the shares may be sold to other and new shareholders. The point is that the organization does not return capital to shareholders in such circumstances. Bankers, however, would not normally supply permanent capital, expecting it to be returned, quite naturally, via the paying back of the loan.

The term **redeemable** means that at some future date(s) this particular form of financing will be *returned* to the investors. Normally, redeemable capital refers to bank loans, or other loans in the form of debentures or bonds. Some shares are specified as being redeemable. Redeemable capital can often be seen on balance sheets with redemption dates specified, e.g. 10% Debentures 2000–2002. This means that at some time during the timespan 2000–2002 the capital sum will be redeemed to the then holder. The exact sequencing of the redemption will usually be specified in the original issue terms. The rights to the funds invested may have been transferred (as happens when shares are sold), and thus the investors who receive funds back may or may not be the original investors.

Fixed and variable reward

With types of funding that have a fixed rate of return, a specific percentage or, to be technical, **coupon rate** is attached to the capital. This is the rate which will be paid relative to the nominal value of the capital. For example, each £100 block of a £1 million 8% debenture or bond denominated in £100 blocks will receive an annual interest payment of £8. This is regardless of the market value of the £100 blocks, assuming it to be a market-quoted loan stock. The market price at which £100 blocks of the loan stock change hands will reflect the market demand for that class of stock, taking into account – among other factors – that the coupon rate of 8% is payable on the £100 *nominal* value, irrespective of the market value. It could thus be an effective higher or lower rate of return depending upon the market price paid or to be paid.

> Thus if a bond has a market value of £120 per £100 nominal value block, the return for anybody purchasing at £120 is (£8 ÷ £120 × 100%) 6.67% and not 8%.

In recent times there has been a growing tendency for coupon rates to be made variable or **floating** by tying them to an external rate. A good example of this is the **LIBOR** scheme, where rates are fixed to a benchmark set by the **London Inter Bank Offered Rate.** Finance directors are understandably reluctant to get their organizations *locked in* to paying a *high* interest rate at any one time. Equally investors are unwilling to have their funds locked in to receiving a low interest rate. A variable rate relative to current market conditions is an answer for both parties, but still requires managing.

In the case of loan capital the coupon rates, fixed or floating, are *obligatory.* This means that organizations *must* pay any loan interest due. The loan providers have the status of creditors to the company and could sue for their interest in the event of default.

Contrasted with this is the major form of variable rate capital: ordinary shares. The dividends paid to shareholders are *variable,* and variable at the *discretion* of the directors. A limited company's Board of Directors, advised by the Finance Director, may decide to recommend that no dividend be paid at a particular time. The shareholders in Annual General Meeting would, of course, be required to ratify that recommendation.

> The above may be illustrated by reference to two real organizations. In 1993, the Trump Corporation in the USA was unable to pay huge amounts of interest due on loan capital. The result was court action by the loan providers and subsequent misfortune for the primary owner of the Corporation, Donald Trump. In the same year, the Midland Bank in the UK declared that no dividend would be paid to ordinary shareholders. Some would argue that it was this move which ultimately led Midland Bank to being subsumed within the Hong Kong & Shanghai Banking Corporation.

Security

Investors and lenders making funds available to a company may require security as collateral in the event of any future default. Whether the loan is secured or unsecured thus plays an important role in the financing decision.

Secured finance in the form of a loan to the company by an investor or group of investors will permit the investor a **charge** on the organization's assets. Such a charge may be either **specific,** nominated to one specific asset like a freehold building, or **floating,** nominated to a group of assets.

Unsecured finance is obtained by the organization without any charge on assets. The best illustration of unsecured finance provided to a limited company is that subscribed for the ordinary shares, although it must be pointed out that the terms secured and unsecured are usually taken to apply to *loan* capital rather than to *share* capital.

Duration of funding period

The duration or **term** of funding is not easy to address, because so much depends upon the nature of the organization's business. For example, companies in the world of personal computing equipment may consider 1 year to be extremely long term, whereas companies engaged in major civil engineering contracts would regard 1 year as short term.

Given that **term** is very much related to a company's particular business activity, the guidelines generally used are that:

- short term is up to 1 year
- medium term is from 1 year up to 5 years
- long term is beyond 5 years.

A common characteristic

One characteristic which any finance source is concerned with is that of **risk.** A lender, i.e. the *investor,* often has to balance the certainty of a specific return against a potentially higher return but which is less certain. The aspect of risk is so significant to potential and existing investors that it is important for the manager seeking or having obtained finance from investors to understand the investor's viewpoint. Thus it deserves fuller consideration.

Risk

Risk is a many-sided subject, and with there being a number of perspectives, is thus somewhat difficult to define. A more detailed look at risk takes place later but initially, in order to gain an insight into the nature of risk, there are a number of aspects to be considered. Not least among these aspects is the degree of **return** which may be expected.

Risk and return

From the investor's viewpoint the level of risk attaching to the funds invested may well depend on the following:

- The form in which the investment is made. The significance here is that funds invested long term/short term, or are secured/unsecured or have any of the other characteristics, will reflect a measure of risk, this risk being termed the **investment risk.**
- Other types of finance from other sources which the organization mixed together in its total funding package. The effect of this mix is termed the **finance risk.**
- The investment decision that the organization makes when utilizing the funds available to it. This gives rise to what is known as the **business risk.**

Of course, it is important to investors that they receive a **reward** for taking a risk. This reward is usually termed the **return.** The return to the investor is represented by the cash flowing from the investment back to the investor, both now and in the future.

Measuring risk

To acknowledge risk as an important factor is one matter, but to measure it is another. A widely applied measurement involves the comparison of: the return the investor expects *with* the return actually realized. Take the example shown in the box.

Suppose you invest £2,000 in a particular company's shares and hold them for 1 year. At the end of the year the market value may have fallen to £1,400. In such circumstances, what would your loss be?

Most people would probably say £600. However, if, when you invested the money, you had expected a positive return, let us say 10%, from your investment it could be argued that you should really include in your calculation that 10% which did not materialize. In such circumstances the loss would be:

	£	£
Original investment		2,000
Amount realizable	1,400	
Actual loss	600	
Expected return	200	
Managerial assessment of loss		800

Of course, given that circumstances are constantly changing, any investment will have a range of returns which it will generate, the spectrum being from excellent to terrible.

The range

The potential range of returns relate directly to the risk of the investment and may be measured by the **dispersion** of the possible outcomes in relation to the expected returns. In the example just considered, the expected outcome was £2,200. This can be represented graphically, as in Figure 3.2. The distribution of area A represents the likely outcomes for an investment in our example. The expected outcome is 10%, but the possible outcomes range between minus 100% (a total loss) and infinity.

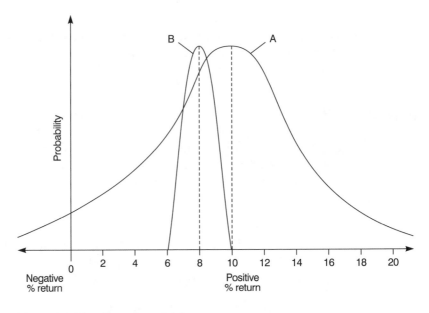

Figure 3.2 The dispersion of risk

Area B profiles perhaps an alternative risk-return profile with, in this case, an average return of 8% and minimum and maximum returns of 6% and 10%, respectively. The narrower the dispersion, the less the risk. The wider the dispersion, the greater potential losses or profits.

Given that a range of returns will apply, it is normal to take the average or mean return as being the return expected. This means is determined by applying a weighting factor involving the probabilities of each potential outcome occurring.

Categorizing risk and return

Any type of investment can be categorized according to the particular blend of risk and return. Some forms of investment are less risky than others. Typical of this category are **gilts** or **government bonds** and **secured** company loan stock. Most risky forms of investment will have higher expected returns on average, but with a wider range of outcomes in any one year. **Shares** are a good example of this type of investment, and the UK stock market *crash* of October 1987 is a good example of the wider range of outcomes!

Of course, in highlighting returns there is a temptation to assume that this is an investment decision factor. Indeed it is, but in raising finance from a range of potential investors it is important to understand the criteria used by those investors.

Categorizing investors in relation to risk

Individual investors' attitudes to risk and return will, of course, vary in relation to a number of aspects such as their existing wealth, their tax positions, their age, health, and so on. The implication is that shareholders are individual people. Some are, of course; the majority however are other organizations, particularly banks, insurance concerns and pension trust funds. Their circumstances will dictate their inclusion in one of two categories, **risk averse** and **risk seeking.**

Risk averse and risk seeking

It is traditional to assume that investors are *risk averse,* as opposed to *risk seeking.* That is, when faced with two equal returns, each with different levels of risk attached (however that is quantified), the investor will logically choose the return accompanied by the lower measure of risk.

The assumption of risk aversion on behalf of investors can lead to the generalized assumption that when faced with an increased amount of risk (investment, finance or business), the investor will seek a compensating increase in return from the investment.

This is illustrated by a simple personal example. If you could invest your surplus cash in a risk-free investment such as government securities, gaining a return of say 5%, why be tempted to invest in a venture (organizations undertake ventures) which might be risky. Being risky it might return 10%, 15% or only 3% – or indeed go under losing everything. In compensation for the greater risk, an investor will thus require appropriately higher returns.

Matching of the finance decision and the investment decision

As a basic principle of arranging a finance package, it is important to attempt to achieve a match between the **finance decision** and the **investment decision.** This is particularly relevant with regard to **risk** and **term**.

For example, Land and buildings, being a long-term, low-risk investment, might be financed by a mortgage type of loan, itself long term, and relatively low cost in terms of interest. On the other hand, motor vehicles will best be financed via some short- or medium-term arrangement, for example leasing. Of course, it would be impossible to achieve an exact one-to-one match between every single investment and finance decision, but as a general rule-of-thumb to be followed and applied, it is appropriate. Certainly, significant violations of this principle – say using bank overdrafts to finance additional buildings or 20-year loan stock to finance vehicles – would need to be avoided. Adverse appraisals by investors of the past financial conduct of an organization's affairs could make subsequent capital-raising a much more expensive business than would otherwise be the case. For example, during the UK hyperinflation period of the mid-1970s many companies raised capital from shareholders and banks simply to fund the increased outlays in monetary terms necessary for working capital purposes. This practice made subsequent raising of capital from shareholders very difficult to achieve.

> Many small firms use overdrafts to fund long-term asset acquisition – a complete mismatch. After all, overdrafts are very short-term sources of funding, and are repayable on demand.

Types of finance

In considering the various characteristics of sources of finances, reference has been made to some of the types. Next you meet those and other types formally.

A non-exclusive list

It would not, of course, be practicable to record here every possible type of finance. The main types considered here are:

- shares
- reserves, as in retained profits
- loan stocks, such as bonds and debentures
- term loans
- bank finance
- leasing
- government finance
- international finance.

Shares

A company registered under the UK Companies Act will have a **registered** or **authorized** capital amount, subdivided into different classes of share, each class denominated with a **nominal or par value**. Companies can then have an **issued share capital** which obviously cannot exceed its authorized limit. The commonest class of shares are **ordinary shares** and the nominal value assumed in, for example, the UK *Financial Times* listing is 25p unless otherwise stated. In setting nominal values, the Finance Director will have an eye to the marketability or transactability of the company's shares. High nominal values and hence high market values do not facilitate marketability in the company's shares. It is worth remembering that share prices can fluctuate. Thus a share with a nominal value of 25p could easily have a market value of 50p one day and 20p on another.

Ordinary shares

Ordinary shares, also known as equity shares, carry voting rights. Each share carries one vote and, under UK company law, resolutions to an Annual General Meeting are carried with a simple majority. Resolutions to an Extraordinary General Meeting require a 75% majority.

Exceptionally, ordinary shares may be issued which do not carry voting rights. Such shares are usually to be found where, for example, the founder of a company wishes to raise risk-bearing capital from subscribers but insists on maintaining voting control of the company. It is possible that the reputation and status of the company are sufficient to persuade investors to subscribe risk capital but forgo the status of voting shareholders. Non-voting ordinary shares are often called **a shares.** Normally though, it is not unreasonable for ordinary shareholders to expect voting rights as they are the ones bearing the risk associated with the company's ventures.

Ordinary shares are an example of *permanent* capital upon which *dividends* are declared, usually as a percentage of the nominal value of the share or in terms of pence per share. In the event of high company profits after tax, the dividend could be very high and conversely could be nothing! (Remember the earlier reference to Midland Bank.) This therefore is the *risk-bearing* capital, attracting variable dividends, with no security, and should the firm fail and be liquidated, the ordinary shareholder will be considered last of all for the return of any capital, and likely to receive little, if anything – a vivid illustration of the risk borne by shareholders.

Preference shares

Preference shares have a specified percentage dividend attached to them and usually rank preferentially for dividends ahead of the ordinary shares. Since their fixed dividend rate makes them very similar to loans, and since their dividends are declared and paid out of *after-tax* earnings, preference shares are not generally popular these days. Loan interest is met from pre-tax profit, and is thus tax deductible; this makes preference shares comparatively expensive. However, they are attractive to Pension Funds particularly, which are tax-exempt and which can therefore reclaim some of the tax deducted. Pension Funds require regular returns, known in advance, from their investments in order to meet their pension payments. Preference shares provide this characteristic and enable the Pension Fund to be a shareholder of the company, not just lenders, and thus to carry some influence with the management. Preference shares can also be found in several forms:

- **cumulative preference shares,** where the right to a dividend accumulates from year to year and cannot be *passed over,* i.e. avoided by the firm
- **convertible preference shares,** with the attached right to convert into other capital forms such as ordinary shares
- **redeemable preference shares,** which, as their name implies, may be redeemed (paid back) in the future.

Reserves or retained profits

It is worth repeating the point made about the flow of finance consideration in Part 1; for most business they are a major source of finance. They are **cumulative undistributed profits,** and thus they do not equate with cash. The cash dimension will already have been utilized to procure and replace the assets of the business. These reserves of course belong to the shareholders who have agreed not to draw them from the business and are often referred to as retained profits. It is usual to show the ordinary shares plus the preference shares, if any, added to the reserves, to comprise the **shareholders' interest** or the **shareholders' stake.** The use of retained profits, it can be argued, enables companies to avoid the discipline of going to the market for finance. In this way companies can avoid disclosing to investors their intentions for the use of funds, and the market does not have the opportunity to scrutinize management's performance and projections in quite such detail as a public issue of shares requires. Obviously the more profitable the organization the better for all concerned; shareholders fare better and management teams need to raise less external finance.

Loan shares and debentures

These are **composite loans,** in that the total amount of the loan, say £0.5 million, is denominated in blocks, each usually with a nominal value of £100. These loan certificates, sealed by the company, can be held by many investors, hence the term *composite loan.* The most common form is *debentures,* also known as *bonds.*

Loan stocks are usually issued for long or medium maturity and attract interest at a stated (fixed or variable) percentage rate. The interest is chargeable by the company in its profit and loss account *before* taxation liability is ascertained. This means that the interest is a tax-deductible charge by the company and the net of tax cost of the interest is lower than the stated coupon rate.

The loan stocks of many major companies are quoted on the Stock Market and investors, attracted by their relatively low-risk returns, may buy and sell blocks of loan stock.

The term **mortgage** is sometimes seen in connection with loan stocks, particularly debentures. It indicates that the debentures are secured by a mortgage against the firm's assets. In fact, in the UK, the term '**debenture**' usually refers to *secured* debt, whereas in the USA it signifies *unsecured!* This question of terminology is an interesting one, and where appropriate we use both UK and US terms. For example, the Americans use the word 'bond' interchangeably with the word 'loan'. However, stock in the UK refers to debts such as bonds and other loan stock, whereas in the USA it refers exclusively to shares or equity.

Loan stock can be issued in a form known as a **convertible.** Basically this is a hybrid of loan stock and equity. Originally issued as loan stock, a conversion may take place into equity after a determined period. Thus, an investor wishing to invest in a new and developing firm can have the complete security of fixed interest loan stock in the early years, but the benefit of converting into equity eventually. In turn, the company is not under pressure to meet high dividend levels initially, neither does it have to provide for the loan to be redeemed, since the debt is usually converted into ordinary shares. The exact terms of a conversion vary greatly from issue to issue, as does the extent of usage of convertibles. Convertibles are, however, an extremely flexible financing instrument. It is worth noting that conversion is at the option of the loan stock holder. The holder can choose when and if to switch into equity – it is not compulsory. Thus, if the share price falls, the investor has the protection of a fixed investor rate and promised redemption at nominal value.

Term loans

These are arranged by the organization from an individual institution such as a Pension Fund, insurance company, bank or other specialist agency. Due to their singular nature, such loans are relatively quick to arrange and they are without the issue costs encountered with a public loan stock issue. Security is almost always given, and the terms negotiated may include a gradual repayment of capital as well as interest. The actual trust deed between the borrower and the lender may, however, impose some stringent and restrictive conditions, particularly with regard to future lending.

Bank finance

The clearing banks are a major source of borrowed funds for organizations. In addition to term loans with specified repayment schedules and overall interest rates, the banks are providers of **overdraft** facilities. Here, the company can draw on its current account up to the limit of its negotiated facility, with interest charged on a daily basis on the amount overdrawn. Theoretically, the bank may *call in* the overdraft on demand, but unless the client organization experiences adverse results it is unlikely that the bank will do so. In many organizations overdraft becomes a sort of 'permanent' temporary source of finance.

Leasing

This is not really a source of funds. It is however a method of acquiring the use of assets, akin specifically to secured lending, hence its inclusion.

Operating lease

Many manufacturers and stockists of equipment will make products available on *short-term* contracts to users whose requirement is temporary or occasional. The user enters into an **operating lease** and agrees to a schedule of lease payments during the use of the item. This has the advantage to the user of allowing all of the lease charge to be charged as a tax-deductible business expense immediately, rather than receiving a series of tax-allowable depreciation charges over a number of years.

Finance lease

The producers of a large capital item may undertake to supply a piece of equipment to a user, but prefer to be paid straight away by the user. This enables Finance Houses, Merchant Banks, etc., to enter into the transactions as providers of finance. They will pay the producer of the equipment and permit the user to enter into a series of leasing payments. This is known as a **finance lease.**

Off balance sheet financing

Leasing arrangements have been particularly popular in the past for two reasons. First, neither the **asset** nor the **obligation** to pay the schedule of lease payments appeared in the actual content of the balance sheet, but merely as footnotes. This gave rise to the term **off balance sheet financing**. This gave the impression that the level of borrowing was lower than it was, a boon for concerns with a lot of existing loans. There were two further advantages to finance leases, both tax based. Organizations which had run out of depreciation tax allowances could not offset the cost of equipment against taxable profits. Instead, by leasing the equipment from institutions such as banks, as indicated earlier, the cost could be offset against taxable profits. This policy enabled the tax benefits of purchasing capital equipment to be maintained, thus reducing the net cost of the equipment to the user. Of course, the bank would remain, technically, the owner.

Appraisal of the organization's performance, at least superficially, could be enhanced by the existence of off balance sheet items. Most operating leases, like any rented items, are still effectively off balance sheet finance, albeit not usually of the size of finance leased items. More recently, changes in accountancy practice have required the lease organization to capitalize their financial leases and to show the liability thereof, as well as the asset, on their balance sheet. The depreciation allowances on the purchase of plant and machinery are no longer generous and the tax efficiency of *equipment leasing* versus *purchasing* has fallen.

Sale and leaseback

The philosophy of *using* an asset rather than *owning* it has led to a series of **sale and leaseback** arrangements as a means of raising finance from assets. Pension Funds especially are agreeable to committing relatively large amounts of finance into the purchase of, say, buildings and the leasing of them to the previous owner for use in return for a regular schedule of lease payments. This provides an opportunity for a company which is short of cash to benefit from the sale of, say, a valuable head office without having to move premises.

Government finance

Acting through one of the many agencies which it has initiated, the UK government makes grant finance available to organizations, usually conditionally, and in selected areas or industries.

The grants are administered through a variety of bodies. The government finances grants in order to encourage certain new industries or companies in areas of high social need. Almost always the discretionary grant-aid is tied to the provision of employment in selected areas.

The international aspect

Before leaving the consideration of the broad types of long-term finance, it should be noted that there is increasingly an *international* aspect to capital availability. As business becomes more international and as communications improve, the organizations have had to broaden the capital-raising activity to encompass capital markets overseas. Commercially, activities in, say, Portugal, could thus be financed by locally-generated Portuguese capital or by established markets in Eurocurrencies existing in Amsterdam and Paris as well as London. Access to Japanese investors may be obtained by making, say, a share issue in the Tokyo market. European Union initiatives towards European-wide markets have already led towards more use of the ECU (European Currency Unit). At the time of writing the debate on European monetary union (EMU) still rages.

Summary

In this chapter you have identified and considered the characteristics of a range of types of financing sources. Having completed the chapter you should now:

- be able to identify the major types of finance sources available to organizations
- be able to attribute characteristics to each type
- recognize the general considerations managers should take account of in opting for one or a blend of particular type(s) of finance.

Self-assessment questions

To assess your progress, attempt the self-assessment questions below. Remember that they represent both assessment and learning mechanisms. After these questions, proceed to Chapter 4 in which you will look closely at the managerial considerations within the blend of differing sources to produce a particular **capital structure.**

SAQ 3.1

Specify in broad terms the major categories of finance available to an organization.

SAQ 3.2

What factors should a management team consider when opting for a financing package?

SAQ 3.3

Detail the main advantages and disadvantages to an organization of raising finance via:

(i)   ordinary shares
(ii) cumulative preference shares
(iii) convertible debentures.

SAQ 3.4

On a recent radio broadcast, you heard a financial specialist say: 'It's essential for the manager raising finance to understand the mind of the investor. Uppermost in the mind of the investor will be the fact that any one investment will display a range of features which, according to the state of the market and the economy, will be attractive to the investor.'

Discuss what you think this statement means.

Further reading

Rutterford, J. and Carter, D. (eds), 1993. *Handbook of UK Corporate Finance*, 2nd edn, Butterworth

4 Capital gearing structures

Introduction

Now that you have an understanding of the various types of finance sources, and their characteristics, you can look more closely at their implications for the capital structure or **capital gearing** of an organization. An organization may well combine a number of sources of finance within its capital structure. To minimize costs – being financed from outside always has a cost – management teams must appreciate what effects different packages of finance will have on their intended operations and reported profits (or losses!). In addition, given the points made in Chapter 3 about ensuring that the financing and investment decisions are matched, the relationship between capital gearing and the use of finance in financing cost structures – **operational gearing** – is certainly worth more than a passing thought. Material in this chapter will lead to such considerations in Chapter 5. In this chapter you will consider questions which have significant implications. These are:

- What is the importance of capital structure?
- What influences management teams and finance specialists in choosing a particular structure?
- Is there some uniquely correct mixture of capital types which can be planned for and implemented?

Obviously, these are very difficult questions to answer unequivocally. Accordingly, given the difficulties and the continuing emergence of new views, it may be appropriate to err on the side of caution and opt for an examination of the more traditional views.

By the end of this chapter you will:

- understand the managerial and financial significance of differing capital structures through **capital gearing**
- be able to calculate the cost of equity capital, the cost of debt capital and the weighted average cost of capital
- be able to trace the impact upon profit generation of differing capital structures
- appreciate some of the differing views which exist regarding capital structures.

The significance of capital structures

Although you have already met the term **capital structure,** it would be as well to make sure that you really do understand what it means. The capital structure of an organization reflects the mix of different finance sources that have been called upon. These finance sources may be divided into two main categories: equity and debt. The divisions are detailed within the box.

Source	Category
Share capital	Equity
Reserves	Equity
Bank loans	Debt
Loan stock	Debt

Debt capital is finance which attracts a *fixed* charge – usually an interest or *coupon* payment – which is obligatory and *must* be paid. Debt capital is that provided to the company by *outsiders* or *lenders.*

Equity capital is funding provided by the shareholders or *members* of the company in the form of their subscribed capital plus the reserves which belong to them but have not been drawn out of the company. (It is worth noting the position of preference shares in that they essentially fall into both categories. On the one hand they represent funds invested by shareholders, but on the other hand they attract a fixed charge – a guaranteed dividend. This of course makes measuring the relationship between debt and equity difficult!)

The relationship between equity and debt within the capital structure is usually expressed through the **gearing** or **leverage** of the structure. Gearing, in other words, is the proportion of debt capital to total capital (although, just to confuse the issue, there are alternative – and acceptable – ways of expressing this relationship). An example of this is shown in the box.

	Company A £ million	Company B £ million
Ordinary shares	185	84
Reserves	29	22
Shareholders' interests	214	106
Loan stock	26	134
	£240	£240
Gearing ratio	$\frac{26}{240} = 10.83\%$	$\frac{134}{240} = 55.83\%$

Company A, at 10.83% gearing, is relatively *low* geared, whereas Company B, at 55.83%, is relatively *high* geared. Notice, however, that accepted high and low levels of gearing vary from industry to industry and from country to country. For example, Japanese companies and German companies have traditionally had higher gearing than their UK counterparts (with a consequence that loan funders such as banks often play an influential role in the management of the organization).

The alternative measures of capital gearing that are used include:

- debt capital: equity capital
- debt capital: total assets (as taken from the balance sheet) with debt capital to equity being the most common of the two.

In the example in the box, the capital structure has been valued on a **book value** basis, i.e. from the balance sheet values. It would be more theoretically correct to measure gearing on a **market value** basis, and indeed you will do so later. For now, however, the book value approach will serve.

Gearing and the costs of capital

Borrowing finance from anywhere or anyone – banks or shareholders or who/where else – has a cost. This cost is usually referred to as the **cost of capital.**

Where external loans are raised the obvious cost is the interest; do not pay it and you are in trouble. Thus **the cost of debt capital** assumes a managerial significance. Funds financed by shareholders also have a cost, albeit a less obvious cost. Shareholders will expect the organization to perform in such a way that enough profits are earned to provide them with an appropriate return – in comparison with what they could earn with their funds elsewhere – via a combination of annual dividends coming into their pockets and increases in the market price of their shares. It is this which, through a variety of mathematical techniques, governs the determination of the **cost of equity capital.**

Overall, **the total cost of capital** for an organization equates with the rate of return that must be earned which is just sufficient to maintain the value of the business. A return above this point, i.e. above the cost of capital, will result in an increase in the value of the business and, of course, vice versa.

Below, you will consider a general introduction to the determination of the cost of capital where the sources are both equity and debt. You will meet the idea of weighted average cost of capital. As you will see, the idea is, at least on the surface, logical. Bear in mind though, as in most matters financial, that there are differing views on how the cost of capital for an individual organization should be worked out. These views invariably place a greater emphasis on the views of the investor. Thus you should reserve judgement until you have considered cost of capital further in Part III of this book.

Cost of debt, cost of equity and WACC

Assume that the cost of an organization's equity capital has been calculated at 14% (do not worry how–yet!); debt capital is available at cost of 10%. At first glance, it would appear that the combined cost of capital is 12% comprising (14% + 10%) divided by 2. In fact it is not. There are two additional factors to be considered, the first of which you met in Chapter 2 when establishing the impact on profits of raising additional finance from shareholders and/or loan providers.

First, you will recall the fact that the cost of debt, as with bank loan interest for example, is a tax-deductible expense. The debt cost is obviously lower than the equity cost. Indeed, given the tax position, it is even lower still. This is because there is only a net cost to the organization after allowing for a reduction in tax. Assuming tax at 30%, the real cost to the organization is 30% lower than 10%, i.e. 7%.

The second factor is the relative weightings of the proportions of each type of capital. If the total capital employed is, say, £1 million, comprising £800,000 equity capital and £200,000 debt capital, the cost of capital calculation must reflect a **weighted average cost of capital – WACC**. The calculation is:

£800,000	× 12%	= £96,000
£200,000	× 7%	= £14,000
£1 million		£110,000 = WACC of 11%
		(being £110,000 divided by £1 million × 100%)

Note that, as per an earlier comment, the balance sheet value of capital is used. If the market value is readily ascertainable and, more importantly, is reliable, then those market values of, say, shares and any debentures/bonds may be substituted into the calculation above. Remember, too, the earlier comment about other views with regard to the determination of cost of capital.

Capital gearing and the effect on profits

Although management teams are obviously interested in the levels of profit achieved, so are shareholders. Shareholders actually own all the profits that are left after interest has been paid to loan providers and tax on profits deducted. Normally this amount left – **earnings attributable to ordinary shareholders** or **EATOS** – is divided by the number of shares to obtain the **earnings per share** or **EPS;** as far as the shareholder is concerned, the higher the better (all other matters being equal, of course!).

The point in the box about any interest payable on debt capital being a tax-deductible expense will have two effects:

- to reduce the amount of reported profit
- to reduce the amount of tax.

On the one hand we have interest reducing profit and thus potentially reducing EPS. On the other we see tax falling and thus potentially increasing EPS. Obviously an appropriate capital structure will need to be adopted if everybody is to be kept happy. This is quantified below.

Gearing effects quantified

Take an example where a company, Dilemma Plc, is considering two alternative levels of gearing (calculated as debt: capital employed), as shown in the table:

	Alternative 1 Nil geared	**Alternative** 2 50% geared
Dilemma Plc: Balance sheet extract	£'000	£'000
£1 ordinary shares	4,000	2,000
12% loan stock	–	2,000
	4,000	4 000
Profit statement extract		
Profit before interest and tax, 20% on capital	800	800
Interest payable	–	240
Profit	800	560
Tax at say 25%	200	140
Profit after tax	600	420
Earnings per share	£600= 15p 4,000 shares	£420 = 21p 2,000 shares

Look carefully at what has happened in the table. The company plans to earn 20% return on its capital employed (this being £800 over £4,000 × 100%). However, note the effect of the two capital structures upon the EPS.

Restating the 50% geared alternative produces:

	Equity £'000	*Debt* £'000
£1 ordinary shares	2,000	–
12% loan stock	—	2,000
	2,000	2,000
Extra profit before interest and tax, 20% on capital	400	400
Interest payable	—	240
	400	160
Tax at say 25%	100	40
Extra profit after tax	300	120
Extra earnings per share	$\dfrac{300}{2{,}000\ shares} = 13p$	$\dfrac{120}{2{,}000\ shares} = 5.2p$

The debt capital subscribers have made their capital available to the company in return for an interest payment of 12%. The company have used these funds in generating a return of 20% before tax. The difference between the two is called the **incremental return**, in this case 8%.

Incremental return

The **incremental return** (20%–12%) of 8% passed to the ordinary shareholders and net of tax 8% (1–0.25) = 6%, supplements their EPS. So long as the debt capital is used to generate a return *in excess* of the after-tax cost of that debt, then the shareholders will gain. Hence the term *gearing* or *leverage:* the capital structure *gears up* the basic EPS once the after-tax cost of the debt capital has been covered.

But caution is required. The converse is also true. The capital structure will *gear down* the EPS if earnings are insufficient to cover the after-tax cost of the debt.

For example, suppose Dilemma Plc earned a return on its capital of only 5%. The table would then change to show the following details.

	Alternative 1 *Nil geared* £'000	**Alternative 2** *50% geared* £'000
Dilemma Plc: Balance sheet extract		
£1 ordinary shares	4,000	2,000
12% loan stock	—	2,000
	4,000	4,000
Profit statement extract		
Profit before interest and tax 5% on capital	200	200
Interest	—	240
Profit (loss) before tax	200	(40)
Tax say 25%	50	—
Profit after tax	150	(40)
Earnings per share	$\dfrac{£65}{2{,}000\ shares} = 3.25p$	$\dfrac{£(20)}{1{,}000\ shares} = (2p)$

Which EPS is preferable now? And which capital structure? In this table note that the 12% interest on the debt borrowed *has to be paid*, it is obligatory. To not make or *pass* the interest payment would almost certainly cause the debt investors to take action against the company, with insolvency a likely outcome.

A return of only 5% on capital results in a loss to the shareholders of 2p per share for *they* pay the interest. It is the pre-emptive nature of the interest payment which creates financial risk for the ordinary shareholders, notwithstanding the enhancement of EPS that gearing promises. Where a company's profit levels are volatile over time, with the risk of low or negative profits, then high levels of gearing should not be built into the capital structure.

Figure 4.1 shows representations of the effects of capital structure upon earnings per share. American writers use the term '**leverage**' and in Figure 4.1(a) the appropriateness of the term is illustrated. The overall length of the lever is the total capital employed with the fulcrum point being at the mix of equity and debt. With profit before interest and tax being applied to one end of the lever, an opposite force (EPS) is created at the other end.

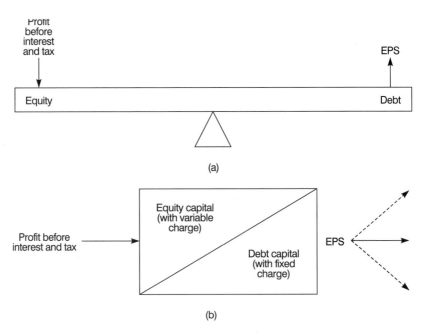

Figure 4.1 (a) The impact of capital structure leverage upon EPS; (b) the inter-relationship of capital structure and EPS

In Figure 4.1(b) we have an imaginary *gearbox* with a *driving gear* (**equity voting capital**) and a *driver gear* (**debt capital**). Profit before interest and tax is fed into the gearbox and EPS power produced from it.

In both cases the rate at which profit is converted into EPS will be a function of the equity/debt proportions and of the corporation tax rate. You have already seen that volatility of profits relative to gearing will induce financial risk, and that increased levels of gearing were likely to bring demands for higher coupon rates from debt capital investors. Return to Dilemma Plc, which had a capital employed of £4 million. Assume that the company wishes to carry up to 60% gearing. To simplify matters, assume also that the company can raise debt capital in discrete blocks of £400,000. Finally, assume that the cost of the debt increases at the rate shown in column 4 of Table 4.1 in response to the increases in gearing and perceived greater risk in the eyes of the debt capital providers (this is an assumption that you will explore further shortly, but it holds for now).

Table 4.1 Measuring the impact of capital gearing from EPS

Equity	Debt	Gearing	Cost of debt	profit	Interest	Profit before tax	Tax (25%)	Profit after tax	EPS
£'000	£'000	%	%	£'000	£'000	£'000	£'000	£'000	p
4,000	–	–	–	800	–	800	200	600	15.0
3,600	400	10	8.0	800	32	768	192	556	15.4
3,200	800	20	8.5	800	68	732	183	549	17.2
2,800	1,200	30	9.0	800	108	692	173	519	18.5
2,400	1,600	40	10.0	800	160	640	160	480	20.0
2,000	2,000	50	12.0	800	240	560	140	420	21.0
1,600	2,400	60	15.0	800	360	440	110	330	20.6
1,200	2,800	70	18.0	800	504	296	74	222	18.5

The appropriate EPS figures stemming from the additional information contained in the table are graphed in Figure 4.2. From this figure you can see that the EPS is maximized at 50% gearing, and begins to decline thereafter owing to the higher interest rates demanded by the providers of debt capital in response to the excessive gearing levels.

Further considerations of the cost of capital

In the first cost of capital calculation in this chapter, it was taken that the cost of equity capital was 14% and the gross cost of debt capital 10%. Here you take a closer look at how such costs may be determined. In addition, given the significance of dividend to equity capital providers, you also look at the importance of a considered managerial approach to setting a dividend policy.

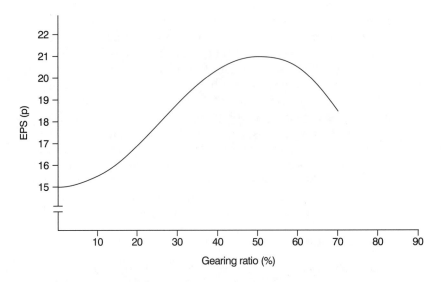

Figure 4.2 EPS with different gearing ratios (see also Table 4.1)

Determining the cost of equity capital

This determination reflects a set of assumptions developed and applied within two approaches which have come to be known as the **Dividend Valuation Model** and the **Gordon Growth Model.** The first model assumes that the market value of shares is directly related to expected future dividends on those shares, with such dividends remaining constant. The second model builds on this, but assumes that investors expect to see dividends grow. Gordon developed a model which showed that the expected return on equity by an investor, and thus the cost of capital to the organization, reflects a combination of dividend yield from the investment and its expected growth. Unlike the first WACC calculation earlier, both models use current market values of capital. For the dividend valuation model it is a relatively simple calculation, comprising:

$$\text{Cost of capital} = \frac{\text{Constant dividend per annum}}{\text{Market value of share}}$$

For the growth model it is adapted to:

$$\frac{\text{The dividend payment one period from now}}{\text{The current value of a share}}$$

with the result added to an expected growth rate of dividends.

The expected growth rate of dividends is usually an average and is normally worked out in one of two ways:

- by calculating the average past growth rate and basing future growth rate on that figure
- by multiplying the average proportion of shareholders' earnings retained each year by the average rate of return the organization earns on its assets.

Calculating the cost of equity capital
Basic Dividend Valuation Model
From the above, with a current share price ex-div of 200p and a most recent dividend payment of 10 p per share, the calculation is:

$$\frac{10p}{200p} \times 100\% = 5\%$$

Gordon's growth model
Assuming the following additional information:

- in recent years, average growth of earnings and dividends has been 10%
- average retention of earnings has been 50%
- normally, a 20% rate of return on assets is achieved, the formula is applied thus:

Return on equity/cost of equity capital
The dividend payment one period from now = 10p × (1 + 0.1)
divided by
the current value of a share = 200p
with the result added to an expected growth rate of dividends = 10% or 0.1
Thus 10(1 + 0.1) divided by 200 = 0.055 + 0.1 = 0.155 or 15.5%
(In this case, by multiplying the average proportion of shareholders' earnings retained each year (50%) by the average rate of return the organization earns on its assets (20%) – the average growth rate still works out at 10%.

Determining the cost of debt capital

As with the equity cost calculation above, the market value of the debt is used in order to reflect the state of reality of the financing and investment world. The calculation produces the current market rate of interest investors require for investing in an organization via debt capital. As with the required rate of equity return equalling the cost of equity capital, so the required rate of debt return equals the cost of debt capital. As with equity capital, it is argued that a more realistic return/cost is obtained using market value of debt. With debentures and bonds, either pre-agreed redemption values or current market values may be used. For fixed interest bank loans it is possible to apply a retail price index based adjustment to the capital sum outstanding. There are two types of debt capital: irredeemable (e.g. example non-redeemable preference shares or a particular form of bond) and reedeemable (e.g. bank loans and bonds/debentures). Consequently there are two approaches to calculating the cost of debt capital.

Calculating the cost of debt capital
Assume the following in relation to an organization:
  Outstanding debt bears 10% per £100 nominal value block
  Debt is non-redeemable
  Current market value is £90 per £100 block
  Tax is currently 25%
Irredeemable debt
The cost of debt capital is relatively easy to determine in such a case. It is:

$$\frac{\text{The coupon in monetary terms (i.e. the interest)}}{\text{The market/purchase price}} \times 100\%$$

Using the details above this becomes:

$$\frac{£10}{£90} \times 100\% = 11.1\%$$

Reedeemable debt
This is harder to calculate as it involves forecasting into the future and the necessity to take account of a need to discount future values back to the present. As a consequence, the calculation involves the use of discount tables or knowledge of discounting using a calculator. In either case, a process of trial and error must be used. Given that the cost of the debt if irredeemable is 11.1%, this other cost will not be too far way. Thus the discounts of 11% and 12% can be used to start matters.

In this case assume that the debt is redeemable at par (the nominal value) after 5 years.

Year		Cash Flow	Discount factor 12%	PV	Discount factor 11%	PV
0	Market value	(90)	1.00	(90)	1.00	(90)
1–5	Interest	10 pa	3.6048	36.05	3.6959	36.96
5	Capital repayment	100	0.5674	56.74	0.5935	59.35
				+2.79		+6.31

Thus the correct discount rate, i.e. the cost of capital, must also be above 12%. Applying 13%, the following results:

Year		Cash flow	Discount factor 13%	PV
0	Market value	(90)	1.00	(90)
1–5	Interest	10 pa	3.5172	35.17
5	Capital repayment	100	0.5428	<u>54.28</u>
				(0-55)

The rate must thus be between 12% and 13%. It is now confirmed as being:

$$12 + \frac{2.79}{2.79 - -0.55} \times 1 = 12.84\%$$

The calculations above may then be used in determining the WACC, as you saw earlier. It is important to note that implicit in these calculations is the premise that the value of the organization increases or decreases according to the capital structure at any one time. This therefore has implications for the cost of capital used in the calculations you will be making in Part III. This is particularly so with the idea of the Capital Asset Pricing Model you will meet in that part of the book. In addition, work by Modigliani and Miller needs to be taken account of.

Modigliani and Miller – the arbitrage theory

In a series of significant research publications since 1958, either jointly or individually, Modigliani and/or Miller (M. & M.) have shown, albeit under sets of restricted assumptions the following:

- gearing has no effect on either the cost of capital or the value of the firm
- it is the total income generated by the organization which is of significance to investors, rather than the way in which the income is divided between providers of finance
- the market value of the organization is independent of its capital structure
- the expected rate of equity return (and thus cost of equity capital) increases linearly with changes in the gearing ratio.

Their research implies that any two organizations with the same cash flows and risks should have the same value. By moving towards such an equilibrium, both may be said to be involved in an **arbitrage** activity. The example in the box, disregarding taxation, illustrates this.

	Ungeared plc	Geared plc
Cost of equity capital, say	20%	22%
	£	£
Operating profits (assume to be constant)	100,000	100,000
less Debt interest, say	–	10,000
Net profit before and after tax (EATOS)	100,000	90,000
Market value of equity, say	500,000	420,000
Market value of debt, say	–	100,000
Market value of company,	500,000	520,000
WACC	20%	17.31%
Gearing ratio, based on market values	nil	23.81%

M. & M. argue that the differing market values would disappear relatively quickly as investors recognize that more could be obtained for less in Ungeared plc. Thus shares would be sold in Geared plc to buy shares in Ungeared plc. This would result in the share price of the latter rising and the share price of the former rising, with consequential changes in cost of capitals.

Taxation footnotes

M. & M. recognize that corporation tax reduces the cost of debt capital and thus the WACC. This does result in an increase in the value of the firm. In addition, Miller recognizes the role played by personal taxation where individuals receive dividends and thus might expect some form of compensation for the tax paid.

Dividend policy

Given the significance of dividend payments in, for example, Gordon's Growth Model earlier, and in organizational life in general, management teams over a long period have sought to set a dividend policy which is attractive to existing and prospective shareholders. This is often achieved by maintaining a balance between the amount of shareholders' earnings distributed as dividends and the amount retained and reinvested. This reflects the premise that it is always the best policy to declare as high a dividend as possible. If by so doing another very profitable project is foregone, some shareholders might argue that a low or zero dividend would have been preferable.

The research contribution

In the early days of significant financial management research, it was held that shareholders liked dividend payments now as opposed to in the future, and that dividends were a mechanism for increasing shareholder wealth. M. & M., however, continued their research and showed that dividends were neutral in their effect. Even more confusingly, research by others showed that the impact of tax on dividends did no more than reduce shareholder wealth!

Despite conflicting research, managers have managed to find the basis of a dividend policy which works for many organizations. Sensible dividend policies would seem to ensure that dividend payments are smoothed from year to year, with increases or decreases in profits being reflected only gradually. Large changes may be perceived by the capital markets as reflecting uncertainty and lead to volatile changes in share prices. Of course, in the background, managers will be ensuring that the organization's liquidity position is not adversely affected and that the tax position is fully taken account of.

Management teams will often try to avoid large increases in dividends, as the market may interpret this as an optimistic sign. Conversely dividend cuts could indicate pessimism about future profit levels. Either could lead to fluctuations in share price, normally unwelcome by managers (and indeed by many investors who themselves need to be able to plan with as much certainty as possible in an already very uncertain world).

Other variables within the finance decision

Before leaving capital gearing, it is important to stress the background matters which managers will be taking account of in opting for a particular structure. There are, in addition to EPS and weighted cost of capital, other aspects which also have to be considered when arriving at the selected finance package. These aspects are:

- cash flow
- security or collateral
- attitudes
- control
- operational stability
- external capital factors.

Cash flow

Interest, dividends and taxation have to be physically paid out in cash and, while trading operations may generate accounting profits, cash flow may not necessarily be available to meet the payment requirements particularly if credit control is weak and debtors do not pay up. In planning the capital structure, due regard for its eventual cash consumption implications is important.

Security or collateral

Only organizations with sufficient assets of suitable type can raise secured debt capital and so, for example, service concerns in rented accommodation and with small asset bases are inevitably low geared. Equally, companies with large holdings of land and buildings available for security can often be highly geared.

Using assets as security for debt capital will inevitably lead to restrictions upon the use of the asset being imposed by the lender. A mortgaged building, for example, cannot be sold and leased back, and perhaps not altered or sublet, without the mortgage holder's permission.

Attitudes

Attitudes towards borrowing are still very *traditional* in the UK and the ethics of 'neither a *borrower* nor a *lender* be' still have some weight. The general levels of gearing in UK industry are found to be lower than in the USA and elsewhere in Europe.

Control

Equity capital issues result in more voting capital being made available which might disturb the existing status quo. Allowing power blocks or even just 'cliques' to obtain voting control may be strongly opposed by the existing ownership.

Operational stability

We have seen that the major aspect of increased gearing is that it may leave the organization very vulnerable to fluctuations in sales and profitability because of the pre-emptive nature of interest payments and fixed costs. Where such fluctuations are possible, high gearing will normally be avoided.

External capital factors

These factors include external capital availability and the cost relative to the firm's needs for replacement and expansion. Shortages in the market place may prompt a retention decision rather than a dividend payout, thus providing internally generated capital. Similarly, high-cost capital in the market place may prompt the use of internal funding.

Summary

In this chapter you have examined the nature, purpose, determination and significance of the capital gearing structure of an organization. In addition you have considered the relationship between differing capital structures and levels of profit and returns to shareholders. Having completed this chapter you should now:

- understand the managerial and financial significance of differing capital structures through **capital gearing**
- be able to calculate the cost of equity capital, the cost of debt capital and the weighted average cost of capital
- be able to trace the impact upon profit generation of differing capital structures
- understand the role played by shareholders' interests in opting for a capital structure
- appreciate some of the differing views which exist regarding capital structures.

Self-assessment questions

To assess your own progress, attempt the self-assessment questions below. Remember that they represent both assessment and learning mechanisms. After these questions, proceed to Chapter 5 where you will look at a particular aspect of the matching (or mismatching!) of the financing and investment decisions in relation to fixed and variable cost structures – operational gearing.

SAQ 4.1

An organization has always operated a gearing ratio of 25%. What do you understand by this? If its appropriateness were challenged, what arguments would you use in its defence?

SAQ 4.2

A finance researcher at a leading business school seminar recently stated that she had evidence to show that the cost of capital at extreme levels of gearing is high. What are the implications of this with regard to the desirability, or otherwise, of an optimum gearing ratio?

SAQ 4.3

A company in which a relative is a shareholder has consistently paid a dividend equal to 10% of the cumulative profits of the previous 3 years. Your relative, knowing you are reading this book, has asked you to comment on the pros and cons of such a policy.

SAQ 4.4

Assume the following for an organization:

Issued share capital – 20 million shares with £1 nominal value each
Market value of 200 pence per share, ex-div
Debt capital of £10 million, nominal value in £100 blocks
Debt coupon is 10%
Current market value of debt is £95
Taxation is at 25%

Calculate the WACC.

Further reading

Gordon, M.J., 1959. Dividends, earnings and stock prices, *Review of Economics and Statistics* (May)

Gordon, M.J. and Gould, L.I., 1978. The cost of equity capital: a reconsideration, *Journal of Finance* (June)

Lanser, H.P., 1983. Valuation, gains from leverage and the weighted average cost of capital as a cut off rate, *Engineering*

5 Operational gearing structures

Introduction

In this (shorter) chapter you will examine another form of gearing. Not capital gearing but **operational gearing.** This is the relationship between investment of financing in fixed costs and in variable costs. It links directly with capital gearing in that it represents the degree to which the type of financing package of an organization matches its types of investment. You saw an earlier reference to the need for there to be a match between the financing and investment decisions, and here you will explore its significance. In this chapter you will consider:

- What is the significance of operational gearing?
- What influences management teams and finance specialists in opting for a particular structure?
- What are the financial implications and consequences of the structure selected?

As with the questions posed at the start of Chapter 4 in relation to capital gearing, these are not always easy to answer, given the differing views of differing management teams, but there are general principles which can be looked at, with lessons drawn therefrom. By the end of this chapter you will:

- understand the managerial and financial significance of differing **operational gearing structures**
- be able to assess the financial consequences of opting for a particular structure
- link operational gearing with capital gearing.

Understanding operational gearing

Just as the term capital gearing represents the relationship between two types of finance, so the term **operational gearing** represents a relationship, but between two types of investment in costs: *fixed* and *variable*. It is sensible for a management team to ensure that long-term finance is used only to finance longer-term costs of the organization and not short-term ones. To understand the significance of this, it is important to appreciate the relationship between the two main categories of costs, and its impact upon reported profits (and thus organizational and shareholder value).

The relationship between costs

You saw in Figure 4. l(b) that, in a sense, *profit is* fed into a *capital gearbox*, with the output being EPS. The actual EPS output, as you saw, then depends upon:

- the level of operating profit fed in
- the gearing of the capital structure
- the cost of debt
- the tax rate.

As then shown in Table 4.1 and Figure 4.2, when the gearing level increases, an increase in operating profit will be followed by a magnified increase in EPS up to the point where high levels of gearing and consequent high debt costs cause EPS to decline. These relationships in the area of capital structure have a parallel in the area of what might be termed **operational gearing structure.**

An organization will have a certain **operating cost structure.** For simplicity, it is usual to assume that each total cost structure is capable of exact resolution into *variable* operating costs – costs which vary with activity – and *fixed* operating costs – those which remain the same regardless of changes in activity (albeit often within a relevant range, on a stepped basis).

Figure 5.1 is a diagrammatic representation of inputs of *sales* activity to the operating gearbox and a resulting output of *profit* before interest and tax (PBIT). The exact rate of output of *profit* relative to the input of sales will be a function of the operating cost gearing structure. This can be expressed as **operational gearing,** with fixed costs being related to the total costs. The significance is that the higher the proportion of fixed costs to total costs, the greater the level of sales required to make sure that these fixed costs are covered; the lower the proportion, the lower the required level of sales. In addition, of course, in respect of each of these cases, the later or the sooner the organization achieves a profit status.

An increase in sales will bring about a magnified increase in profit relative to the operating cost gearing structure, assuming that the volume of activity is sufficient first to cover the fixed costs. (This last point is identical to the necessity to cover the interest charges in the capital situation.)

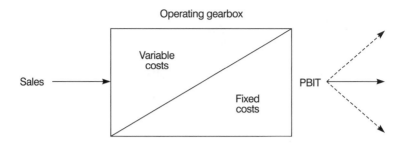

Figure 5.1 Effects of operational gearing

Operational gearing quantified

This relationship may be illustrated thus. Return to the example of Dilemma Plc on page 65 in Chapter 4 and take the 50% level of capital gearing. An extract from the figures relative to profit shows:

	£'000
Operating profit before interest and tax (PBIT) 20% return of capital	800
Interest payable	240
Profit before tax (PBT)	560
Tax at say 25°O	140
Profit after tax (PAT)	420

The EPS at this level was 21p. If fixed costs have already been covered, it is reasonable to expect a (higher) disproportionate increase in EPS in light of this. Thus if it is assumed for the purposes of illustration that the only fixed cost in Dilemma Plc is the debt interest, a measure of the likely increase in EPS in light of increasing profits may be determined.

One way to measure the effect of changing profits, based on the 50% capital gearing situation selected, is:

$$\frac{PBIT}{PBT} = \frac{£800,000}{£560,000} = 1.4286 \text{ times}$$

This factor measures that rate of change in EPS relative to a given change in PBIT. Thus, at 50% gearing level, an increase in PBIT of, say, £80,000 on the existing £800,000 (a 10% increase) would result in a (10% × 1.428) 14.28% increase in EPS. You can confirm this by checking the figures shown next.

	£'000
PBIT	880
Interest	240
PBT	640
Tax at say 25%	160
PAT	480

Revised EPS $= \dfrac{480}{2,000 \text{ shares}} = 24.0\text{p}$

Previous EPS $= 21\text{p}$

Increase in EPS $= 3\text{p}$

$\dfrac{3}{21} \times 100 = 14.28\%$ increase

Knowing the degree of operational gearing to be 1.428 at 50% gearing, you can project the EPS for any percentage change in profit before interest and tax, provided that fixed costs have already been equalled or exceeded, where the breakeven level – in this case £140,000 and equivalent to the pre-emptive interest payment – has been achieved.

The situation above, using Dilemma Plc, assumes that debt interest is the only fixed cost. In reality there are likely to be many other types and categories of fixed costs. The approach using such a more realistic scenario is detailed in the box.

Calculations for variable and fixed cost example

Assume that the £800,000 profit before interest and tax had arisen in Dilemma Plc as shown below:

	£'000
Sales	3,600
less Variable costs (33.3% sales)	1,200
Contribution (C)	2,400
less Fixed cost (F)	1,600
Profit before interest and tax (PBIT)	800

From the above, the operational gearing may be determined:

	£'000
Variable cost	1,200
Fixed cost	1,600
Total cost	2,800

i.e. $\dfrac{1,600}{2,800} \times \dfrac{100}{1}$

$= 57.143\%$

The contribution (C) may be related to PBIT so:

$\dfrac{C}{\text{PBIT}} = \dfrac{2,400}{800}$

$= 3$ times

This factor measures the rate of change in PBIT relative to a change in the level of sales, given the level of operational gearing and assuming that C exceeds F, the fixed costs.

If sales in Dilemma Plc increase by 6⅔% then the PBIT will increase by 20%, this being (3 × 6⅔%). You can check this as follows:

		£ 000
	Revised sales	3,840
	less Variable costs (33.3% sales)	1,280
	Contribution	2,560
	less Fixed costs (remain the same)	1,600
	PBIT	960
	Revised PBIT	960
	Previous PBIT	800
	Increase in PBIT	160

$$= \frac{160}{800} \times 100$$

$$= 20\% \text{ increase}$$

Knowing the degree of operating gearing to be 3, at 57.143% gearing it is possible to project the PBIT for any percentage change in sales, providing of course the breakeven level of contribution equal to the pre-emptive fixed cost has been achieved.

Mixing operational and capital gearing

Taking the calculations made earlier, in which:

- the ingredients of both capital gearing and operational gearing were identified, and
- the relationships between the ingredients within each of the two gearing structures were illustrated

it is not unreasonable to assume that the two gearing structures have an effect upon each other, given that they exist within the same organization.

The amalgamation

The operational gearing, based on variable and fixed costs, will help to determine the operating profit before interest and tax. It is this profit which is fed into the capital gearbox in Figure 4.l(b). Based on the calculations made earlier for Dilemma Plc, Figure 5.2 illustrates diagrammatically the relationship between the two figures.

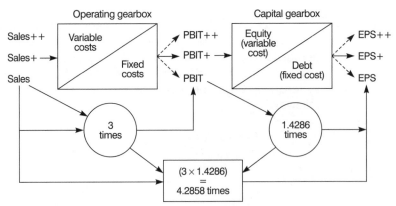

Figure 5.2 The interrelationship of operating gearing and capital gearing (using the Dilemma Plc example figures for illustration)

The diagram quantified

The operating gearbox, with its factor of three times conversion of percentage increases in sales into percentage increases in PBIT, has been linked to the capital gearbox with its factor of 1.4286 times conversion of percentage increases in PBIT into percentage increases in EPS. The product of these two conversion factors (3 × 1.4286 = 4.2858) can be used to relate percentage changes in sales and EPS.

For completeness, the two rates of change relating to Dilemma Plc may be verified:

(Sales increase × Joint gearing factor) = Increase in EPS
(6.67% × 4.2858) = 28.57% increase in EPS

This increase is shown more fully in the following:

	£'000
Sales	3,840 being 6⅔% increase
less Variable costs (33.3% sales)	1,280
Contribution	2,560
less Fixed costs	1,600
PBIT	960
Interest	240
PBT	720
Tax at say 25%	180
Profit after tax	540

Present EPS   £540/2,000 = 27.0p
Previous EPS   = 18.2p
Increase to EPS   = 5.2p
$$= \frac{5.2p}{18.2} \times \frac{100}{1}$$
= 28.57% increase in EPS
which equals 6⅔% × the gearing factor of 4.2858 times

Operational and capital gearing in perspective

There are certain simplifications built into this analysis which should lead to a cautious use of the model relating to operating and capital gearing. For example, very few concerns have one single product or service, their fixed/variable cost structure reflecting an amalgam of the sales mix of a range of products or services.

This process links the financing decision and the investment decision areas very strongly. There will however, need to be some level of 'trade-off' between operating and capital gearing in order to achieve the optimum conversion of sales to EPS. As a manager contemplating the introduction of, say, new advanced technology equipment, you can appreciate that the introduction of such equipment may alter the company's fixed/variable cost structure – its operational gearing – and, further, if this investment is not appropriately financed, then the optimum conversion of sales to EPS can be missed. Even less desirable is the possible mismatch of the two sections of gearing so that a neutralizing effect results. Operational managers must be aware that their involvement in investment decision-making has implication for the financing decision simultaneously.

Summary

In this chapter you have considered the nature and significance of operational gearing – the relationship between fixed and variable costs as part of the cost structure of an organization. Having completed this chapter you should now:

- understand the managerial and financial significance of differing cost-operating structures through operational gearing
- be able to calculate the operational gearing ratio
- be able to trace the impact upon profit generation of differing operational capital structures
- understand the interrelationships between capital and operational gearing structures, particularly in relation to profits, EPS and shareholder value.

Self-assessment questions

To assess your own progress, attempt the self-assessment questions below. Remember that they represent both assessment and learning mechanisms. If you have the opportunity, follow up on some if not all of the Further reading references cited below. Thereafter, proceed to Part III of the book.

SAQ 5.1

> Explain in general terms the significance of an organization having a high fixed costs to total costs ratio. More specifically, what do you imagine is its significance in time of recession?

SAQ 5.2

> Explain how, illustrating with your own figures, operational gearing and capital gearing interrelate. Show how, in given circumstances, they might cancel each other out.

Further reading

Rybczynski, T., 1989. Corporate restructuring, *National Westminster Bank Quarterly Review* (August)

Sizer, J. and Coulhurst, N., 1984. A Casebook of British Management Accounting, Institute of Chartered Accountants in England and Wales

Miller, M.H. and Modigliani, F., 1961. Dividend policy, growth and the valuation of shares, *Journal of Business* (October)

Miller, M.H. and Modigliani, F., 1958. The cost of capital, corporate finance and the theory of investment, *American Economic Review*, reprinted in *Archer and D'Ambrosio* (1983)

Part III The Investment Decision

6 Investing in the future

Introduction

The success of any organization, whether it be measured in terms of levels of profits, value for money or whatever, is inextricably linked to the success of management teams in investing scarce resources in the assets, be they human or otherwise, used in activities. When management teams make a decision about investing funds in activity areas they are said to be making, not surprisingly, an *investment decision.*

As part of the flow of finance you met in Part I, the investment decision is one of a number of important interlocking decisions which any organization must make and, as you will see, make correctly, if long-term survival (let alone success) is to be achieved. Although making the right investment decision is not a sufficient condition for survival or success, it most certainly is a necessary one. Successful investment decisions provide the basis for future solvency and profitability. As such, the managerial significance of the investment decision is high indeed.

By the end of this chapter you will:

- understand why managers should be concerned about longer term investment appraisal
- recognize the significance of the factors to be considered in managing investment appraisal decisions
- be aware of the concern for shorter term, ad hoc decisions, particularly of a cost-saving/profit-enhancement nature.

Looking to the future

Managers will understandably be concerned, after any investment decision, with a review of how matters have fared post-decision. But in considering the decision to be reviewed, managers, perhaps rather obviously, also need to be concerned with the future – at the time the decision is being made. What is important is to establish that the future can be, and is, divided into the short term – figuratively speaking today and tomorrow – and the long term – beyond tomorrow. In financial terms the short term is usually viewed as being within the next year, whereas the longer term is any period longer than a year. (It is important to recognize that this financial definition may differ from an organization's planning and strategy cycle; some concerns may view long-term planning as being 6 months, whereas others might view short-term plans as being up to 3 years.)

Making a long-term investment decision is commonly termed *capital budgeting* by financial specialists. The short-term investment decision is usually concerned with the *management of working capital*, which you will consider in Part IV. To set the scene for both this part and Part IV, a consideration of some of the general features and characteristics of investment decisions will help to place matters in context.

Perspectives of the future

Any decisions concerned with the future will have certain common features. These include:

- the objective(s) or aim(s) articulating the decision-maker's (i.e. the investor's) own preferences
- beliefs and expectations about what the future holds both generally and in relation to the range of choices open to the decision-maker.

Although these features can never be prescribed against (nor indeed perhaps should), the establishment of a framework or model to help with the processing of decision-making is likely to help. Even though organizations can and do develop often quite sophisticated models for investment decision-making, you should not be surprised if the conclusions generated by those models both differ from organization to organization and are not heeded. This lack of surprise stems from the fact that:

- investment decisions are usually made in a particular context with different individuals holding:
  (a) vested interests in the outcomes
  (b) different beliefs about the costs and benefits of alternative options
- as management rewards are often based upon performance measures (such as profitability or sales turnover), individual managers may wish to make decisions on bases which are different from those which will be best for the organization as a whole
- many, particularly longer term, investment decisions require investment now but with benefits and returns only appearing at some stage in the future; consequently managers make decisions which look good now but are, in fact, suboptimal.

Model criteria

To minimize these effects, most organizations insist on two important elements being present if the investment decision is to be good. These are that:

- a realistic assessment about the possible outcomes and the risks attached to those outcomes are made
- a formal decision-making framework is developed which allows predicted outcomes to be assessed.

It is worth remembering, however, that a framework is really only a model and that models have limitations. A model is really only an abstraction of beliefs about reality, and decision-making models in particular really only abstract those elements that individual managers perceive to be important. It is therefore important to select a model which facilitates the quantification of the effect of decisions. It is also important to recognize two consequential features. The first is that different managers may arrive at differing conclusions despite applying the same decision-making model. The second is that as the decisions are about the future, even the application of the most rigorous model can never guarantee an outcome: reality and forecasts rarely coincide.

Forecasting: profit or cash based?

In forecasting to assess the impact of following one particular course of action as opposed to another, it might seem appropriate to look for outcomes which show appropriate levels of profits. Profit, however, is a variable in the sense that it is subject to the interpretation by management teams of what, under accounting convention, is deemed to be true and fair. This was illustrated in Chapter 2. What is much less variable is cash. As a consequence, financial decision-making should be, and indeed usually is, concerned with establishing the future cash flows to arise as a result of an investment decision. This point is not only important because it is cash which determines the survival of an organization. It is important because it links the long-term decision to the management of working capital. As you discover later, high levels of profits can be generated but only effective working capital management will help to convert them into hard cash. Thus for the investment decision, be it of a longer term focus, for ad hoc decision-making or working capital management, cash flow is of the essence.

In the rest of this chapter you will consider the essentials of two major types of decision: the long-term capital investment decision and the cost-saving profit-enhancement decision. You may be relieved to discover that the inevitable numerical quantification is reserved for Chapters 7 and 8.

Understanding the framework for the capital investment decision

Whatever the organization's overall objective – pursuing success or surviving in the short-term or whatever – both long-term and short-term investment decision-making are important and need to be managed as processes side by side. You concentrate here on the long-term decision, looking at:

- the significance of the decision to the organization
- the types of decision
- the essentials of a number of investment appraisal models and techniques
- the complications of:
  (a) inflation
  (b) taxation
  (c) limited availability of financing risk
- the significance of the decision to you as a manager.

It is worth reiterating that the purpose is not to make you a finance expert. What is important is to equip you with the knowledge to enable you to participate more fully and effectively in the management of an organization's financial resources. Consequently, as opposed to 'number crunching', the initial emphasis here is on understanding the whys and wherefores of the framework of the capital investment decision, an area that financial specialists often refer to as *capital budgeting*.

Deciding the future

Managers make many decisions in the course of a day's work. The decisions they make in respect of longer term investment in activities are probably the most significant factors affecting the level of profitability – a prerequisite to cash flow through effective working capital management. The reasons such bold statements can be made are because long term capital investment decisions:

- involve the commitment of usually fairly substantial portions of an organization's scarce funds
- require commitment of funds over at least a year and often longer periods of time, thus increasing the uncertainty of outcomes
- are frequently virtually irreversible
- often determine the survival or otherwise of an organization.

The significance of the capital investment decision is thus clear. The reasons rationalizing the significance apply to longer term investment decisions in general although their degree of significance, and thus their degree of influence upon decision-making, will vary according to the particular type of decision and organizational activity being looked at. A common feature that all capital budgeting decisions have with shorter term investments is that managers are looking at making investments which will (hopefully!) produce returns. The distinction is that the longer term investment decision will produce returns over a number of future time periods rather than the current period returns which arise from other types of decisions.

Capital investment decisions will generally be concerned with the planning for and management of activities such as:

- the acquisition of fixed assets such as land and buildings, plant and equipment and vehicles (be it a first-time or replacement acquisition)
- investment in a special project such as a marketing/advertising campaign or research and development
- the expansion of current facilities, be they production or administrative or in relation to any other
- entry into new product/service provision
- investment in development of managers, such as yourself, through training and education.

Such investment decisions are never easy. Often, given the long-term nature of the decision consequences, the projected outcomes and associated returns are at best uncertain and at worst unpredictable and/or intangible. Given this scenario it is understandable that many managers seek advice from all quarters as an aid to reducing the risk of making the wrong capital investment decisions. What they invariably seek is a framework, at least from a financial angle.

A framework for predicting the future

If you as a manager had the opportunity to design an appropriate advisory framework from scratch, it is likely that you would wish the design to help you to solve certain key problems which might hamper your effective decision-making. Perhaps the two key problems needing remedies might be:

- the reduction of the uncertainty associated with longer term decision-making

- the establishment of all known relevant factors affecting the decision, together with an assessment of the possible effects of them.

As ever, these key problem areas are compounded by the specifics of the context in which the decision must be made. For example, there may be:

- competing alternatives with differing features
- differing management viewpoints and attitudes
- shareholder and other stakeholder pressures
- the entanglement of two or a number of decisions.

Given their complicating influence, it is appropriate to consider them further.

Competing alternatives

It may be, of course that competing alternatives have differing features and characteristics. For example:

- initial investment monetary outlays may differ in size and timing (particularly where phased investment is required)
- there may be differing timings for and sizes of operational maintenance payments
- no two alternatives may have exactly the same length of operational life
- the rates of return may differ over the total lifespan of the investment and during each year of the life span.

Important aspects of the above are given in Figure 6.1, which shows three scenarios of fairly typical types of investment decisions, highlighting the problems presented by competing alternatives with some of the differing characteristics identified above. Figure 6.1 (a) shows the typical cash flow profile from a major capital investment decision such as the purchase of a major item of plant; Figure 6.l(b) shows the repetitive cycle of a routine replacement decision; Figure 6.l(c) shows the cash flow profile from an investment producing returns on a cyclical basis. This last figure is quite typical of many industrial and commercial projects, and creates the need for the creation of a portfolio of differing types of investments to smooth out the pattern of annual cash returns to the organization.

Figure 6. l(c) illustrates a common characteristic of all types of long-term investment decisions. Each type can be seen to be proceeding through three distinct phases:

- *The investment phase.* This is where the principal cash outlays are

met either all at one go or, as in the figure, over a number of years.
- *The return phase*. This is where the flow of benefits and returns are earned over a number of years.
- *The disinvestment phase*. This is where the investment is wound down, with money being spent on decommissioning, and perhaps with returns being made from sales of scrap.

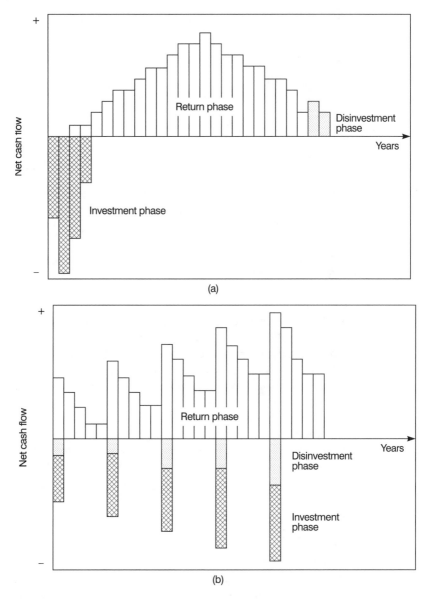

Figure 6.1 Typical investment decisions: (a) cash flow profile from a major long-term capital investment project; (b) periodic replacement with increasing prices

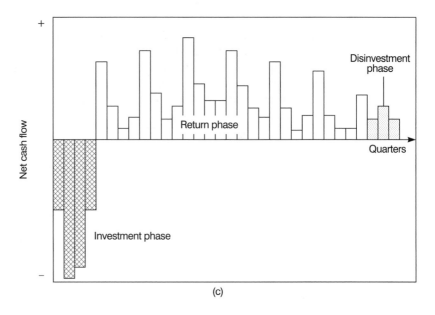

Figure 6.1 Typical investment decisions: (c) project investment with cyclical cash flows

Management attitudes and priorities

All investment decisions, including long-term ones, will be influenced by the views of individual managers. Each manager is likely to hold certain beliefs about the costs and benefits of alternative options. On top of this, the particular contexts in which the need for a major investment decision arises will differ and they may compound the differences between different managers.

An additional complicating factor arises where individual managers have vested interests in the outcomes of decisions. For example, it is not uncommon for management rewards to be based upon performance measures. Individuals may consequently make decisions which are different to those which are in the best interests of the organization.

Shareholder pressures

The calculations for increasing EPS you saw in Part II enable managers to make decisions which maximize shareholders' wealth. A decision to make large-scale investments over a number of years may ultimately reap huge rewards for an organization. However, given that information about investment decision-making is made public at best through press releases, company bulletins and financial statements, there is plenty of scope for misinterpretation. As a consequence, heavy cash outflows may cause anxious investors to react in a way which reduces the market price of the shares. Managers who are aware of this might well opt for what could be regarded in the absolute sense as a suboptimal decision, with the short-term effects appearing favourable in conventional accounting terms.

Families of decisions

It is often difficult to disentangle one decision from another. For example, new capital investment may require new funding sources to be found. In practical terms, the two decisions are understandably linked. It might be appropriate for managers to build a framework for decision-making which separates the costs and benefits of one decision from another, but also allows for the fact that there is bound to be some reciprocal influence. All of the above would need to be incorporated within a financial framework which will provide information to managers to enable them to improve their investment decision-making.

The actual framework devised and adopted by any one management team will, understandably, be influenced by a number of factors peculiar to that one organization (in addition to the more general factors).

The aspects revealed above require a quantification. This happens in Chapter 7, but it is important to recognize that, in planning for the long-term future, the factors taken account of may well change as the future becomes now, and does not turn out in the way a management team might have thought it would. As a consequence the impact of the factors needs to reassessed on a regular and ongoing basis.

The disinvestment phase

So far in this chapter it appears that appraising the investment opportunity is all important. Also of significant importance is the decision that management teams often have to make regarding the closing down of a project or removal of a brand – indeed, cessation of any major activity.

The decision not to continue with a particular activity can have a wide-ranging variety of consequences. These include:

- the loss of profit and incoming cash flows
- the spending of additional cash to pay for associated decommissioning costs
- the possible adverse consequences of losing a particular brand image by ceasing to deal in it.

This is where the principal cash outlays are met, either all at one go or over a number of years.

Of course, although the above consequences appear to concentrate on the negatives, account would need to be taken of any (particularly longer term) perceived advantages. In so doing the identification of any (what you will come to know as) opportunity costs would also need to be achieved and the impact on that notoriously difficult-to-measure area of quality. In essence, management teams will be concerned with assessing the future costs and benefits of continuing with a particular activity *vis-à-vis* the likely benefits from exiting from that area, but not forgetting any decommissioning costs. Again it is common to express as far as is possible the alternative impacts in cash flow terms.

The other important investment decision area, introduced next, the cost-saving/profit-enhancement decision, also takes account of cash flow and opportunity costs.

An introduction to the framework for the cost-saving/ profit-enhancement decision

For many managers the pressure to reduce costs now, in the short term, is very real. However, this may be at odds with the desire to improve profitability (and thus, theoretically at least, cash flow) in the longer term. A typical result is where training and development or research expenditure is cut now – saving cash immediately and perhaps ensuring short-term survival – but with a likely impact on the long-term future of the organization. In such cases, as far as is possible, the immediate savings should be compared with an assessment of the longer term impacts.

As with longer term capital investment appraisal, an accepted framework to help manage such situations has been developed. This involves the understanding of a set of particular views of costs, not least:

- relevant and non-relevant costs
- sunk and committed costs
- opportunity costs.

Each is identified in Chapter 7 and their roles within the framework considered.

Summary

In this chapter you have been introduced to the nature of investment decisions and some of the factors usually considered. In the rest of this part you will focus on the nitty-gritty of making longer term and ad hoc decisions.

By now you should:

- understand why managers should be concerned about longer term investment appraisal
- recognize the significance of the factors to be considered in managing investment appraisal decisions
- be aware of the concern for shorter term, ad hoc decisions, particularly of a cost-saving/profit-enhancement nature.

Self-assessment questions

To assess your own progress, attempt the self-assessment questions below.

SAQ 6.1

Discuss why organizations and their management teams might be concerned with the development of models to help in planning ahead.

SAQ 6.2

Imagine that you have been asked to brief other managers in your organization on the specifics of developing a model for long-term investment.

Further reading

Coase, N.R., 1968. The nature of costs, *The Accountant*, London (October-December) reprinted in Solomons, D. (ed.) *Studies in Cost Analysis* (2nd edn, 1968) Sweet & Maxwell

Davis, E. and Pointon, J., 1991. *Finance and the firm*, 2nd edn, Oxford University Press

7 Quantifying the long-term investment decision

Introduction

There are a number of techniques available to managers which quantify the impact of the variable elements which need to be taken account of in investment decision-making. Some are, in financial and mathematical terms at least, relatively basic, whereas others are a little more sophisticated. What they all have in common is that they can help to reduce the odds against poor decision-making.

By the end of this chapter you will be able to:

- identify the specific factors to be taken account of in quantifying the investment decision
- understand the rationale of and apply the techniques of:
  (a) payback
  (b) discounted cash flow and net present value
- rank competing projects in terms of a profitability index
- understand the complicating variables of taxation, inflation and funding shortages.

The impact and significance of the specific factors you identify are considered in both this chapter and in Chapter 9.

Specific factors in quantifying the decision

In addition to the general aspects identified in Chapter 6, there are more specific decision-related factors which must also be taken account of when endeavouring to quantify the decision. These include:

- the amount and timing of the initial outlays
- the amount and timing of subsequent investment outlays
- to end-of-life scrap or salvage values
- the amount and timing of operating cash flows, both into and out of the investment
- the economic life of the project
- the impact of taxation and taxation allowances
- the effect of inflation

- the impact of shortages of funding availability.

The relevant data relating to each of these elements would need to be gathered and screened. The screening process should aim to assess the influence of each element upon the investment, thus converting general data – possibly useful, possibly not – into most certainly useful information.

History shows that they will all, to a lesser or greater degree, have an influence on the final decision. In light of this, each is considered individually within the next two chapters as you set about quantifying the investment decision. The factors of taxation, inflation and funding shortages require particular attention and are considered in depth at the end of the chapter. Meanwhile, the first five on the list above are introduced below.

> Before each is introduced, it would be as well to address one of those financial jargon areas which can cause managers so much confusion. It is usual for the injection of funds into an investment to be termed *outfows*, with the returns back to the organization being termed *inflows*. Some management teams reverse these and, of course, that is their prerogative. For our purposes, however, we will adhere to funds into an investment being an *outflow*, and funds back as *inflows,* funds equating with cash.

Initial outlays

In general. there are three factors which need to be considered here. They are:

- the total cash (or equivalent) required to implement the proposals
- working capital costs
- the possible use of existing facilities.

The total cash required to implement the proposal

This is understandably important. Any preliminary design, survey or consultancy fees that may be involved must be included if they have not yet been incurred but will be. This is very significant in that any expenditure already incurred no longer has any relevance to the future, and the future is the only time dimension of our interest in making better investment decisions. Thus, intended cash expenditure is a vital and essential consideration.

Working capital costs

This involves consideration of any additional cash expenditure over and above the initial outlay. Thus, cash spent on, for example, maintaining adequate stock levels, or paying additional wage and other operating costs, should be included as an outflow. In addition, the cost of running higher levels of account sales customers in the form of debtors must also be included, together with any consequential increases in bad debts. On the other side of the coin, any benefits of additional credit obtainable from suppliers might well be regarded as a form of compensatory inflow.

The use of existing facilities

This can sometimes have a significant role to play when viewed as a relevant cost for decision-making. For example, if existing facilities would have been sold but for the considerations of a new project, the sacrifice of the potential sale value should be regarded as a chargeable outflow in the same way as if the facilities concerned had needed to be purchased at that price. Conversely, the disposal price of other facilities which could be sold as a result of the introduction of the new project would be equivalent to an inflow.

> For instance, a new project may call for the use of particular facilities. If these existing facilities, having a book value of £10,000, could be adapted for use at the cost of £2,000, then, all else being equal, only the modification cost would be chargeable to the project.

Subsequent investment outlays

Investments will usually require injections of funds (other than working capital funding) on an ongoing basis. It is one thing to buy a machine, for example, but there may be periodic additional outflows for major overhauls, or phased capital payments. Any such additional costs should all be forecast as outflows during the period in which they are expected to occur.

Scrap/salvage values

Many investments involve the purchase of fixed assets which may have a value once a project has run its course. It may be that such assets are still useful in the operating sense and could be sold on to a third party, either internally or externally (vehicles might fit here). Alternatively, they could be sold as scrap (the metal contained in plant machinery is a good example.) Whichever is the case, if there is anticipated value at the end of a project's life, i.e. an anticipated cash inflow, then this should be quantified and included as an inflow in assessing the viability of the project.

Operating cash flows

With all the ins and outs of funds during the life of an investment it may be appropriate to divide such flows into two (fairly predictable) categories:

- sales volumes and revenues
- operating costs.

Sales volumes and the associated revenues

These are very sensitive and crucial areas in investment appraisal. It is essential that the marketing specialists do their forecasting homework properly, as the cost of error in this area can be lethal. Overestimating will result in the commitment of costly and scarce resources which may never be recovered. Underestimating could result in the provision of inadequate facilities which may need to be enlarged or replaced, perhaps at an inflated cost, long before the end of the project's economic life.

Sales revenues are, of course, only a function of sales volumes and their associated unit prices. It is thus equally important for the marketing specialists to recommend that prices are pitched at the right level. Even then, it does not finish there. How much is spent on promotion may also be very significant, as may the effect of a new product or service on existing offerings from the organization.

Operating costs

These should be analysed into as many groups as a management team feels necessary. They could be divided into functional groupings such as *production, administration, selling* and *distribution,* with subsequent subdivision into *variable* and *fixed costs* categories. As with the use of existing facilities met earlier, only new costs should be charged as an outflow into the investment. A point to note is that depreciation charges and the reallocation of existing general overheads are irrelevant in this context. This is because they represent past expenditures of cash and already exist. As such, they are outside the embrace of the investment decision as they have no connection with *actual future movements of cash.*

Once the additional costs have been identified and isolated they should be charged to the relevant accounting period in which it is anticipated they will be incurred.

The economic life

The economic life of a project may be defined as being: the interval between the time the investment starts and the time at which the combined forecast of obsolescence and deterioration will justify the cessation of the project.

This period will not necessarily be the same as the individual life of any one of the assets required by the project. The project's economic life is not determined by the anticipated life of facilities, but by the duration of the *earnings stream* generated by the project. The economic life could come to an end as a result of:

- the cost of major replacements or renovation of facilities being greater than the benefits likely to result
- market obsolescence rendering continuation of the project no longer viable
- rising maintenance costs exceeding the estimated disposal value
- the availability of new facilities justifying new investment (at which time a new investment appraisal exercise will be necessary).

In general, the longer the life expectancy of a project, the better the return will be.

Risk

You have already identified in this book that risk is something we would need to take account of in the management of financial resources in both our own personal lives and within organizations. Because risk is so important, it is equally important that the investment decision-making model attempts to capture the degree of risk and to measure the effects of the differing probabilities of certain events that may take place during the life of any investment being considered. This is achieved via a range of approaches to *sensitivity* and *probability analyses* which are considered specifically later. For the meantime the risk dimension should not be forgotten. After all, all investment decisions concern predicting the future – and nothing in life is certain!

Having outlined the ins and outs of an appropriate framework for investment decisions, you can now proceed to quantify the elements and variables which are relevant to effective appraisal.

The techniques

There are a range of techniques available to help in quantifying the investment decision. They are rarely used singly but rather as a group to develop a profile of the possible outcomes of the potential investment. The techniques considered here are:

- the payback period
- the accounting rate of return
- discounted cash flow techniques:
  (a) net present value
  (b) internal rate of return
- sensitivity and risk analysis.

The payback approach

This is a very logical approach to the measurement of how long it takes for an investment to recoup or *payback* its initial investment. It involves calculating cumulative cash flows until the initial investment is accounted for. Using the detail in the first box, the relevant calculations are shown in the second box.

An organization intends to invest £300,000 now and anticipates the following returns:

Year 1	50,000
Year 2	160,000
Year 3	120,000
Year 4	80,000
Year 5	40,000
Year 6	20,000

In year 3 the cumulative cash flow becomes positive. Assuming an even return over each 12-month period, an average return or payback period of 2 years, 9 months can be calculated based on:

$$2 \text{ years } + \frac{\text{Negative cash flow at start of year 2}}{\text{Cash inflow in year 2}}$$
$$= 2 \text{ years} + (£90,000/£120,000) \times 12 \text{ months}$$
$$= 2 \text{ years, 9 months}$$

This figure represents the period required for the recovery of the invested funds. You might well think that this is a somewhat simplistic approach, and you would not be wrong in doing so.

Year	Annual cash flow £	Cumulative cash flow £
Now	(300,000)	(300,000)
1	+ 50,000	(250,000)
2	+ 160,000	(90,000)
3	+ 120,000	+30,000
4	+ 80,000	+ 110,000
5	+ 40,000	+ 150,000
6	+ 20,000	+ 170,000

Payback disadvantages

There are a number of disadvantages associated with this technique, including:

- it assumes regular and even cash flows during each accounting period (usually a year)
- it ignores events that take place after the calculated payback point in time. It thus ignores later positive cash flows and tax payments and disinvestment costs
- it does not take account of the fact that money to be received in the future will have a different value to the current value of money. This means that a positive accounting payback could well, in economic and real terms, be a negative figure.

To compensate for such deficiencies, the annual net cash inflows/outflows may be discounted back to the present time of the initial investment, time 0 (zero). This is achieved, normally, by applying a technique of **discounted cash flow**, discounting future cash flows back to the **net present value** at the time of the investment. Thus **DCF** is used to obtain **NPV**.

Discounted cash flow and net present value

The rationale of this technique, as outlined immediately above, has an intrinsic degree of logic. For many managers, the challenge is under-standing which discount rate is used and why. The rate is that which is equivalent to the required return on the project. This will normally be the WACC percentage (however determined) or, to reflect any per-ceived additional risk associated with the project, higher – a risk premium.

Using, again, the figures in the first box above, the annual cash flows may be discounted by a discount factor of, in this case, say, 10% p.a. (The discount factor may be calculated using a calculator or taken from pre-prepared discount tables.) These calculations are shown in Table 7.1.

Table 7.1 NPV calculation

Time/year	Cash figure £	Discount factor for 10% p.a.	Discounted cash flow (DCF) £
0	(300,000)	1	(300,000)
1	50,000	0.909	45,450
2	160,000	0.826	132,160
3	120,000	0.751	90,120
4	80,000	0.683	54,640
5	40,000	0.621	24,840
6	20.000	0.564	11.280
	170 000		58.490

The £58,490 is the discounted (at 10%) equivalent of the undiscounted £170,000. On the surface, the project appears to be making a substantial surplus of £170,000; when adjusted through discounting it drops sub-stantially to £58,490, although in this case it is still very positive.

Assessing the NPV

- If the NPV is positive it reflects a quantified assertion that the cash inflows will yield the organization a return in excess of the cost of capital (or higher required return).
- If the NPV is negative it reflects a quantified assertion that the cash inflows will yield a return below the cost of capital.

The NPV may also be calculated from a slightly different perspective, resulting in the **internal rate of return** or **IRR**.

The internal rate of return

As you saw above, the NPV approach to discounted cash flow involves calculating net present values by discounting at a target rate of return or cost of capital and establishing the difference between the present value of costs and present value of benefits. The internal rate of return approach still involves the application of a discount rate, but that which is derived from the exact rate of return the project is expected to achieve if the resulting NPV were to be zero. In a sense, the IRR approach establishes a quasi-break-even point. If the expected rate of return exceeds the target rate of return, the investment would appear, on paper, to be viable.

The methodology of calculating the IRR involves the determination of at least two NPVs relating to the proposed investment which are as close to zero as possible. This requires a hit-and-miss approach and, indeed, may require a number of attempts. Ideally, the two NPVs settled upon should be either side of zero. Then, via extrapolation, the exact discount rate between the two resulting in the NPVs may be established.

Experience has shown that often, although not always, selecting a discount rate which is equivalent to about two-thirds of the accounting rate of return on investment can be an appropriate starting point.

Comparing competing investment alternatives

It is not unusual for managers to have to choose between two or more investments which are competing for their scarce resource of funds. There are a number of ways in which making the right (or should it be the more appropriate?) choice can be pursued and we will consider some of them here. To help us, the figures shown in Table 7.2 will be used. In both cases each set of figures has been discounted by 10%.

Table 7.2 Comparing competing investment alternatives

| Time | Investment A | | Investment B | |
	Undiscounted cash flow £	Present value £	Undiscounted cash flow £	Present value £
0	(300,000)	(300,000)	(300,000)	(300,000)
1	50,000	45,450	160,000	145,450
2	160,000	132,160	50,000	41,300
3	120,000	90,120	120,000	90,120
4	80,000	54,640	20,000	13,660
5	40,000	24,840	40,000	24,840
6	20,000	11,280	80,000	45,120
	170,000	58,490	170,000	60,490

The figures in Table 7.2 can help to solve a dilemma. If a management team used an undiscounted cash flow assessment, both investments return the same net inflow of £170,000. The same applies to an undiscounted payback assessment with both investments paying back in 2.75 years. When the time value for money is considered however, a discounted NPV cash flow assessment, Investment B is favoured, returning £60,490 as opposed to £58,490 for A. On a discounted payback assessment however, Investment A pays back in 3.6 years, whereas B takes 4.4 years. Clearly, the dilemma facing the management team here is great. It is compounded by the fact that, on an IRR basis, A has a rate of 12.2% and B 11.4%.

In **ranking** situations like this, where funds may be inadequate to finance all potentially profitable projects, or where a choice needs to be made between a number of contenders, a further method of evaluation called the **profitability index** could be used. This is based on the same data as the NPV method, in that a target rate of return has to be established and the NPV calculated. What then happens is that the present value of an investment's inflows is related to the present value of its outflows in the form of a ratio, this being:

$$\text{Profitability} = \frac{\text{Present value of cash inflows}}{\text{Present value of cash outflows}}$$

Under this criterion, the two investments would be ranked as follows:

$$\text{Investment A} = \frac{£358,490}{£300,000} = 1.19$$

$$\text{Investment B} = \frac{£360,490}{£300,000} = 1.20$$

The profitability index shows us the net present value of each £ invested. Under this criterion, investment B shows up better than A.

It is quite common for the profitability index to be misused. This is because the term *cash outflow* is often interpreted as relating solely to the initial outlay at time 0. It is not unusual for net outflows to be encountered in subsequent years and these must be incorporated as outflows within the index calculation.

In summary, what we can say is that the common aim of discounted cash flow techniques is to translate a projected stream of cash flows into one single index number that is then capable of comparison with other index numbers.

If the projected net cash flows are discounted back to present values at a predetermined target rate of return, then the sum of these plus or minus discounted values will be the **net present value** of the project in *absolute* terms. If, on the other hand, they are discounted at a rate which results in the sum of the present values of the projected inflows equating exactly with the sum of the present values of the projected outflows, then the net present value will be nil and the rate that needs to be applied in order to achieve this balance is the **internal rate of return** of the project. This is consequently a *relative* measure, since its comparative base must be the target rate of return.

The **profitability index** is also a relative measure. It relates the present values of a project's inflows to the present value of its outflows in order to establish the net present value per £ of investment.

Both the internal rate of return and the profitability index are dependent upon the existence of negative cash flows – or investments of capital – into the projected earnings stream, otherwise they cannot be calculated. It is quite possible, however, to measure the net present value of a projected earnings stream which contains no net outflow.

These are the main individual characteristics of the three discounting measures, but they do have their quirks and idiosyncrasies. What we will do next is to examine the variables that you managers should consider when interpreting the figures.

The complicating variables

The impact of taxes and tax allowances

As they say, the only two certainties of life are death and the tax authorities, and the latter at least, surely applies to many organizations. In a healthy profit-making environment, a limited liability company (in whatever country) will be liable to pay some form of taxation on its net reported profits. Many countries operate a specific system which compensates for the vagaries and inconsistencies of the traditional accounting reporting mechanisms. Consequently, charges such as depreciation, which could vary between companies depending upon their management team's viewpoint, are added back to the reported profits and a special system for taxation allowances applied. These allowances will alter the reported profit to a taxable profit upon which the company will be taxed.

These tax allowances are accounted for in a particular accounting year relative to the year in which profits arose or investments are made. What is important for you to remember is that the amount of tax that is to be paid is very likely to be in a different year (usually the following year). This cash flow aspect means that, when working out investment appraisals, the tax on any profits should be accounted for in the year it is actually paid rather than the year in which the liability arises.

Inflation

Inflation tends to occur, and consequently must be taken into account in investment appraisal, in two ways. First, there is *general inflation,* which relates to a statistical average of price increases over a wide range of goods and services. Secondly, there is *specific inflation,* relating to specific price increases for a particular type of product or service.

As far as investment appraisal is concerned, inflation affects the analysis process in (at least) two ways:

- through price changes in specific elements of cash flow projections
- by changing the perceptions of providers of funds in relation to the value and prospects of the organization.

You will see later how both effects are quantified.

Shortages of funding availability

It is quite easy to fall into the trap of making forecasts about investment appraisal on the basis that the funding required is freely available. In addition, many managers assume, either through ignorance (in the nicest sense of the term) or for convenience, that funds are borrowed or lent at one single rate of interest. In the real world, neither of these assumptions actually exists. Any framework for investment decision-making must try and account for the reality of the situation associated with what is termed in financial jargon *capital rationing.*

There are many, many variables which might need to be considered in making what appears to be the best decision regarding an investment. Some of them will be industry and/or investment specific and we will not be able, obviously, to look at those. What we can look at are those which are more common. These will include:

- the impact of taxation
- the impact of inflation
- competing investments with differing life expectations
- integration of new projects into existing activities
- capital shortages or **rationing.**

Each is considered in turn below.

The impact of taxation

Taxation is a complex topic. Indeed, the UK tax system is notorious for its complexity. However, as far as investment appraisal is concerned it impacts upon investment analysis in just two ways:

- it introduces a new relevant cost to take into account as one of the cash outflows to be considered in the investment decision

● it may have some impact upon the discount rate considered appropriate when discounting those cash flows.

The peculiar difficulty as far as the cash flows of a new project are concerned is that taxation can severely distort the timing of anticipated cash flows. An implication of the mathematical rationale of discounting is that the discounting procedure favours earlier rather than later cash flows. A marginal project will appear more favourable if a tax regime displaces the incidence of costs further away in time, and less favourable if it brings those cash flows forward.

Below is illustrated the effect of three simple taxation systems upon investment appraisal. The UK tax system is more complicated than any of the three that we show here, and always presents a difficult modelling problem in practice. For example, special rules govern particular allowances and the treatment of losses. However, the three cases shown here provide the basis of such a modelling exercise and bring out some very important principles. The three cases are:

(i)   where a percentage tax rate is paid in the year in which the liability for tax arises

(ii) a system where the payment of tax can be delayed relative to the date on which the liability arises

(iii) a system where a writing-down allowance is given for capital investment over the life of the project. (A writing-down allowance enables a percentage of the cost to be charged against tax – in a sense it is a special tax depreciation system.)

In all cases it may be assumed that the organization will distribute all net surpluses from its projects to its investors, and that the company pays taxes on its other activities (i.e. will not incur net tax losses on its total operations in any year during the project).

To illustrate the cases we will consider a very simple project consisting of a single outlay now of £90,000 and two subsequent net cash inflows of £80,000 and £50,000 at the end of Years 1 and 2, respectively. The discount rate for this project we will set at 10%.

The net present value calculation of this project is shown in Table 7.3 and shows that the project is worthwhile.

Table 7.3

Time	Undiscounted cash flow £	Discounted at 10% £
0	(90,000)	(90,000)
1	80,000	72,727
2	50 000	41,322
Total	40,000	24,049

Tax liability paid in the year in which it arises

Let us consider a very simple tax regime where tax is levied on all net cash surpluses at a rate of 40% and a first-year allowance of 100% of initial capital expenditure is allowed for tax purposes. In addition, we initially assume that tax must be paid as soon as it is incurred.

The point about the first year is that 100% of the investment outlay is allowed as an expenditure for tax purposes, i.e. as a deduction before the overall liability for Corporation Tax is calculated on the company's profits. As a result of this investment, the company will save tax (at assume 40%) of the full amount (100%) of the expenditure made at that time. However, each subsequent year's tax bill will be increased by 40% of the net cash surpluses from the project, as no further charges will be allowed, the whole cost having been allowed in Year 1. This saving of 40 per cent and the subsequent additional cash charges are laid out in Table 7.4.

Table 7.4

Time	Undiscounted cash flow £	Discounted at 10% £
0	(90,000)	(90,000)
	36,000	36,000
1	80,000	
	(32,000)	43,636
2	50,000	
	(20,000)	24,793
Total	24,000	14,429

You will notice that all that has happened is that the net present value has been reduced by 40%. A tax system of this type is **investment-neutral** in that no matter what the rate of tax (provided that it is not 100%), the project will remain worthwhile if it has a positive net present value without tax.

Payment of tax delayed

We now look at a slightly more realistic example where the incidence of tax is delayed for 1 year beyond the date in which it is saved (in the case of a first-year allowance) or the date on which it falls due. The revised project cash flows are shown in Table 7.5.

In this case, the tax regime has worked in favour of the project relative to the tax-neutral system described previously. Everything else being equal, the delay in the impact of taxation is (relatively) beneficial as cash flows moved further into the future have less effect when discounted.

Table 7.5

Time	Undiscounted cash flow £	Discounted at 10% £
0	(90,000)	(90,000)
1	80,000	
	36,000	105,454
2	50,000	
	(32,000)	14,876
3	(20,000)	(15,026)
Total	24,000	15,304

Writing-down allowance given for capital investment

We can now look at the effect of withdrawing the 100% first-year allowance and replacing it with a writing-down allowance (this is the tax authority's form of depreciation allowance).

In this example we assume that the organization can depreciate the project for tax purposes over the project's life on a straight-line basis. In practice, in the UK the situation is not as favourable as this, as companies may only charge a set percentage of their capital investment on a reducing balance against tax. Assuming, as before, that payment is delayed for 1 year and that all net cash flows are distributed, Table 7.6 shows the relevant calculation with a tax rate of 20%.

Table 7.6

Time	Undiscounted cash flow £	Discounted at 10% £
0	(90,000)	(90,000)
1	80,000	
	(18,000)	89,091
2	50,000	
	(18,000)	29,752
	(32,000)	
3	(20,000)	(15,026)
Total	24,000	13,817

In this case the tax system has worked adversely relative to the neutral system and will, in marginal cases, be a disincentive to investment. Indeed, any taxation system which defers capital allowances reduces the value of an investment project relative to the neutral position.

Taxation in perspective

To summarize, taxation will always have the effect of reducing the net present value of a project, although in the neutral system (excluding a

completely confiscatory tax of 100 per cent) a project which is worthwhile before tax will always be worthwhile after tax. This may not be
the case, however, where tax flows are deferred relative to the point in
time when the liability arises.

The real tax system is complicated because, under the current
'imputation' system, a company's annual Corporation Tax liability
is paid in two instalments:

- as soon as a distribution is made, the shareholders' tax component of the dividend (assessed at the basic rate) is deemed to
  be part of the settlement of the year's Corporation Tax liability
- the balance (if any) is paid 9 months later.

This produces nasty timing problems and is where computer software comes into its own. If you are interested, an analysis of the
effects of the imputation system are worked out in the reference
given in Further reading, below.

The impact of inflation

In order to understand the impact of inflation upon investment
appraisal it is important to understand the nature of inflation itself.
Specifically, two types of inflation may be described:

1 *Specific inflation.* This relates to specific price increases for particular goods or commodities. Thus, over a period, if the supply of a particular type of component rises in price from £200 per unit to £250,
   there is a specific price rise of 25%. Prices change for specific
   goods for a variety of reasons, causing changes in the relative levels
   of supply and demand. Generally, according to economic theory, if
   the capacity of an economy to produce a particular good or com-
   modity is less than the demand for that good at the current price,
   then its price will rise: correspondingly, if capacity is more, then the
   price will fall.
2 *General inflation.* This relates in the UK to the statistical average of
   price increases over a wide range of goods and commodities. The
   Retail Price Index, for example, is an index consisting of price
   changes of a range of goods and commodities in the economy.
   Changes in the UK government's Retail Price Index are taken as
   proxy for the general economy-wide changes in average prices. In
   the long term, increasing inflation is a symptom of under-capacity in
   the economy to produce (through investment) or by cutting back the
   level of demand (by increasing tax or by restricting borrowing).

As far as investment appraisal is concerned, inflation affects the investment described in two ways:

- through price changes in specific elements of cash flow projections
- by changing the level of the discount rate used by investors to appraise the value of the firm.

The first impact can be handled quite easily by taking account of all anticipated price increases in our future cash projections. The second impact is also fairly easy to handle as well because, as you will see later, if market values are used to input the appropriate discount rate, then investors' anticipations of future inflation will be automatically incorporated.

Adjusting for inflation: money rates and real rates

A problem arises, however, in that many managers attempt to eliminate the effect of general inflation from their projection to create what are termed **real cash flows,** i.e. cash flows expressed at today's price level. This is perfectly satisfactory, provided that the inflation component is eliminated from the discount rate adopted. This adjustment from what may be termed a *'money'* discount rate to produce the *'real'* rate is thus important. A fully-worked illustration is shown in Tables 7.7 and 7.8.

Assume a company invests £24,800 today, expecting net cash returns of, respectively, £11,435 in Year 1, £7,034 in Year 2 and £10,264 in Year 3. When discounted at 10% the figures are as shown in Table 7.7.

Table 7.7 Discounting at a money rate of 10%

Time	Non-discounted £	Discounted £
0	(24,810)	(24,800)
1	11,435	10,395
2	7,034	5,813
3	10,624	7,711
NPV	3,843	(881)

Table 7.7 shows that under a standard discounting approach at a rate of 10%, the project yields an NPV of (£881) and is therefore not worthwhile. Of course, this calculation takes no account of inflation.

Assuming an inflation rate of 6% p.a., the *real* cash flow can now be calculated by discounting money flows at 6%. This is shown in Table 7.8.

Table 7.8 Discounting at an inflation rate of 6%

Time	Non-discounted £	Discounted £
0	(24,800)	(24,800)
1	11,435	10,783
2	7,034	6,260
3	10,264	8,618
Real cash flows	3,843	(866)

These *real* cash flows do not yet represent fully discounted present values because only one component of the time value of money has been eliminated (the inflationary component). To create the *true* **net present value** further, the real cash flow must be further discounted by the real discount rate. This is achieved thus:

$$(1 + \text{real rate}) = (1 + \text{money rate})/(1 + \text{inflationary rate})$$

Thus, as the money rate is 10% and the rate of inflation is 6%, and calling the real rate r:

$$(1 + r) = (1 + 0.1)/(1 + 0.06)$$
$$= 1.03774$$

thus,

$$r = 0.03774 \, (= 3.774\%)$$

If the real rate of 3.774% is used to discount the real cash flows above, the figures shown in Table 7.9 are obtained. This value is, of course, the same as that produced by discounting the money flows by the money rate.

Table 7.9 Discounting at the *real* rate of 3.774%

Time	Non-discounted £	Discounted £
0	(24,800)	(24,800)
1	11,345	10,395
2	7,034	5,813
3	10,264	7,711
	3,843	(881)

It is natural to query why this process should be undertaken, particularly if the answer is the same as the first calculations. The reason is that it is important to understand the mechanics of performing the analysis in order to avoid two very common errors:

ERROR 1

Often, managers discount the *real* rate at the *money* discount rate. Research carried out by Carsberg and Hope for the Institute of Chartered Accountants in England and Wales as far back as 1976, supported the fallacy of this, stating:

> Our study provides strong support for the hypothesis that investment appraisal practices used by large British firms tend to lead to investment below the optimal level. A large number of firms use a *money target rate* of return in association with *cash flows estimated in current prices* (with the added disadvantages of failure to predict the effect of differential inflation as it affects their resources).

ERROR 2

As indicated in the quotation above, many firms ignore the effect of specific price changes on individual elements of their cash flow budgets, assuming that by so doing they are computing cash flows in real terms (which they then proceed to discount using a money rate!). If this were applied to the example used in Table 7.9, a completely different NPV of £2,904 would be obtained.

This mistake clearly overestimates the value of the project in this case, and could lead to an investment decision which will not generate a level of return sufficient to reward the firm's investors at the required level. In this case, ignoring the effect of price changes understates the money value of costs and misrepresents their real level as well. The use of the money rate of discount serves to confound the issue further.

Having said that, there is certainly a practice of ignoring the effects of inflation. The argument is that the overall effects of inflation are bound to be reflected very quickly in interest rates – or, conversely, that interest rates will fully reflect anticipated rates of inflation or changes in price levels. It is, after all, changes in price levels which combine together to make up the rate of inflation, and Carsberg and Hope maintained that, generally speaking, market forces react together, and interest rates move with them – a phenomenon now known as the 'Fisher effect', after the eminent economist Irving Fisher who proposed this as long ago as 1930.

Different project life expectations

The results of calculations for NPV, payback period and IRR can be very confusing, even where investment lives are the same. It can be even more confusing where the lives of a number of projects differ. Table 7.10 illustrates the challenge.

The results shown in the table seem to indicate that any one of the three projects could be favoured depending upon which criterion you decided to use. Project D has the highest net present value, although this is achieved at the cost of a higher initial investment outlay than Project E – as indicated by the profitability indices. The profitability index points to Project E and yet, if you compare these indices with the internal rates of return, you will find that they are in completely the reverse ranking order. So what are you to decide?

Table 7.10

Project	Initial investment	Net annual cash flow in	Project life	Total NPV after discounting at 10%	IRR	Profitability index
	£	£		£		
C	–20,000	9,500	for each of 3 years	3,618	20%	1.18
D	–18,500	6,000	for each of 5 years	4,240	19%	1.23
E	–15,500	4,000	for each of 7 years	3,968	17%	1.26

The reasons for this apparently paradoxical situation lie in the different project lifespans that are involved, and the way in which the internal rate of return reacts – or fails to react – to this situation. The implication of IRR is that funds can be reinvested after the end of a project's life at exactly the same rate of return as that achieved during its actual active life. The net present value and the profitability index criteria, on the other hand, assume that funds will be reinvested at the *target* rate – in this case 10% – after the end of the project's life. So, if you were to take these three new projects, and compare them over the 7-year term of the longest running one, you can see that what actually happens is described in the following.

Now, assume that during the third and final year of Project C's original forecast life it was decided that it could be extended by a further 4 years by investing a further £24,500 in Year 3 to maintain the present steady earnings stream of £9,500. Similarly, in the fifth and final year of Project D's planned life expectancy, it was decided that it, too, could maintain its earnings stream of £6,000 per annum for a further 2 years – provided that a further £9,000 was invested at that point. (In practice, these project extensions would be evaluated separately from the main project, but that requirement is being overlooked for the purposes of this example, and all of the projects are being regarded as continuing operations.)

In this way, all three projects would then have an equal life expectancy of 7 years, but Project C would now have a net outflow of (9,500 – 24,500 =) £–15,000 in Year 3, and Project D would have a net outflow of (6,000 – 9,000 =) £–3,000 in Year 5. Project C's profitability index would rise to 1.25 and Project D's to 1.25.

So the life extensions have improved the prospects of both of these projects. But that is not the message that you would get by looking at the internal rates of return which have not even moved. For Project C, the IRR would remain 20%, and for Project D at 19%.

Learning the lessons

Now that all three projects are on an equal lifespan, however, the three measures do at least appear to be much more in agreement with each other. The first lesson to be learned from this example is that the internal rate of return cannot be used as a reliable comparison between projects of different life expectancies.

The second point is that one should always ensure that any DCF evaluation is linked to the expected lifespan of the project, so that there can never be any misunderstanding about what the figures are telling you. In the original version of the current example, where the project lives were different, it would be quite misleading to claim that Project E had an IRR of 20% and an NPV of £9,500, compared with only 17% and £4,000 for Project E. This would have to be qualified quite clearly by saying that Project C had an NPV at 10% of £9, 500 and an IRR of 20% *over 3 years*, compared with an NPV of £4,000 at 10% and an IRR of 17% for Project E *over 7 years*.

This would not necessarily lead to the rejection of Project E – it might well be a valid selection if a manager wanted to generate a fast, high rate of return in the short term in order to build up sufficient capital for future, longer term projects. The ultimate decision would depend on the company's overall philosophy and business strategy.

Before finally leaving this example, it is worth reflecting for a moment on the significance, if any, of the profitability indices in Table 7.10. Apparently, if the lives of Projects C and D are both extended to 7 years, then the profitability index would be 1.25 for both. If you were able to invest in both of these projects, then you would obviously take both. If you had to choose one rather than the other because funds were scarce, then C would be better on the grounds that the biggest – in NPV terms – is the best. More often than not, however, many projects are in operation side by side and often on a staggered basis. Such projects, understandably, need integration.

Project integration

An important investment appraisal point to remember constantly is that cash flows are *not* the same as reported profits. This is because:

- the period in which taxation capital allowances and any investment grants are received is almost certainly going to be different from that in which the investment is made
- the general effect of investment will be reflected in the organization's accounts throughout the anticipated life of the project via the depreciation charges that are made
- actual cash flows will differ from the purchases and sales recorded in the accounts because of the time-delay effect introduced by debtors, creditors and stocks.

These points are reinforced where more than one project applies, and particularly with regard to the effects of a new project upon the pattern of a company's existing cash flow. This is illustrated in Table 7.11 which indicates a steady cash flow over the next few years from existing activities, together with projections relating to three new proposals.

Assume that you are in Year 0, and that Project 1 is already underway. On the face of it, a straight choice between Projects 2 and 3 would indicate a preference for Project 2, because this has a positive net present value, whereas Project 3 has a negative one.

However, for the purposes of minimizing capital outlay or maintaining a steady earnings stream it may well be preferable to adopt Project 3, because this integrates more smoothly with the existing cash flow plus Project 1. The integration of Project 2 would result in an erratic cash flow situation, and could possibly create future liquidity problems.

Table 7.11

	Year 0 £	Year 1 £	Year 2 £	Year 3 £	Year 4 £	NPV
Existing activities	25,000	24,000	22,000	20,000	20,000	
Investment proposals:						
Project 1	−(6,000)	+1,000 X.909	+2,000 X.826	+4,000 X.751	+5,000 X.683	= 5,029
Project 2	−(10,000)	6,000 X.909	1,000 X.826	X.751	8,000 X.683	= 1171
Project 3	X.909	−(5,000) X.826	1,500 X.751	2,200 X.683	2,400	= (15)
Existing activities combined with:						
Projects 1 and 2	19,000	15,000	30,000	25,000	33,000	
Projects 1 and 3	19,000	20,000	25,000	26,200	27,400	

Of course, not all projects can be undertaken, not least because not enough capital is ever available for investment. Given this, the aspect of capital rationing and techniques for assessing appropriate ways forward should be considered.

Summary

You should now be familiar with a number of techniques available to managers which quantify the impact of the variable elements which need to be taken account of in the longer term of capital investment decision-making. The variable elements include taxation and inflation and you should now be in a position to recognize their impact on the investment appraisal decision.

Specifically, you should now be able to:

- identify the specific factors to be taken account of in quantifying the investment decision
- understand the rationale of and apply the techniques of:
  (a) payback
  (b) discounted cash flow and net present value
- rank competing projects in terms of a profitability index
- comment on the impact of taxation and inflation upon the investment decision.

Self-assessment questions

Before proceeding to Chapter 8 to consider further background knowledge to the investment appraisal decision, attempt the self-assessment questions below. Where appropriate undertake the Further reading.

SAQ 7.1

Return to the figures in Table 7.1. See if any other combination of projects generates a total NPV of greater value than that calculated.

SAQ 7.2

What can you say about the IRR – is it a better guide to the ranking of projects than NPV alone? If so, why? Refer to the figures in Table 7.1 if you wish.

SAQ 7.3

A project is being considered as an addition to the above five projects. Its initial capital outlay will be £20,000, followed by 4 annual cash flows of £6, 500 in each of the following 4 years. Without reworking the original plan and assuming a discount rate of 10%, determine whether this project should be included as part of the capital budget.

Further reading

Gitman, L.J. and Mercurio, V.A., 1982. Cost of capital techniques used by major US firms: survey and analysis of Fortune's 1000, *Financial Management* (Winter)

Pike, R.H., 1983. A review of recent trends in capital budgeting processes, *Journal of Accounting and Business Research* (Summer)

Drury, C., Braund, S., Osborne, P. and Tayles, M., 1993. *A survey of management accounting practices in UK manufacturing industries*, The Chartered Association of Certified Accountants

8 Complications in the investment decision

In this chapter you will meet some of the realities associated with making investment decisions and thus build upon these areas where investment decisions can only be guided by the simple net present value techniques considered earlier.

These areas include that of *capital rationing* which you met at the end of the last chapter, the often overlooked *post-implementation audit* and revisiting the cost of capital idea you explored in Part II. In addition, the notion of managers having vested interest and preferences highlighted earlier will be re-emphasized.

By the end of this chapter you will be able to:

- apply methods to short-term capital rationing decisions
- recognize the significance of what is termed the marginal investment project
- understand better the concept of risk and techniques for assessing risk
- understand how risk can be accounted for in determining the cost of capital idea you met earlier.
- place investment decision-making in the context of organizations without a ready market for shares, for non-profit-making concerns and for the public sector.

The challenge of capital rationing

In Chapter 7, you considered a number of approaches to investment decision-making, among other techniques. Underpinning each approach was a basic assumption: that any amount of money, large or small can be borrowed or lent at a single rate of interest. Clearly, in the real world in which organizations exist, this condition does not hold – all financing institutions offer a lower rate of interest on deposits to that which they demand on loans. In addition, there is a clear upper limit on the amount that a firm or its investors will be able to lend given particular levels of security and risk. It may be, therefore, that an organization will come up against an absolute limit concerning the amount of cash that it can raise and hence the amount of investment that it can undertake. Indeed, the firm may well have to forgo projects with positive net present values because of this situation of **capital rationing.**

The capital rationing framework

In formulating a framework to respond to the capital rationing challenge, you start with a scenario where capital is limited to one investment period only. There are good reasons for this (apart from the considerable simplicity of the analysis compared with the multiperiod case). First, most organizations which experience capital rationing difficulties only perceive it as a one-period problem. Financing decisions are invariably made on a year-by-year basis as part of the annual capital budgeting process, and management teams will work hard, as a matter of priority, to obtain funding in subsequent periods for any project which is ostensibly worthwhile. In addition, capital investment projects are rarely funded as single entities, but as programmes – seeking balanced portfolios, if you like, of risky and not so risky projects.

In Table 8.1 are shown details of five projects. Each has a different capital outlay, the total requirement being £6,250,000. Unfortunately, available capital is limited to £6,000,000 in the first year only. The cost of capital is 10% p.a. and this has been applied to produce the NPV of each project. In addition, the IRR has been calculated, as has the NPV per £1 of capital expenditure. On the far right is shown the capital balance left after investing in the projects in order of greatest NPV benefit.

Table 8.1

Project	Capital investment	Net inflow at end of year				NPV	IRR	NPV/ outlay	Balance
		1	2	3	4				
	£m	£m	£m	£m	£m	£m	%		£m
1	(4.0)	3.2	2.1	0	0	0.644628	22.76	0.161	2.0
2	(0.675)	0.342	0.400	0.400	0	0.267014	30.70	0.396	1.325
3	(1.2)	0.550	0.400	0.300	0.300	0.060877	12.63	0.051	0.125
4	(0.450)	0.223	0.320	0.050	0	0.054756	17.88	0.122	(0.325)
5	(0.080)	0.020	0.050	0.050	0	0.017070	20.23	0.213	(0.405)

In line with your earlier NPV considerations in the last chapter, the projects have been ranked in terms of their net present value. Patently, with not enough capital for all the projects there is an understandable temptation to opt for Projects 1 – 3 and as much of Project 4 as possible.

However, in terms of the most effective usage of capital which is rationed, this ranking (which implies accepting Projects 1–3 and part of Project 4 – if we can) is not the most beneficial. A higher overall net present value can be calculated if we rank according to *net present value per pound of outlay*. Reordering thus produces the new ranking in Table 8.2.

Table 8.2

Project	NPV/outlay	Capital investment £m
2	0.396	(0.675)
5	0.213	(0.080)
1	0.161	(4.0)
4	0.122	(0.450)
3	0.051	(1.2)

By ranking by NPV per pound of outlay, all projects except Project 3 would be fully accepted. This would consume £5,205,000 (£675,000 + £80,000 + £4,000,000 + £450,000). This would leave £745,000 to be used for as much of Project 3 as possible, or another project.

Project 3 is thus in a limbo – marginalized if you like. And such situations concerning the **marginal project** often demand particular attention from management teams.

The significance of the marginal project

In the NPV/outlay ranking above, Project 3 lay on the margin of acceptability. In other words, minor changes in the availability of capital would entail reductions or expansions in the proportion of this project which could be undertaken. Indeed, the addition of £1 to the availability of capital would increase the net present value of the firm by £0.051. This number provides a benchmark by which all additional investment opportunities can be appraised. If a new project has a net present value per pound of outlay which is in excess of £0.051, then that project can be added to the investment plan, replacing Project 3 in our list. If it generates a net present value per pound of outlay, which is less than this value, then it need not be considered further.

The value of £0.051 for this project plan represents the marginal return on the marginal project. It is sometimes referred to as the **dual** or **shadow price of capital.**

> *Multi-period capital rationing*
> Multi-period capital rationing represents a much more complex problem which cannot be solved without recourse to linear programming, using the net present value of each project as the objective function and the period-by-period cash flows as a series of annual constraints. If you are particularly interested in exploring this aspect, study the Carsberg (1974) reference in the Further reading at the end of this chapter. His text has an excellent chapter on the topic of capital rationing.

So far it has been assumed that all future cash flows are known accurately. In reality this is rarely the case. Indeed, in many cases, management may feel considerable uncertainty concerning the size of future cash flows if different circumstances arise.

The problem of risk

Earlier, in Part II, you met the idea of assessing risk and return via a graphical illustration (Figure 3.2) showing the standard deviation. The statistical measure of standard deviation is used to gauge the extent to which a particular variable (such as an annual cash flow) may deviate from its most likely value. A variable which has a high spread relative to another is said to have a higher risk; consequently, if two projects are compared, the project with the highest standard deviation of returns is said to be the more risky.

Before proceeding further, it is important to note that, from the investors' point of view, the risk of a new project cannot be considered in isolation. From their point of view, what will be important is how undertaking that project alters the risk of their overall investment in a number of projects in a previously balanced portfolio. This difficulty of managing *portfolios* of investments, is addressed shortly.

Accounting for uncertainty

Consider two projections of next year's cash flow from two independent projects, only one of which can be undertaken (for whatever reason). Both are estimated to give the same expected value, but one, Project B, has a higher standard deviation of possible cash returns than Project A. In this sense there is a much higher probability, with Project B, of either very high or very low results than with Project A. Project B can be said to be more 'risky' than Project A. This is captured graphically in Figure 8.1.

In capital investment appraisal, uncertainty such as that captured in the graph can be accounted for by adjusting the discount rate in light of the manager's perception of the degree of associated risk inherent in the proposed project. This in itself is not too difficult. The discount rate will be adjusted increasingly to take account of greater or lesser risk. Thereafter, the NPV is determined as in your earlier calculations.

An alternative approach involves, with greater difficulty, attempting to estimate the impact of risk on future cash flows through sensitivity analysis or simulation. It is this you consider next.

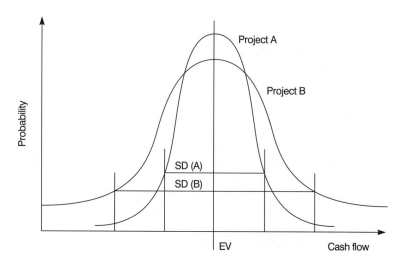

Figure 8.1 Projected cash flows for Project A and Project B

Sensitivity analysis

Sensitivity analysis is a technique which seeks to determine the effect on the net present value of the changes in various assumptions built into estimations of future cash flows. As such, it endeavours to measure by how much the variables might change and then ask 'what if'?

Take, for example, a project which has an expected outlay of 1.1 million and a productive life of 5 years. During that time, initial sales of £450,000 in the first year are expected to grow at 6% p.a., and variable costs of £120,000 are expected to grow at 8% p.a. The fixed costs directly attributable to this project are expected to be £50,000 p.a., growing at 2% p.a. The company's cost of capital is currently 8%, although fluctuations in money market rates have caused some uncertainty about this figure. Ignore taxation.

Using the standard NPV calculation approach, the relevant figures are shown in Table 8.3. When discounted at appropriate discount factors relating to cost of capital of 8%, the project NPV is determined as being £144,882 (and thus positive).

Table 8.3

Detail	t_0	t_1	t_2 (all in £m)	t_3	t_4	t_5
Outlay	(1.1)					
Sales		0.450	0.477	0.505620	0.535957	0.568115
Variable costs		(0.120)	(0.129600)	(0.139968)	(0.151165)	(0.163259)
Fixed costs		(0.050)	(0.051)	(0.052020)	(0.053060)	(0.054122)
Net cash flow	(1.1)	0.280	0.296400	0.313632	0.331732	0.350734

Although the NPV in Table 8.3 is predicted as being positive, it is only so and at that value in relation to the detail shown in the table. If any of the details were to change, so would the NPV. Given that predictions are about the future, it may be that one or more of the details may well change, with consequences.

To enter the uncertain world of the future, a management team must consider the impact of changing assumptions concerning:

- the magnitude of the capital outlay
- changes in growth variations on sales, variable costs and fixed costs
- changes in the assumptions concerning initial sales levels and costs levels
- changes in the anticipated cost of capital
- changes in the life of the project.

By using sensitivity analysis, a manager can identify those variables to which, if changed, a project may be most vulnerable. The analysis is usually judged by measuring the degree to which NPV (or accordingly) IRR is affected.

Illustrating sensitivity analysis

Assume that a proposed project about which a management team is uncertain has been subjected to analysis to establish how sensitive the outcome is to changes in any of the variables. Using the details in Table 8.3, the research shows, say, the following pattern of sensitivities.

If the variable below changes, then the impact on NPV will be:

Sales	13% +
Variable costs	(3.8%)
Fixed costs	(6.2%)
Cost of capital	(8.1%)
Interest rates (funding working capital)	(1.02%)

By applying further computer modelling, each of the percentage changes in NPV above may be assessed cumulatively. It may be that this is done many times over in light of likely changes in the organization's external environment.

The individual sensitivity factor is calculated thus:

$$\text{Sensitivity factor} = \frac{\text{Percentage change in NPV}}{\text{Percentage change in variable}}$$

From the example above, you can see that alterations in sales level has the most significant effect followed by (in order) capital cost, fixed cost, variable cost and interest rate. Variations in sales level appear to be the most significant, and interest rate the least significant, variable in determining NPV.

Sensitivity analysis in practice

As a practical illustration, look at Figure 8.2 which shows just how sensitive the projections of Eurotunnel Plc are to a range of selected variables. (This schedule has been taken from Eurotunnel's original prospectus for prospective shareholders in 1987. The analysis is ongoing with regular revisits being made.)

A footnote

There are two important problems with the use of sensitivity analysis:

- sensitivities are estimated on individual variables, one by one
- it is assumed that changes in different variables in the net present value formula are independent of one another.

The first problem we can overcome by the use of **simulation** techniques. The second requires a much deeper understanding of risk, which you will pursue shortly.

Simulation

This technique facilitates the analysis of the effects of risk (measured as variations in outcomes) on the net present value of a project. With this technique it is possible for managers to:

- identify the most likely project cash flows and the appropriate discount rate
- identify the distribution of each variable in the cash flow projection and the discount rate
- using random numbers and an algorithm for translating random numbers into values from each distribution, take specimen values of each variable (a **trial)** and compute the net present value
- repeat this trial procedure until a distribution of net present values for the project can be generated.

Simulation as a technique overcomes one of the most important difficulties of sensitivity analysis in that it allows more than one component of the net present value calculation to be varied at once. It does, however, suffer from the following deficiencies:

1 It misses an important aspect of risk which is caused by the interrelationships between different variables. In the example above we would, for instance, expect there to be some relationship between changes in the value of the cash flows and changes in the cost of capital (through inflation).

Returns and sensitivity analysis

The following table sets out Eurotunnel's projected returns and the effect, for illustrative purposes, on those returns of varying revenue levels and certain of the key assumptions underlying Eurotunnel's financial projections.

		1994	1998	2003	2013	2023	2033	Net value in 1995 of gross dividends per Unit discounted at 12% (note 4)	Gross dividend yield over life of project (note 5)
		Net dividend per – Unit £ (notes 1 and 2) (Gross dividend yield per Unit at the UK Offer price – %) (notes 1 and 3)							
	Eurotunnel's projections:	£0.39 (16%)	£0.85 (34%)	£1.46 (60%)	£3.80 (155%)	£7.70 (315%)	£14.44 (591%)	£24	17.7%
Sensitivities									
(i) **Increased revenue:**	assuming an increase in revenues of 10% and in operating costs of 5%	£0.67 (27%)	£0.82 (33%)	£1.67 (68%)	£4.21 (172%)	£8.53 (349%)	£16.13 (660%)	£28	18.8%
(ii) **Reduced revenue:**	assuming a decrease in revenues of 10% and in operating costs of 5%	£0.15 (6%)	£0.67 (27%)	£1.22 (50%)	£3.32 (136%)	£6.77 (277%)	£12.75 (522%)	£20	16.6%
(iii) **Increased inflation:**	(a) assuming 7% inflation from 1993 and unchanged real interest rates	£0.31 (13%)	£0.92 (37%)	£1.65 (67%)	£4.69 (192%)	£10.37 (424%)	£21.32 (872%)	£30	18.6%
	(b) assuming inflation increased by 0.5% in 1988 and 1% from 1989 to 1992 and unchanged real interest rates	£0.33 (13%)	£0.87 (35%)	£1.50 (61%)	£3.96 (162%)	£8.02 (328%)	£15.06 (617%)	£25	17.9%
(iv) **Reduced inflation:**	(a) assuming 5% inflation from 1993 and unchanged real interest rates	£0.49 (20%)	£0.70 (28%)	£1.29 (53%)	£3.07 (126%)	£5.69 (233%)	£9.74 (399%)	£20	16.9%
	(b) assuming inflation reduced by 0.5% in 1988 and 1% from 1989 to 1992 and unchanged real interest rates	£0.46 (18%)	£0.80 (32%)	£1.41 (58%)	£3.65 (149%)	£7.38 (302%)	£13.84 (567%)	£24	17.6%
(v) **Lower real interest:**	assuming real interest rates 1.5% lower throughout	£0.64 (26%)	£0.73 (30%)	£1.53 (62%)	£3.81 (156%)	£7.66 (314%)	£14.36 (588%)	£25	18.2%
(vi) **Higher real interest:**	assuming real interest rates 1.5% lower throughout	(note 6)	£0.75 (30%)	£1.38 (57%)	£3.79 (155%)	£7.73 (316%)	£14.53 (595%)	£23	17.2%
(vii) **Increased construction costs:**	assuming construction costs increased by 10%	£0.17 (7%)	£0.76 (31%)	£1.38 (56%)	£3.74 (153%)	£7.63 (312%)	£14.37 (588%)	£23	17.3%
(viii) **Delay:**	assuming a delay in commencement of operations of 6 months and increase of £30m (at July 1987 prices) in corporate and other costs	(note 6)	£0.81 (33%)	£1.42 (58%)	£3.77 (154%)	£7.67 (314%)	£14.43 (590%)	£23	17.4%

Note:
1. These amounts include an allowance for inflation, as indicated in note 4 to the profit projections above.
2. This represents the net dividend per Unit payable in respect of the relevant year.
3 This represents the gross dividends per Unit (including the associated UK and French tax credits) payable in respect of the relevant year, divided by the UK Offer price of a Unit.
4. This represents the value in mid-1995 of all dividends paid from the project in respect of one Unit (including the associated tax credits) discounted to mid-1995, the expected date of payment of the first dividend, at an illustrative rate of 12% per annum. If the rate of discount used were 10% or 15% then the corresponding net values on the basis of Eurotunnel's projections would be £35 and £16, respectively. It should be noted that the discount rate used for each sensitivity case is constant, although the inflation and interest rates applied in certain sensitivities vary.
5. This represents the average rate of return over the life of the project, based on gross dividends, to a purchaser in the issue who also exercises his New Warrants in November 1992.
6. In these cases the first dividend would be declared in respect of the year ending 31 December 1995.

Figure 8.2 Extract from Eurotunnel Plc prospectus – financial projections

The sentitivity of the revenue projections to changes in the assumed rate of growth of UK gross domestic product and
to assumed corresponding changes in UK consumer expenditure is shown below:

	1985–1993		1993–2003		2003–2013	
		Consumer		Consumer		Consumer
Rates of growth in UK (% p.a.)	GDP	expenditure	GDP	expenditure	GDP	expenditure
Eurotunnel's projections	2.15	2.05	2.15	2.05	2.00	1.90
Lower growth	1.50	1.50	1.50	1.50	1.40	1.40
Higher growth	2.50	2.30	2.50	2.30	2.35	2.15

	1993	2003	2013
Changes in revenue projections			
Lower growth	–7%	–13%	–16%
Higher growth	+3%	+5%	+8%

Figure 8.2 Extract from Eurotunnel Plc prospectus – financial projections (continued)

2 It can be computationally very complex where many different variables have to be brought into account. This problem has been
reduced in recent years through the availability of cheap computing
power and specialist computer packages which make the modelling
of the processes much easier than before.

Sensitivity analysis and simulation in perspective

From the above you should now appreciate the deficiencies of the net
present value model when capital is in short supply and the methods
for handling risk in projections of cash flows.

It may appear that the modelling methods that are being employed
are complex – especially in our treatment of risk. Indeed, it would be
only natural to ask if there is an easier way to incorporate the effects of
risk into our analysis without having to calculate its effects on each
and every element within the analysis. Fortunately there is, as you will
see in the next section as you build upon your earlier considerations of
risk in Part II. There, you may recall, the required rate of return by a
funder equates with the cost of capital, and it is with the cost of capital
that you will begin a deeper understanding of risk.

Managing the cost of capital and risk

Here you will revisit the all-important problem of estimating the cost
of capital which is appropriate for a particular project, but in particular consider the cost of capital and risk.

The cost of capital

In Part II you established that any providers of capital funds to an
organization require a reward and that the reward required is the cost
of capital to the firm. A complicating reality is, however, that the

providers' relationship with the organization is mediated through the capital market. As far as any investors are concerned they view their investment as a source of cash (in the form of dividends and eventual capital sale proceeds) and are unlikely to have any other financial interest in the firm. With larger companies especially, the notion of 'ownership' is quite separate from that of management. Investors are free to buy and sell their ownership stake through the market without let or hindrance from the firm whose shares they hold. As a consequence, existing and/or potential investors, viewing an organization as a long-term investment, will wish to focus on:

- alternative rewards from alternative and competing investment opportunities
- where a portfolio of investments is required – a balanced portfolio to balance out differing degrees of risk from differing investments.

This has the following consequences:

- investors see their pay-off in terms of the straight cash reward that they earn from the firm
- they will only be concerned with the most likely return that they can earn (their average return) and the risk attaching to that return
- sensible investors will hold well-diversified portfolios in which non-systematic, firm-specific risk is diversified away
- as well-diversified investors, they will only be concerned with their exposure to common 'market' risk and the effect which changes in their portfolio of investments will have on this exposure.
- diversification for firms (by acquisitions, mergers or simply by expansion into new areas) will only be worthwhile to their investors if it can be achieved at a cheaper cost than they can achieve through their own diversification into different shareholdings
- the risk of a new project is of itself unimportant – what matters for investors is the degree to which the acceptance of the new project alters the firm's exposure to market risk.

The economics of investor behaviour and its implications for firm policy come to some quite startling conclusions. Radical diversification by companies into new projects is unlikely to be a sensible strategy for investors (they can do it more cheaply). The merits of any new project should be judged in terms of (a) the level of return it offers, commensurate with (b) its influence upon the exposure of the firm, *as a whole*, to market risk.

You may wonder, however, why the firm should be concerned at all about what its current investors think about a new project. Surely, the firm is independent of its investors – they buy and sell in the market. What possible effect can that have on the firm?

The answer is tied up with the notion of opportunity cost. If an organization uses up a resource such as raw materials from stock, then the opportunity cost of its use will be the cost of its replacement (assuming that its realizable value is less than its economic value to the firm). With investment, the same concept holds; if a firm uses up capital by way of investment, then the opportunity cost of that capital is the cost of its replacement from the market. This will normally be taken to mean the minimum rate of return required by the market to reinstate the capital position of the firm to that which held before the investment took place. So, if a firm uses up (say) £1 million from its current cash resources, then the opportunity cost associated with the use of those funds is the average rate of return that it would have to offer to the market in order in order to secure their replacement. (In addition, it is normally assumed that the firm will secure replacement in its existing gearing ratio to avoid confusing a decision about change in gearing with a decision on the merits of investment.)

The cost of equity capital

Where greater levels of risk exist, it is not unreasonable for investors to expect a higher average rate of return for holding higher levels of market risk. They cannot expect to be rewarded, by the market, for holding random, firm-specific risk which they can easily eliminate by sensible diversification. In essence, therefore, they have a right to expect an average rate of return which consists of:

- the return that they would get if their investment was entirely risk-free, plus
- an additional component of return which is their reward for holding the level of market risk attached to the share concerned.

This can be expressed thus:

Average expected return = Risk free rate + Risk premium

Of course, what is important is to assess how the level of market risk exposure of a particular share, and hence the amount of risk premium due for that share, is measured. The simplest way is to look at how the share responds when compared with the market as a whole, as reflected in the performance of some market-wide index. The best candidate in the UK is the *Financial Times* All-share Index, which is published daily and provides a comprehensive indicator of changes in the general price level of all quoted equity shares.

Theoretically, because investors invest in a much wider market than just equity shares, we should use an indicator for the total capital market. However, for most purposes the FT All-share Index (because of the very wide degree of internal diversification of its constituent companies) may be taken as quite a good indicator of the total capital market. The level of the index can be regarded as a surrogate for the price of the equivalent portfolio of shares.

The market index may then be used as a 'benchmark' against which the comparative riskiness of individual investments may be measured. For example, if a share's periodic return measurements fluctuate exactly in line with those of the index, then it has, to use the technical term, a **market beta** (β) of 1.

Betas

Consider, now, a share which fluctuates in line with the market. If such a share increased its return at a rate (say) 30% greater than the market on upturns, and decreased 30% faster on downturns, then its beta would be 30% greater than the market, i.e. 1.3. Similarly, if a share was less sensitive to market risk (say, 20% less than the index), then it would have a beta of less than 1 (in this case 0. 8).

The notion of the **beta-value** *is* very important and, apart from the price, is the most important item of information which can be obtained about an investment in a company. It is a difficult statistic to compute, and the only reliable listing of betas in the UK is provided by the London Business School Risk Management Service. However, their coverage of UK equities is exhaustive and copies of their quarterly publication can be obtained from the London Business School or major libraries. For US stocks, beta-values are published by a number of the principal investment houses.

The Capital Asset Pricing Model

It is possible to apply very useful formulae to capture the utility of betas. This is through what is known as the **Capital Asset Pricing Market**. This tries to establish an appropriate (to say correct might be over-ambitious) equilibrium market value of a company's shares and the cost of equity capital taking account of risk. In essence, it may be seen as alternative to the dividend valuation cost of equity model you met in Part II.

If a share (i) has unit market risk, then its expected level of return should be the same as the return on the market index, i.e.

$$\text{Er}_i\% = \text{Er}_m\%$$

where $\text{Er}_i\%$ is the expected return on the share, and $\text{Er}_m\%$ is the expected return on the market index. The additional premium of return which is earned by a unit beta share is

$$\text{Risk premium} = \text{Er}_m\% - R\%$$

The premium expected from a share which bears 20% more risk than the market should be

Risk premium $= 1.2(Er_m\% - R\%)$

We can generalize the return formula, as follows:

Average expected return = Risk free rate + Risk premium
$Er_i\%$ $= R\%$ $+ ß(Er_m\% - R\%)$

The **Capital Asset Pricing Model** asserts that this return-market risk-trade-off is essentially linear and this, in fact, accords with a number of empirical studies concerning the market risk return relationship. In Figure 8.3 this mode is shown in graphical form.

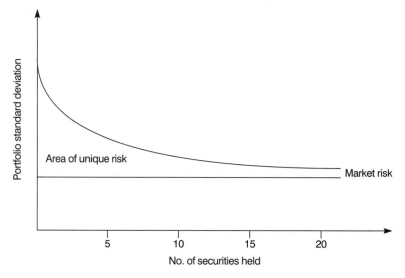

Figure 8. 3 The Capital Asset Pricing Model

CAPM betas in operation
A company's beta-value is 0.96. The risk-free rate of interest (found from the discount currently offered on government short-dated stock) is 4% p.a. and the annual rate of return on the FT All-share Index currently stands at 9%.
    The minimum rate of return required by this company can easily be derived from the Capital Asset Pricing Model:

$Er_i\% = 4\% + 0.96(9\% - 4\%) = 8.8\%$

Once the required rate of return has been found for a share, the rate of return which the market requires for new equity investment in the company concerned has been established. Thus the opportunity cost of equity capital which can be used as the discount rate in capital investment projects which leave the exposure of the firm to market risk (as measured by the firm's beta) undisturbed, is determined. However, not all investments fall into this class. Some will move the beta-value of the firm into a more defensive risk class, whereas others will move the firm into a more aggressive risk class.

Another CAPM beta example
A company is examining the cost of its finance for project appraisal purposes. The minimum rate of return on its equity is 4% higher than its debt. It also has an irredeemable preference share issue in circulation which offers a rate of return exactly half-way between that of its equity and its debt. The company's beta-value is reported at 1.05, the market risk premium is 6.5% and the rate of return on short-term government stock is 4%. The proportions of the market values of each of these items of capital to the company's total market capitalization is 4:2:2 for equity, debt and preference stock respectively.
  The cost of equity capital is:

$r_e = 4 + (1.05 \times 6.5)$ (from the Capital Asset Pricing Model)
      $= 10.825\%$

Thus $r_d = 6.825\%$ and $r_p = 8.825\%$ are the rate of return for debt and for preference capital respectively. The weighted average cost of capital is, therefore,

WACC $= (0.5 \times 10.825\%) + (0.25 \times 6.825\%) + (0.25 \times 8.825\%)$
        $= 9.325\%$

The cost of capital in a geared firm

The opportunity cost of capital concept developed earlier can easily be applied to a geared firm, i.e. a firm which has more than one form of capital in its capital structure. In such a firm, a project should be able to offer a return which is better than the market weighted average of the different classes of capital in its capital structure. For example, if a firm is financed by equity and debt in equal market value, and the returns required for its equality and debt by the market are 12% and 9%, respectively, then its 'weighted' average cost of capital will be

$$\text{WACC} = w_e r_e + w_d r_d$$

where

w_e = weight (in terms of total market value) of equity in the firm's capital structure

w_d = weight (in terms of total market value) of debt in the firm's capital structure

r_e = the minimum market rate of return on equity (specified by the Capital Asset Pricing Model)

r_d = the minimum market rate of return on debt (measured by its market yield).

Each of the weights can be specified as the proportion of market value of the respective capital component (equity or debt) to the total market capitalization of the firm:

$$w_d = \frac{\text{Total market value of debt}}{\text{Total market value of equity + debt}}$$

This ratio is also termed the market **gearing** ratio, and it gives a measure of a firm's exposure to financial risk.

Substituting the values given above in the weighted average cost of capital formula:

$$\begin{aligned} \text{WACC} &= (0.5 \times 12\%) + (0.5 \times 9\%) \\ &= 10.5\% \end{aligned}$$

The cost of capital for unlisted and non-profit-making companies

The concept of the 'opportunity cost of capital' has been most clearly worked out in those situations where a company has securities which are traded in an active market setting. It is also based upon the assumption that the interests of the investor group are dominant. In many organizations either or both of these situations may not be true.

In the case of a small company, the estimation of the cost of capital must be carried out in a context where there is little or no market evidence to support the estimation of yields or prices. Two strategies for dealing with this are:

1 The use of 'proxies', where a similar company can be found which does have a full listing. Clearly, the closeness of the proxy in terms of capital structure, market, technology, etc., is a matter of judgement. However, as a first approximation this approach can give acceptable results.
2 The use of 'internal' proxies – estimates of the variation of earnings on a monthly or quarterly basis with variations in the market index

may give a beta-value to a first degree of approximation. Current interest rates on lending from financial institutions may give an estimate of the debt component, and so forth.

With non-profit-making institutions, the use of discounting techniques is much more questionable. For example, the use of cash flow analysis assumes that the residual cash flow should be optimized, whereas other items such as labour charges are regarded as a 'cost' which should be minimized. This may well run counter to the objectives of the organization. Similarly, even though a publicly funded project, such as the recent development of the cross Channel link, may be constructed with the intention that it should be 'profitable', a great proportion of the social benefits and costs may not be captured by the analysis of cash flows described in this book. Even assuming that a reasonable analysis of the relevant cash flows can be conducted, the problem of how to interpret those flows via a single discount rate remains.

Most appraisals of large-scale projects in the public sector rely on the calculation of what is sometimes called the 'social time preference rate' as an analogue of the time preference rate of the investor groups within a market-financed firm. The calculation of the social time preference rate takes us into the area of cost–benefit analysis, which is beyond the scope of this book; suffice it to say that there is considerable debate among economists concerning the calculation of such rates. Some argue that market rates can be used, whereas others argue that the instabilities of market systems mean that administrative decisions have to be made concerning the appropriate rate for a given project. This latter approach is the one usually followed by the UK government when making its investment decisions.

Summary

You have now examined in some detail, the estimation of the appropriate discount rate for net present value analysis. The methods shown have followed the notions of an 'opportunity cost of capital' which have been used to define costs for different types of finance. Finally, the fuller implications of cost of capital in a geared firm have been considered.

Having considered the techniques available for appraisal and the associated managerial issues, the management consideration of post-implementation audit and appraisal is addressed.

Self-assessment questions

SAQ 8.1

Calculate the weighted average cost of capital (WACC) in the two scenarios shown in (a) and (b) below:

(a) where £1 million total capital employed comprises:
  (i) shareholders' equity at book value is £500,000 with an expected rate of return by shareholders of 10%
  (ii) debt capital of £500,000 with a coupon cost of 15%
and
(b) where the £1 million total capital employed as shown on the balance sheet and referred to in (a) above may be restated in market value terms thus:
  (i) shareholders' equity has a market value of £2.50 per share, there being 500,000 shares
  (ii) 15% coupon debt capital has a market value of £300,000.

After you have completed your calculations, comment on which of the two WACC figures you have calculated might be more appropriate for management to consider in its planning and decision making.

SAQ 8.2

A company is considering a diversification into a new product line which is expected to reduce considerably the seasonality it normally experiences in its cash flows. The project cash flows are expected to be:
Outlay: £(1,5000,000)
Year 1: £420,000
Year 2: £570,000
Year 3: £550,000
Year 4: £200,000

The discount rate on short-term Treasury stock is currently 5.5% and the market rate of return is currently 10.8%. The company's beta-value, as reported by the LBS Risk Management Services is 1.15. A consultant risk analyst estimates that the 15% over exposure to market risk specified by this level of beta could be reduced to 12% by the acceptance of this project.

Calculate this project's net present value using (i) the pre-project discount rate, and (ii) the adjusted discount rate. Should the project be accepted or rejected, and why?

Further reading

Carsberg, B.V. (1974) *Analysis for Investment Decisions*. Accountancy Age Publications.

Coulthurst, N.J., 1986. Accounting for inflation in capital investment: state of the art and science, *Accounting and Business Research* (Winter)

Lorie, J.H. and Savage, L.J., 1955. Three problems in rationing capital, *Journal of Business Finance* (October)

Wengartner, H.M., 1997. Capital rationing: authors in search of a plot, *Journal of Finance* (December)

Allen, D. 1996. High hurdles, *Management Accounting* (October)

Pike, R.H., 1982. *Capital Budgeting in the 1980s*, CIMA

Neale, C.W., 1991. A revolution in post-completion audit adoption, *Management Accounting* (November)

Gadella, J. and Jones, J., 1996. Post completion review, *Management Accounting* (September)

9 Cost savings, profit enhancement and ad hoc decisions

Introduction

In this chapter you will look at typical financial frameworks used by management teams to assess the viability of individual and relatively short-term decisions. They are often concerned with cost cutting or one-off or ad hoc decisions which may increase or save cash flow. As was established in Chapter 6, there still remains the need to balance any projected shorter term outcomes against longer term implications. However, the appropriate frameworks must be applied to produce the likely short-term outcome before any comparison may be made. You will thus concentrate on such frameworks.

Specifically, you will be looking at decisions concerned with:

- assessing the profitability and viability of particular areas of activity, be they product or service lines or units or departments
- undertaking an activity in-house or subcontracting it externally, often referred to as make or buy decisions
- the best utilization of scarce resources.

In so doing you meet the idea of contribution (which has links to operational gearing from Chapter 5) and the notion of relevant costs for decision-making, involving particularly opportunity and sunk costs.

By the end of this chapter you will:

- understand the principles adopted in assessing the impact of short-term decisions
- be able to apply those principles to assess the liability of activities
- be able to undertake make or buy decisions
- be able to make the best use of scarce resources, particularly in the short term.

Understanding costs

In Chapter 5, in considering operational gearing, you became accustomed to the idea of accountants making an assumption for decision making that costs may be divided broadly into two categories – fixed (at least within a range) and variable. There are, however, other ways of viewing costs – dividing them into relevant and non-relevant costs, in relation to the decision under consideration. In such a division the recognition of what are termed opportunity and sunk costs are paramount.

Categorizing costs for decision-making
Imagine a manager working for British Airways who is thinking of leaving and setting up a business. The manager is earning, say, £40,000 p.a. A feasibility study which the manager has paid for, costing £5,000, indicates that over a 3-year period the consultancy could earn gross fees of £150,000, incurring directly associated costs of £25,000 (excluding car costs). The manager would need to invest £25,000 as capital, using money currently invested in a special bank deposit account earning 10% p.a. interest. In addition, a detached annex at home, currently rented out to students for £5,000 p.a., would be used as an office base. By leaving British Airways, the manager would save travel to work costs of £3,000 p.a. although car costs of £5,000 p.a. would remain unchanged and the car would be used for the new business.

In assessing the viability of the proposal, as with capital investment appraisal, the manager should concentrate not on profit but on cash flows. In so doing, the principle adopted will be to include as a relevant cost any amount or value which, as a result of going ahead, represents an additional cash flow in or out and/or an outward cash flow saved or an incoming cash flow forgone. Applying these categories to the situation in question:

Detail	Additional cash flow		Cash flow	
	In	Out	Saved	Forgone
	£	£	£	£
Consultancy fees	150,000			
Direct costs		25,000		
Salary × 3 years				120,000
Bank interest × 3 years				7,500
Rent from students × 3 years				15,000
Travel saved × 3 years			9,000	
Totals	150,000	25,000	9,000	142,500

The above may be interpreted thus:

	£
Fees	150,000
less direct expenses	(25,000)
add savings	9,000
less amounts forgone	(142,500)
Net cash deficit	(8,500)

In arriving at the net figure it is important to note that accounting convention ignores the cost of the survey – £5,000 – on the grounds that the cash flow has already taken place. It is therefore a sunk cost and as such has no bearing now on whether or not to proceed. (Note, however, that in any subsequent profit measurement, the sunk cost would need to be accounted for, perhaps as a one-off charge to Year 1's profit statement or, more likely, as a depreciation charge to, say 3 years' profit statements.) The car costs, too, of £15,000 over 3 years are ignored in this assessment as they already exist and no future cash flows or savings arise; they are not relevant. There are, however, also valid costs in preparing any subsequent profit statement. In addition, each of the three values tagged as forgone represent opportunity costs and should be taken account of, although in any subsequent measurement they are ignored.

Of course, the manager in the box would not wish to be guided by the calculation alone. The accuracy of the forecast would need to be considered, as would any qualitative factors, such as the value of working for oneself. In addition, an assessment of what might happen after 3 years would need to be assessed.

Included in any such further assessment might be a return to the division of costs into fixed and variable. Such a division, as shown in Chapter 5, can facilitate the use of the contribution mechanism (sales less variable costs). You will recall that if fixed costs are already covered and a proposal incurs no additional fixed costs, then any proposal resulting in a positive contribution should be adopted as in such circumstances all of that contribution will be profit.

The categorization of costs can help in assessing a variety of proposals and more often than that the principles illustrated are to be found in decisions concerning:

● product/service line profitability/viability
● internal/external propositions (such as make or buy decisions)
● utilizing scarce resources.

The decision framework is applied to each in turn, in the rest of the chapter.

Profitability/viability of product/service lines/activity areas

In a sense, decisions in such areas are a hybrid of the cash flow principles exposed above and the associated reported profitability of the area under review. The framework here demands that an assessment is made of the reported profit impact upon the organization as a whole, having taken account of any additional cash flows out or cash savings made. An additional problem usually arises in the guise of fixed overheads shared with other activity areas. This will result in the contribution principle re-aired above being employed, as you see below.

Practical illustration 1

Assume a small UK domestic airline (perhaps a partner of British Airways) has three routes, coded A123, B456 and C789. The latest profit statements show, in £000s, the following:

Detail	A123	B456	C789	Total
Sales	300	600	900	1,800
Direct costs – variable	150	300	450	900
Fixed costs	180	180	180	540
Net profit/(loss)	(30)	120	270	360

Understandably the airline's management may be concerned about route A123, apparently making a loss. Of course, it may be that the loss arises only because of the proportionately greater charge for fixed costs it receives as opposed to the other routes. After all, there may be alternative – and more importantly, more valid – ways of dividing up the overheads. The problem is that we do not know which might be more appropriate. The answer lies in:

- establishing the contribution to see if it is positive
- establishing whether or not any fixed costs are saved by closing down the route.

On this latter point we discover that of the airline's total £540,000 fixed costs only £60,000 would be saved. Thus, restating on a contribution basis we establish:

Detail	A123	B456	C789	Total
Sales	300	600	900	1,800
Direct costs – variable	150	300	450	900
Contribution	150	300	450	900
Fixed costs				540
Net profit/(loss)				360

A123 currently produces a positive contribution of £150,000 towards covering the airline's fixed costs, and, once covered, thus towards profit. If the route is closed down, the saving of £60,000 in cash spent on fixed costs when offset against the contribution of £150,000 means that the business as a whole would lose £90,000 contribution. It would thus, all other factors being equal, be inappropriate to close down the route.

Clearly, in practical illustration 1 there would be a range of other factors which might need to be considered before any final decision were made. For example, curtailing A123, or another line, might have an impact on another route. There may be a loss of customer allegiance or a marked effect on staff morale. Whatever the other factors, the cost analysis will play a key role.

Internal/external propositions

Another decision, particularly in modern times, often facing management teams is that of having to decide between carrying out an activity internally or contracting it out externally. The detail in the next box illustrates this.

Practical illustration 2
A public sector concern provides a staff training and development function. It is about to be, in the jargon, market tested, i.e. compared with, among other factors, the cost quoted by an established private sector training consortium. It has been established that the level of quality is likely to be the same whether training originates internally or externally. The following cost information is available in relation to a financial training course which has traditionally been run in-house:

	£
Direct costs – variable: bought-in lecturers	600
Training equipment depreciation	50
Administration cost charge	350
Total cost	1,000
Number of delegates per course	20
Cost per delegate	£50

The external consortium has offered to run the course at a cost of £45 per delegate, subject to there being 20 delegates per course.

At first glance it would seem that £5 per delegate, £100 per course, could be saved. However, when the notion of relevant and non-relevant costs is considered, a different picture emerges. To begin with, the depreciation of £50 per course can be treated as a sunk cost because the equipment has already been purchased and will continue to exist (unless a resale value equivalent to its net book value can be obtained, for which there is no evidence). This must thus be treated as a sunk cost and thus ignored. The administration costs, too, will remain as no redundancies are likely.

So only the direct costs (£600 per course) will be avoided if the course is sub-contracted. It will, therefore, in relevant cost terms, cost £400 (comprising £350 + £50) to operate the course, as opposed to £900 (£45 × 20 delegates) externally.

Of course, the situation in practical illustration 2 might change if redundancies were to be made and/or the training equipment sold. In such cases, the calculation would need to be made again, taking account of new information.

Utilizing scarce resources

A commonality between all organizations, large or small, private, public or voluntary sector is the fact they are all likely to have limited resources. As a consequence they will not be able to undertake all the activities they might like to. Important management decisions are required about the use of scarce resources to ensure efficiency, effectiveness and value for money. The key factor in such decisions is the scarcity of the particular resource concerned. The decision framework here involves maximizing the contribution per unit of scarce resource. This is illustrated in the following box.

Practical illustration 3
Assume a business manufactures and sells two products, Nice and Notso, in equal amounts. The total fixed costs are £40,000 p.a. The contribution per unit of Nice is £12 and of Notso £8, producing, given the equal production and sales, an average contribution of £10. Nice takes 4 machine-hours to produce and Notso 2 machine-hours, and there are only 16,000 machine hours available per annum. The company's management team is looking at maximizing its scarce resource of machine-hours. What should it do?

In such a case, with the scarce resource being machine-hours, the solution lies in determining the contribution per unit of scarce resource, i.e. per machine hour. This results in:

Nice   £12/4 hours = £3 contribution per hour
Notso   £8/2 hours   = £4 contribution per hour

With 16,000 hours available, concentrating on Nice produces contribution of (16,000 x £3) £48,000 and on Notso of (16,000 x £4) £64,000. Deducting the fixed costs of £40,000 results in Nice producing a profit of £8,000 and Notso of £24,000. All other factors being equal, the management team should opt for maximizing production of Notso.

Again, as with the earlier scenarios, it is important that any other relevant factors in practical illustration 3 are taken into consideration. It may be that the potential for sales of one or both of the products is limited. In such circumstances the team should first attempt to sell as many of Notsos as possible, and then concentrate on Nice. Also, any complementarity between the two products would need to be taken account of. And finally, in this case in particular, if production and sales are to be concentrated on Notso, perhaps consideration should be given to changing the name!

Summary

In this chapter you have considered decision frameworks to help in assessing what to do when particular – and not unrealistic – scenarios might arise. The notion of relevant and non-relevant costs is, as you have seen, important. A problem is, as you have also seen, that the notion can be difficult to grasp given the emphasis on opportunity costs, sunk costs, contribution, not to mention cash and profit flows.

Now you should be able to use a financial framework to:

- assess the profitability and viability of particular areas of activity, be they product or service lines or units or departments
- undertake an analysis of the appropriateness of subcontracting an activity externally or to maintain it in house
- make the best utilization of scarce resources.

Before you proceed to Chapter 10 and explore the management of investment in working capital, undertake the following self-assessment questions.

Self-assessment questions

SAQ 9.1

A manufacturing firm normally sells a product for £11,000 producing a normal profit of £1,000.

It has received a request for a variant on its standard product and the customer has offered to pay only £10,000.

The variant product would have the following cost profile:

- material A would be used which is also in the standard product. This costs £2,000
- another material, B would be required. There is currently enough on hand although if it were not used in the variant product it would be scrapped as it has no other use. When purchased it cost £2,000 and disposal costs if scrapped would amount to £500
- direct labour is normally £3000 and this would remain unchanged
- a supervisor currently earning £20,000 per annum would be allocated to the product manufacture and devote 10% of her time to it
- overheads are normally charged in at 100% of direct labour

In the light of the above, the firm is considering rejecting the offer as the cost statement would appear to show a cost of:

	£
Material A	2,000
Material B	2,000
Direct labour	3,000
Supervisor	2,000
Overheads	3,000
Total	12,000

Advise the firm to accept or reject the contract.

SAQ 9.2

Explain the rationale used in determining whether to carry out an activity internally or to contract it out externally. Justify your explanation with an appropriate numerical illustration.

SAQ 9.3

Explain the rationale used in making the best use of a scarce resource when there are competing alternatives which would also make use of that scarce resource. As with SAQ 9.2, provide an appropriate numerical illustration.

Further reading

Arnold, J. and Hope, T., 1983. *Accounting for management decisions*, Prentice-Hall International

Part IV Other Investment Decisions

10 Understanding and managing the working capital decision

Introduction

In this chapter you will look at the management of investment of funds into working capital. Working capital management is concerned with the balance between current assets and current liabilities and the individual components of both of these. For many organizations the investment of finances into shorter is as important as that for longer term assets. It is one matter to forecast ahead using investment appraisal techniques, but another to manage the ongoing financial management required to ensure that a project or investment that looks good on paper turns out to be so in reality.

You will look specifically at:

● the nature and significance of working capital
● the monitoring of liquidity and cash management
● the assessment of debtor, creditor and stock control.

By the end of this chapter you will:

● recognize the importance of working capital and its management
● understand how to measure and monitor liquidity
● be able to calculate and interpret the current and quick ratios, and ratios to measure and monitor credit and stock controls.

Working capital in perspective

As a departure point, it is appropriate to define working capital. In its simplest form, working capital – or more accurately net current assets – may be defined as the excess of current assets over current liabilities. It is important to note at the outset that on occasions current liabilities may exceed current assets. In such cases the negative working capital may be termed net current liabilities. You are reminded that the balance sheet layouts you met in Part I show the net current assets (or equivalent) as a matter of routine information.

In contrast to the investment appraisal decisions you met earlier, involvement in working capital and its management is more widespread throughout most organizations and on much more of a day-to-day basis. Given less associated emphasis on specialism, it is tempting to assume that working capital management is less important than investment appraisal. The facts belie such an assumption. Many organizations have greater investment in working capital for day-to-day purposes – in short-term current assets – than in longer term fixed assets. Indeed, when viewed as a short-term source of finance, current liabilities take on as great if not greater significance than conventional longer term financing sources. Thus, for these reasons alone, working capital assumes a degree of significance. This is compounded when the need to maintain an appropriate level of net current assets to ensure operations is taken account of.

Again, in contrast to longer term investments, working capital as a management area is more easily approachable in that is has the advantage of being short term, more easily assessable and thus more suited to flexibility, with the need for corrective action quickly ascertained and implemented. In addition, the management of working capital involves decisions which are routine and frequently made, resulting in the facility of a set of defined working practices throughout an organization. In essence, such management requires the establishment of a working capital policy geared towards the minimization of committed finance to day-to-day needs. Working capital management recognizes this, but seeks to balance minimization against the optimization demanded by operational requirements, not least liquidity and continuing survival.

Working capital: policy v. management

The implication of the foregoing paragraph is that there is a tension between policy and management. As ever, the soothing of such a tension may be found by establishing an appropriate balance between the demand for minimizing investment in working capital but ensuring that operations and even ultimate survival are not threatened. In striking this balance, the management of the policy must seek to:

- meet the operational requirements of the organization
- minimize financial mismatching in the sense that long-term financing should not be used for short-term investment
- control the costs of managing working capital by taking account of such matters as stockholding costs, costs of reordering and raising invoices, and credit control costs.

Such a balance is not always easily and readily struck. Later in this chapter you will consider in greater depth some of the cost items in particular.

The working capital flow

The determination of net current assets, as shown in the balance sheet layouts in Part I – current assets minus current liabilities – produces a figure which, as with all balance sheet values, represents a book value at the moment in time that the balance sheet is drawn up. It is thus tempting to assume that working capital is nothing more than a static figure. On the contrary, it is by its very nature dynamic. This is reflected in Figure 10.1, which shows the complexity of the cash circulation route into, through and out of, for the purposes of illustration, a manufacturing company.

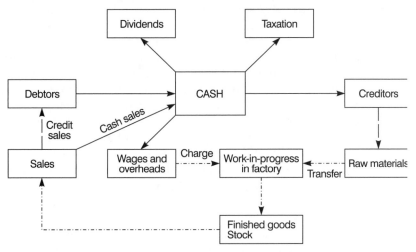

Figure 10.1 The dynamic nature of working capital: cash circulation in a manufacturing concern

In this figure you see that creditors supply materials and overhead items which pass through various checkpoints in the organization. At one checkpoint, work-in-progress, the values of wages and manufacturing overheads are added, with a transfer of the cumulative value into finished goods. Such goods are held there until sold, with such sales being for cash and/or on account terms. Cash is collected from customers, be they cash or account customers (debtors), whereas additional cash payments leave the route to pay other overheads, loan interest and where appropriate, taxation and/or dividend payments.

As with any circulatory route it is important to ensure that it is kept free from blockages, to ensure the free and unhindered flow of cash into, through and out of the organization. A number of practicalities need to be considered, however, with this aim in mind.

For example, it may be that blockages occur in areas such as raw materials and/or finished goods stockholdings. In such case, values build up and will take longer to be transferred into cash inflows into the organization. Similarly, in the manufacturing example, hold-ups in production may occur, for whatever reason, again delaying the ultimate inflow of cash. Even when goods (or of course services) have been sold, debtors may take some time to pay, perhaps deliberately so or perhaps through an inefficient credit control system. Balanced against this build-up of values which block cash inflow are any time delays affecting payments to creditors, to taxation authorities and to shareholders for dividends. In most organizations, such delays do exist legitimately but do not usually counterbalance let alone out-balance the potential blockages detailed earlier. Nevertheless, management teams continually seek to reduce the time length of the cycle from investment in stocks and other costs and taking account of payments, to the generation of net cash inflow.

Figure 10.2 shows the significance in general terms of continually seeking a more appropriate balance between the timings of cash inflows and outflows. In this figure are detailed the alternative scenarios relating to an organization which starts by investing £100,000 in working capital, but then succeeds in making that capital work harder by increasing cash flow throughput by decreasing the cash flow cycle.

In Figure 10.2(a) the organization concerned has committed £100,000 to its working capital cycle, but with the somewhat lengthy (and unrealistic) duration from investment in working capital to return of 1 year. It would be in everybody's interest to cut down this duration both to minimize the overall level of investment and to minimize risk. By cutting the duration in half, as shown in Figure 10.2(b), the risk is halved and the investment reduced to £50,000 at any one time. In Figure 10.2(c) the duration has been cut still further, with the rate of throughput increasing to four times and the commitment of investment reduced to £25,000. At this point we can see the meaning of the phrase 'making working capital sweat' – cutting both investment and duration by as much as possible. There will be a point, however, at which the working capital may be sweated too much, raising the possibility of danger to the organization in not having enough current assets to carry on trading or cash to survive. Thus working capital does need careful and constant monitoring.

The reality of duration and commitment is illustrated in the box and shows what may be termed the working capital cycle: You can see that a table is bought for cash on day 1 for £50. It is held in stock for 20 days before being sold, but on account, not for cash. Debtors then take a further 40 days to pay (despite the bill stating payment terms of 30 days!). Thus £50 is invested in the system for a total of 60 days. This means that the organization is forgoing the use of that money for perhaps more fruitful purposes for 60 days, or indeed borrowing it from the bank and paying interest for 60 days. Of course, £50 over 60 days in reality does not amount to much. But if the organization actually holds 50 tables at any one time, together with 50 chairs plus a range of other items, the average investment over an average duration becomes very high. In such circumstances both investment and duration need careful monitoring, particularly when the not so obvious costs of stockholding and credit control are considered. Such monitor-

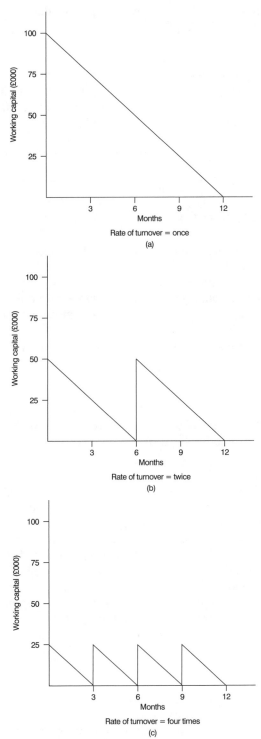

Figure 10.2 Working capital: increasing the rate of turnover in the cycle

ing is usually achieved via the calculation and application of a series of working capital ratios.

Time (day)	Transaction
1	Table bought for £50 for cash
20	Table sold for £100 on account
60	Debtors pay £100

Thus the company finances the cost of the table for 60 days.

Working capital ratios

There are five key ratios which are used. These are:

- the current ratio
- the liquidity ratio (also known as the quick or acid test ratio)
- the debtors and creditors and stock turnover ratios.

These are considered in turn below, followed by a worked example.

Current ratio

This ratio is sometimes referred to as the working capital ratio. This is understandable in that it is measured thus:

Current assets : Current liabilities

In essence, this ratio asks the question, 'If we pay off current liabilities, will we have enough current assets left over with which to carry on trading?' It should not be too high, as that would be a poor use of the scarce resource of finance, but nor should it be too low, as that would be risky and put the survival of the organization at risk. As stated earlier, an appropriate balance would need to be struck, not least in light of the nature of the organization and its specific operating cycle characteristics together with those of its competitors. There is, however, a flaw in the question being answered.

Liquidity ratio

The flaw in the question considered by the current ratio is that it begs another perhaps even more important question. That is, 'Can we pay off current liabilities?' After all, it is one matter to have lots of stocks which mathematically are in excess of current liabilities, but if there is not enough cash available to pay off immediate debts, the organization may never get the chance to sell such stocks as it will be out of business.

The liquidity ratio is measured thus:

Very liquid current assets : Current liabilities

with such liquid assets normally comprising cash/cash at bank plus debtors plus any marketable securities and investments. Again, as with the current ratio, it should not be too high or too low and should take account of firm specific and industry-wide characteristics.

Debtors turnover ratio

This ratio measures how long, on average, debtors take to pay. It is measured thus:

$$\frac{\text{Closing or average debtors for a period}}{\text{Account sales for the period}} \times 365 \text{ days}$$

This enables a comparison to be made with the stated payment terms.

Creditors turnover ratio

Although the debtors turnover measures how long on average debtors take to pay, the creditors ratio measures how long on average it takes to pay creditors. It is measured thus:

$$\frac{\text{Closing or average creditors for a period}}{\text{Account purchases for the period}} \times 365 \text{ days}$$

Not only is a comparison with stated payment terms facilitated, but the debtors and creditors turnovers may also be compared. An analysis of the balance sheets of a range of financially troubled businesses often reveal that there is no cash because creditors are being paid on time, but collections from debtors have been allowed to become longer and longer.

Stock turnover ratio

Referring back to the previous box, you saw that the table was held in stock for, on average, 20 days. This figure would have been derived from the stock turnover calculation which is:

$$\frac{\text{Closing or average stock for a period}}{\text{Cost of stock used or sold during the period}} \times 365 \text{ days}$$

This may also be applied to stocks used in, say, administration and is not limited to stocks which are resold.

Managing through working capital ratios – a worked example

Below are detailed summarized financial extracts from the last 3 years' accounts of Messy Ltd.

Detail	Year 1	Year 2	Year 3
		(all in £000s)	
Year end stocks	50	50	80
Year end debtors	60	60	135
Year end cash	40	40	5
Year end creditors	50	50	25
Account purchases for year	200	200	300
Cost of stock sold during year	360	360	440
Account sales during year	720	720	880

The management of Messy Ltd is concerned that, despite sales rising, cash is falling. The bank manager has advised that attention be given to the working capital situation.

The following calculations have been made for Years 2 and 3:

		Year 2	Year 3
Current ratio:	$\dfrac{\text{Current assets}}{\text{Current liabilities}}$	$\dfrac{50 + 60 + 40}{50}$	$\dfrac{80 + 135 + 5}{25}$
		= 3:1	= 8.8:1

Liquidity ratio: very liquid

	$\dfrac{\text{Current assets}}{\text{Current liabilities}}$	$\dfrac{60 + 40}{50}$	$\dfrac{135 + 5}{25}$
		= 2:1	= 52:1
Debtors t/o:	$\dfrac{\text{Average debtors}}{\text{Account sales}}$	$\dfrac{(60 + 60)/2}{720} \times 365$	$\dfrac{(60 + 135)/2}{880} \times 365$
		= 30.4 days	= 40.4 days
Creditors t/o:	$\dfrac{\text{Average creditors}}{\text{Account purchases}}$	$\dfrac{(50 + 50)/2}{200} \times 365$	$\dfrac{(50 + 25)/2}{300} \times 365$
		= 91.25 days	= 45.6 days
Stock t/o:	$\dfrac{\text{Average stock}}{\text{Cost of stock used/sold}}$	$\dfrac{(50 + 50)/2}{360} \times 365$	$\dfrac{(50 + 80)/2}{440} \times 365$
		= 50.7 days	= 53.9 days

The above figures reveal the following:

Current ratio – in answer to the question, 'If we pay off immediate debts, can we carry on?', the answer is an unequivocal 'Yes!' However, a comparison should be made with, say industry averages to discover whether Year 2 was too low or too high, with consequential implications for the interpretation of Year 3's much higher ratio. In addition, of course, the current ratio begs the question, 'Can we pay off immediate debts?'

Liquidity ratio – on the surface, with both years showing positive (above 1:1) ratios here, it would appear that all is well. It is, however, important to delve beneath the surface of the make-up of the constituents of very liquid current assets. In Year 2, with immediate debts of £50,000, we can see that there is, in fact, only £40,000 in cash which may cause problems. This is accentuated in Year 3 when, despite creditors falling to £25,000, cash in hand has fallen to only £5,000. It is worth noting that some organizations, particularly in times of recession, apply an adapted liquidity ratio using only cash: current liabilities – a true acid test.

Debtors turnover – this has moved from a cycle of making the sale, issuing the invoice and collecting the money once every 30.4 days to once every 40.4 days. It serves only to lengthen the duration of the working capital cycle and must contribute towards the worsening cash situation, with monies being collected more slowly.

Creditors turnover – this has moved in the opposite direction to debtors, with account purchases being made and paid for now once every 45.6 days as opposed to 91.25 days. With debtors paying more slowly and creditors being paid much more quickly, no wonder there are problems at the bank with cash!

Stock turnover – this has not changed very much, having moved from holding stock on average for 50.7 days to 53.9 days, but it has of course moved in the wrong direction and this can only accentuate the deteriorating cash situation.

Working capital ratios in context

From the above you witness that the lower the investment in working capital and the shorter the duration invested for, the harder the working capital is made to work. As a general principle, subject to ensuring the safety of the organization, increased throughput and shorter duration are keys to successful working capital management. However, as indicated earlier, such management needs to take account of the reality of the organization's own world.

For example, it is perfectly feasible for large retailing companies to have a negative working capital cycle. This is because they usually take delivery of goods and sell them before they are required to settle payment to creditors. In addition, the cash nature of the retailing business means that large organizations such as Tesco and Sainsbury have liquidity ratios often well below 1:1, and yet on the surface we might imagine ratios below 1:1 as signalling danger. In contrast, manufacturing companies often have long working capital cycles with, say, shipbuilding concerns requiring very high current and liquidity ratios (although in reality, unfortunately, the latter one turns out to be too low!).

There is no such figure as an average level of investment in working capital or a target generic liquidity ratio. It all very much depends on the nature of the business activity as to the level of the working capital necessary to operate it. For example, as desirable as it is to collect money in very quickly from debtors, if industry practice is to allow lengthy credit periods an organization bucking against this practice might find itself isolated and losing customers. A current ratio of 2:1 seems to have entered folklore as the target for the average organization. First, of course, there is no such entity as an average organization, and secondly, a ratio of 0.6:1 might be acceptable for one organization but disastrous for another requiring say 3:1. The necessity to carry working capital is a function of the cycle time of the organization and its industry and the level of activity. Hence the emphasis earlier on, comparing with industry norms.

Changes in working capital needs

A necessary evil associated with working capital management is that, having achieved working capital nirvana, the world changes through natural and/or engineered evolution. Such changes can occur naturally or through specific management actions. This can be considered in the context of Figure 10.3, where the organization depicted has a balance sheet which comprises the optimum division of financing and investment in assets for its world at the moment, this being represented by the present level of sales, termed S. The fixed and current assets are in optimal relationship and are the long-term and current liabilities.

If the level of sales were, however, to change then it follows that the balance sheet composition would need to reflect this change towards a more optimal balance to suit the new circumstances. Even if the exact relative relationships between sales and debtors and sales and stocks were maintained, the absolute values would need to change accordingly. At sales level S^+ more working capital would be required and at S^- less so. Unfortunately the adjustments to the levels do not happen automatically. They can only result from specific and intended management team action as a result of constant monitoring of the situation and careful balancing of working capital cycle duration with required investment.

Changes in working capital needs: investment and financing decisions

The changes in activity depicted in Figure 10.3 require management attention to be directed, understandably, towards the investment decision – how much more or less needs to be invested in working capital. But such changes also require attention to be paid to the corresponding financing decision, as to how the changes in investment relate to their financing.

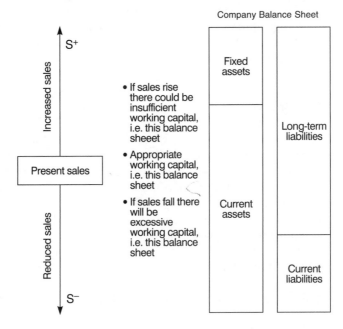

Figure 10.3   Impact of activity changes on working capital needs

It is, for example, a feature of rapidly expanding organizations that they experience short- to medium-term liquidity problems. They are usually described as over-trading in that their balance sheets – i.e. the summarized financing and investment decisions – are not sufficient to support the increased activity in the short to medium term. In such cases, if the increased activity is to continue, longer term finance may be needed in light of the accompanying increases in both working capital investment and duration.

In times of decreasing activity, the balance sheet would need adjustment with even, perhaps, the extreme of assets being disposed of.

The costs of working capital management

Part of management's responsibility in the area of working capital management is to minimize the cost of investment in working capital. As such, a highly visible cost of working capital is the cost of finance. The lower the level of investment, the lower the cost of financing required. Against this, however, must be balanced the operational and ongoing costs of working capital. For example, average stockholdings may be reduced (thus lowering cost of financing as less is invested), but if more orders have to be placed to achieve, say, just-in-time stocking, the operational ongoing cost may outweigh the financing costs saved. As with working capital management in general, a balance needs to be struck, finding a trade-off between the cost benefits of working capital management and the cost of achieving those benefits. Next, you will look at a range of the associated trade-off issues needing to be taken account of.

The costs of stockholding

Any stock control activities must be set against the background of the specific organization and its industry. Manufacturing companies require stocks of raw materials, work-in-progress and finished goods, whereas, a retailing firm will require only stocks of goods for resale. Seasonality will add complications, as will consumer demand patterns, all adding to the practicalities of everyday life, with associated complications for stockholding.

Whatever the scenario, the implementation of a stockholding policy will need to balance:

- the cost of holding stocks and hence the cost of holding too much stock
- the opportunity cost of not carrying enough stock
- the vested interests of managers which can cost the organization in many ways.

Stockholding costs include such items as the cost of capital, storage space, security costs, insurance, the risk of deterioration and/or obsolescence and stock control system costs. Carrying insufficient stock can result in lost sales, owing to lack of supply and/or choice, or expensive hold-ups in production, or having to hold emergency stocks at non-discounted prices. The vested interests of managers can cost the organization, in that some managers may fly in the face of good policy just because it makes life easier for themselves.

An ideal working capital policy in this area will seek to maximize stock turnovers in order to minimize the commitment of finance to the stockholding process. Operationally, however, the ideal will never be achieved as the practicalities of day-to-day life must be taken account of to arrive at a series of practices to effect policy. With regard to stock-holding, this has resulted in the development of models for economic order quantities involving the establishment of maximum/minimum/reorder levels, with many going as far as minimum stock or indeed just-in-time policies.

The costs of debtor and creditor management

Credit control involves ensuring that monies from debtors are collected when due and that bills are paid when due. It is important to manage the associated cash flow of credit control for both debtors and creditors.

In so doing, credit control management of debtors should endeavour to achieve a trade-off between the cost of granting credit terms and carrying debtor balances, and the cost of denying credit or at least making it very restricted. This is an area in which custom and practice in the industry as a whole can overrule desirable policy. If all competitors grant credit and you do not ... !

Whatever, the costs of granting credit include:

- the credit control process from approving applications, setting credit limits, monitoring account balances and payment patterns and, of course, extracting the cash from debtors!
- the accompanying accounting and recording process
- discounts for early settlement
- bad debts
- both the real and opportunity costs of capital locked up in debtor balances.

On the other hand, the costs of not granting credit include:

- loss of sales, as customers may see no credit as a lack of inducement
- the necessity to collect and physically handle cash, ensuring its banking and security
- the protection of cash from theft and associated increased insurance premiums.

Given the need to strike a balance, perverse it may seem, taking steps to ensure rapid debtor turnover may be disproportionately expensive and thus not cost-effective.

It is just as complicated a picture when creditors are considered. On the surface it may appear that being able to take credit from a third party is good news – they finance your organization for the length of non-payment period. However, even taking credit has its costs, including:

- discounts on offer may be forgone
- unhappy creditors may refuse further supply
- after initial problems an organization may have its published or available credit rating reduced.

An approach often adopted is that of **factoring**, where debts can be converted into cash by being sold on to a third party, with either a lump sum (below full value of course) being accepted in exchange, or a lump sum taken in advance with the collector deducting a fee from the outstanding sum when the debt has been collected.

Again, highlighting the need to strike a balance, by not taking credit costs are incurred:

- the interest which could have alternatively been gained from the use of finance is lost
- cash handling costs and inconvenience.

The costs of cash management

Just as with the other components of working capital, cash too needs to be managed within the overall framework of working capital policy, with excessive cash holding being as undesirable as insufficient cash.

The costs of holding cash include:

- physical security measures
- insurance premiums
- increased internal audit and system checks and controls
- the opportunity costs of lost returns from other investments or, indeed, reducing existing loans and overdrafts.

Having insufficient cash may incur costs related to:

- the late settlement of creditors' accounts with loss of discount and/or bad press with subsequently restricted or no credit facilities
- lack of flexibility to take advantage of opportunities as they arrive
- short-term borrowing charges.

As with the other components, the pattern of trade-off continues, with balance being the key issue but demanding constant attention from management.

Working capital management in perspective

Given the often high level of investment in working capital, as an area it needs managing as a matter of course. The complexities of achieving a balance between desirable policy and pragmatic practice is everywhere. The use of ratios as a favoured approach to helping monitor the working capital situation is appropriate, but only if the ratios are placed in the contexts of the organization's activity pattern and its own industry. The challenge to management through ratios and any other means is to look after both the specific components of working capital and the residual working capital or, put formally, net current assets.

Summary

In this chapter you have looked at the investment of funds into those assets which are used on day to day business within the organization. Such investments are normally referred to as being investments into working capital.

The investment seeks to balance the investment in current assets and current liabilities which more often than not fund such investment. This is important for three reasons. First, the management of an organization should seek to ensure that the balance is neither too high nor too low. The former could result in an unproductive use of funds and the latter in skating on thin ice, with the possibility of not being able to carry on after current liabilities have been met. The second reason reflects the need for the organization to remain liquid and be able to meet its due debts. The third is that an optimum balance will enable the cash tied up in working capital to remain in such an investment for as short a period of time as is practicable.

In seeking to achieve the above, management will calculate and monitor current and quick ratios, and receivables/payables and stock ratios.

By now you should:

- recognize the importance of working capital and its management
- understand how to measure and monitor liquidity
- calculate and interpret current and quick ratios
- be able to calculate and monitor credit and stock controls.

Self-assessment questions

To assess your own progress, attempt the self-assessment questions below.

SAQ 10.1

Explain why, on the one hand, it is important for an organization to invest in working capital but on the other hand to minimize such investment.

SAQ 10.2

Distinguish between the current and quick ratios.

SAQ 10.3

The manager/owner of a small manufacturing business has, according to the latest profit statement, been operating profitably. A letter however, has, just been received from the bank asking for the management of working capital to be improved with a view to helping to reduce the overdraft.

The only information the manager/owner has is detailed below. Explain what the figures mean and what should be done.

Working capital ratios – Year to 31 December ...

	Last year	*This year*	*Latest industry average*
Current ratio	4:1	6:1	3:1
Quick ratio	1:1	0.7:1	1.6:1
Debtors turnover	60 days	80 days	45 days
Creditors turnover	60 days	45 days	80 days
Stock turnover	30 days	40 days	15 days

Further reading

Lee, G.A., 1970. Working capital: theory of control, *Accountancy* (July)
Smith, K.J., 1979. *Guide to Working Capital Management*, McGraw-Hill
Moyes, J., 1988. The dangers of JIT, *Management Accounting* (February)

11 Business valuation

In this chapter you will identify and consider the issues relating to the valuation of a business. Included in these issues are the range of techniques available to attach financial figures to the issues considered.

As you work through this chapter you will revisit the idea, established in Part I, of the balance sheet value of an organization reflecting nothing more than the book value – the value in the records of account are usually very different to the market value. As you discover, however, despite the limitations of the balance sheet book value, accounting data based calculations such as book value and adjusted book value per share do have a role to play in assessing the value of an organization. The roles of current asset values and future profit and cash flows need to be considered, and those of market price per share and price-earnings ratio.

The chapter concludes with the connection of the range of valuation techniques to a range of valuation scenarios including acquisitions, management buy-outs, flotations, liquidations and the complexities of valuation across international borders.

By the end of this chapter you will:

- understand the issues of significance in valuation
- be conversant with a range of valuation techniques including book value, market value and cash flow based approaches
- be able to identify the advantages and shortcomings of each valuation technique
- be able to select and apply the most appropriate technique to a particular scenario demanding valuation
- recognize the complications caused by international considerations in assessing valuation.

Issues in valuation

Perhaps the relevant issues are best identified and illustrated by using the scenario outlined in the box.

> In 1992 the chain of Nationwide Estate Agencies was sold to Hambro Countrywide for £1, and this despite there being 304 locations throughout the UK .

The Nationwide estate agency scenario reflects the tension that exists between the book and market values of physical assets, and between such values and the likelihood of future profit and cash flows. The organization possessed property – freehold and leasehold – owned office equipment and vehicles and had experienced and valued staff, yet was valued at just £1. The emphasis in this valuation was on the fact that the business was generating losses rather than profits, and to turn this situation around any prospective new owner would need to invest cash while still incurring ongoing losses until such time as the business achieved that turnaround. Even the book value of the business was way above £1.

An examination of the Nationwide scenario reveals that the issues detailed below in the next box are of significance. Such issues need to be considered before any attempt at valuation may be undertaken.

> Issues to be considered in valuation include:
>
> - the book value (balance sheet derived)
> - the market value of assets and liabilities
> - the intangible assets (such as goodwill of customers, quality of, say, manufacturing and/or information systems, motivated and efficient staff)
> - the off balance sheet items
> - the historic and projected profit and cash flows
> - the track records and trend analysis of dividend payouts and market share price movements.

The issues identified are reflected within the considerations of the specific valuation techniques considered next. These are:

- Accounting based valuation
- Stock market valuation
- Cash flow valuation.

After considering these, you will link these to a range of specific scenarios, including the international perspective.

Accounting based valuation

The term 'accounting based' refers to valuation techniques derived from the balance sheet or book value of an organization. There are two you will consider here. The first is the *book value* technique, which focuses very directly upon balance sheet values. The second is the *adjusted book value* technique which attempts to move the balance sheet values closer to market values. You will consider both in turn, together with associated issues.

Book value

The standard balance sheet layout in the UK results in a figure at the bottom of the vertical layout which represents the shareholders invested in the organization. This is also referred to as the *net worth* of the organization. It thus also represents the value of the firm, assuming all assets realize their book values and all liabilities are settled at book values. Where, as is normal, the book values of assets, exceed those of liabilities, the net worth shows the book value of the business. When divided by the number of issued ordinary shares, a book value per share is obtained.

This may be illustrated by referring to Figure 11.1, which shows the balance sheets of British Airways Plc at the end of March 1985 through to 1994. The shareholders' equity is shown as £1,827 million. The number of issued shares at that date was 954 million, producing a book value per share of £1.92 per share, but the market price was £4.04. The movement between 1990 and 1994 is shown below.

		1990	1991	1992	1993	1994
Shareholders' equity	=	912	958	1.284	1.214	1,827
N. of issued shares		720.7	721.4	727.6	741.7	954.0
	=	1.27	1.33	1.76	1.64	1.92
Market price multiple	=	1.5	1.7	1.9	1.8	2.1
(all in times)						

An examination of the market price multiples shows the discrepancy between the two values. For a whole variety of reasons, at the end of each of the financial years, the UK stock market valued the business at a price well in excess of the balance sheet or book value. These reasons include, of course, those influencing issues earlier highlighted.

An additional challenge to book valuation is that, at different times throughout any one year, the stock market places greater or less emphasis upon the influencing issues. This is illustrated by a comparison of the year end book value of British Airways and the highs and lows of the market price during the years.

	1990	1991	1992	1993	1994
Book value	1.27	1.33	1.76	1.64	1.92
Price:					
Highest in year	2.58	2.10	2.64	3.02	4.95
Lowest in year	2.26	1.79	1.20	1.51	2.15

Issues in book valuation

Whereas all the assets and liabilities of British Airways and other organizations as shown in the balance sheet represent book values, it is as well to understand that each individual component may be recorded using differing approaches and assumptions.

For example, in depreciating fixed assets, the accounting rationale is merely to ensure that the cost of a fixed asset is spread over and charged to the profit statements of the years benefiting from the use of that asset. There is no compulsion to use one method or another.

An asset costing £ 100,000 and with a 4-year life could be depreciated using the *straight line* approach. This would result in equal annual depreciation charges of £25,000. However, applying the *declining* or *reducing balance* approach could result in a charge of £50,000 to Year 1, £25,000 to Year 2, £12,500 to Year 3 and £6,250 to Year 4. (The remaining undepreciated portion of £6,250 would be matched against any resale value achieved, producing a profit or loss over book value.)

Some fixed assets such as land and buildings may reflect a cost less depreciated charge based value and all that that entails. It may be, however, that the property has been revalued and shown in the balance sheet at a conservative market value.

The UK Companies Act 1985 recognizes the gap between historic/book and current market value of properties and requires that directors bring such gaps to the attention of shareholders.

Another type of asset which can distort book value is the *intangible*. Examples of such include expenditure on goodwill, research and development and the value of brands.

SUMMARY FINANCIAL STATMENTS
GROUP BALANCE SHEETS

£ million	1985	1986	1987	1988	1989	1990	1991	1992	1993	**1994**
Fixed assets										
Tangible assets	1,247	1,320	1,300	2,165	2,467	2,464	3,134	3,472	4,230	**4,648**
Investments	4	5	5	40	111	108	108	93	546	**575**
	1,251	1,320	1,305	2,205	2,578	2,572	,3242	3,565	4,776	**5,223**
Current assets	710	593	777	901	916	1,295	1,057	1,687	1,577	**2,357**
Creditors: amounts falling										
due within one year	(998)	(988)	(1,140)	(1,471)	(1,748)	(1,816)	(1,600)	(1,706)	(,851)	**(1,928)**
Net current assets										
(liabilities)	(288)	(395)	(363)	(570)	(832)	(521)	(543)	(19)	(274)	**429**
Total assets less current										
liabilities	963	925	942	1,635	1,746	2,051	2,699	3,546	4,502	**5,652**
Creditors: amounts falling due										
after more than one year	(591)	(340)	(270)	(851)	(896)	(1,075)	(1,686)	(2,208)	(3,219)	**(3,759)**
Provisions for liabilities										
and charges	(85)	(103)	(66)	(150)	(100)	(64)	(55)	(54)	(69)	**(66)**
	287	482	606	634	750	912	958	1,284	1,214	**1,827**
Capital and reserves										
Called up share capital	180	180	180	180	180	180	180	182	185	**239**
Reserves	106	300	425	453	569	732	778	1,102	1,029	**1,588**
Shareholders' equity	286	480	605	633	749	912	958	1,284	1,214	**1,827**
Minority interests	1	2	1	1	1					
	287	482	606	634	950	912	958	1,284	1,214	**1,827**

Following the adoption of Financial Reporting Standard 4 in 1994 the Convertible Capital Bonds have been reclassified within creditors falling due after more than one year and corresponding amounts have been restated.

Figure 11.1 British Airways Plc – group balance sheets

Goodwill is the generic term applied to the difference between the book values of shares and the market values. If a business is a going concern and is likely to continue creating a future profit and cash flows, the market price (or indeed actual price paid by an acquiring company) may well exceed the book value: the goodwill has been ascertained.

In paying for goodwill, an acquiring company may be faced with having to show a large sum for goodwill on its balance sheet immediately after acquiring another business. For example, the acquiring company may have paid out £10 million and acquired a business with a book value of £5 million. To keep the balance sheet in balance, a goodwill sum of £5 million would need to be accounted for. In the UK, such acquiring companies may either revalue the assets of the company acquired or immediately write off the goodwill sum against reserves.

Another intangible is the money spent on and the resulting quality and application of research and development. While not representing a tangible asset such as a building or land, nevertheless it represents cash spent – in the hope of generating future profits and cash flows. Unfortunately there is no realistic way of forecasting future revenues and hence no way of linking general research and development expenditures to unknown future income.

> It is worth noting that some companies do capitalize a portion of research and development expenditure, but only after identifying a specific market for a specific project which is very likely to generate future cash flows. Thereafter, the capitalized research and development expenditure is written off against revenues as they are realized.
>
> IBM, for example, regularly capitalizes portions of investment in research and development expenditure on new information systems, but only after the project looks as though they are certain to be up and running.

In the late 1980s and early 90s, companies began to pay greater attention to the value of another intangible – the past and potential revenue generation derived from owing a number of brands. Such brands are obviously of value to an organization, but traditionally historic balance sheets have not accounted for them. This is not surprising as, along with associating research and development expenditure with future revenues, forecasts are only ever as good as the assumptions made.

> In 1989, Allied Lyons added 'overnight' £0.5 billion to its balance sheet by revaluing its brand values. The group Grand Metropolitan, too, increased its balance sheet book value by valuing its brands. A bonus for both groups was a readjustment of low valuations, making them vulnerable to takeover bids.

Brands are, in essence, *off-balance sheet*. There are, however, other assets which are not, conventionally at least, shown on the balance sheet. These include, typically, pension fund surpluses which, as a result of sheer size and volume, can generate huge surpluses even with only mediocre fund management.

At present, despite moves in the 1990s to tighten up the rules governing pension fund disclosure, it is still possible for finance directors to boost, on paper, company earnings by variation of company contributions in response to huge existing surpluses. The Mirror Group, under Robert Maxwell, went way outside the legitimate boundaries but, for example, BTR, when acquiring Dunlop with a pension fund surplus, quite legitimately postponed company contributions and thereby boosted reported earnings. UK Statement of Standard Accounting Practice (SSAP) No. 24 now prevents this, but other manipulations are still applied.

Adjusted book value

This approach attempts systematically to compensate for the misvaluations and undervaluations which are inherent in the book value approach. This is achieved by moving from the book value of the firm to an adjusted book value by comprehensively assessing the impact of reality on each group of assets and liabilities. A pro-forma is detailed in Figure 11.2.

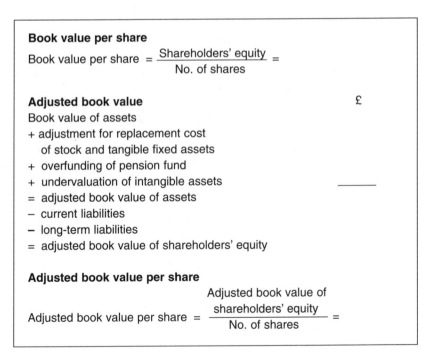

Book value per share

Book value per share $= \dfrac{\text{Shareholders' equity}}{\text{No. of shares}} =$

Adjusted book value   £

Book value of assets
+ adjustment for replacement cost
  of stock and tangible fixed assets
+ overfunding of pension fund
+ undervaluation of intangible assets   _____
= adjusted book value of assets
− current liabilities
− long-term liabilities
= adjusted book value of shareholders' equity

Adjusted book value per share

Adjusted book value per share $= \dfrac{\text{Adjusted book value of shareholders' equity}}{\text{No. of shares}} =$

Figure 11.2 A pro-forma for determining adjusted book values

> The post World War II years have generated trends which are
> interesting as points to note. These include:
>
> • for companies quoted on the New York and London stock
>   markets, the ratio of market to book values is, on average, rel-
>   atively high
> • if market to book value is low, acquisitions are more appropriate
>   than starting from scratch ...
> • if market to book value is high, starting a business from scratch
>   is more attractive.

The limitations of book and adjusted book values are clear enough.
After all, book values are nothing more than that and adjustments are
only best 'guesstimates' and take no account of future earnings potential. It is particularly in relation to this last point that stock market valuation techniques are favoured.

Stock market valuation

It is tempting to think that any techniques under this heading might
solve valuation problems. Unfortunately, even the techniques you are
about to consider cannot provide a 100% guaranteed and definitive
valuation. In cognizance of this, the UK International Stock Exchange
has the following to say about the market prices quoted on the Stock
Exchange at any one time:

> We desire to state authoritatively that Stock Exchange quotations are not
> related directly to the value of a company's assets or to the amount of its
> profits and consequently these quotations no matter what dates may be
> chosen for references, cannot form a fair and equitable or rational basis for
> compensation.
>   The Stock Exchange may be likened to a scientific recording instrument
> which registers not its own actions and opinions, but the actions and opin-
> ions of private and institutional investors all over the county and indeed, the
> world. These actions and opinions are the result of hope, fear, guesswork,
> intelligence or otherwise, good or bad investment policy, and many other
> considerations. The quotations that result definitely do not represent a val-
> uation of a company by reference to its earning potential.

The significance of the above is self-evident and should constantly be
kept in mind as you consider:

• the Stock Market price per share valuation, and
• the price–earnings ratio (PE ratio) valuation.

Stock market price per share valuation

At any one moment in time, a company quoted on the Stock Exchange will have its share price valued at a particular price by the mechanism of the Stock Market. It is not unreasonable to expect that such a price reflects what might be termed a 'fair market price'. Unfortunately this *is not the case.*

A 'fair market price' would only ever result from a stock market which as a mechanism is particularly efficient. This implies that a 'fair' price reflects all publicly available information about the company and the share price adjusts very quickly to any new relevant information. However, potential inefficiencies and sources of distortion are legion. Not least as an inefficiency is the already stated undervaluation of and/or not visible assets. In addition is the possibility of someone having prior information of a takeover bid for a company – hence privately but not publicly available.

A problem arises with the implication that the publicly quoted price share reflects that the share is marketable. This in turn implies that an investor can always be found who is willing to buy the share at the quoted price. However, prospective purchasers of large, indeed controlling, volumes of shares may have to pay a premium for the privilege, whereas anyone wishing to sell may have to do so at a discount.

A further problem can arise in that any share price quoted is at a single moment in time in relation to a specific deal with a specific intermediary – known as a market maker – between buyer and seller. As one moment moves into another, be it minutes or literally seconds later, the nature of the proposed transaction may change, resulting in a different, higher/lower, price. Thus the essentially temporary nature of a quoted price results in market prices being relatively volatile, again distorting the value of an organization. You saw earlier, for example, how British Airways' shares had widely varying highs and lows of share prices during a year.

Other distortions may arise as a result of, for example, shareholder loyalty and a reluctance to sell, benefits to shareholders such as cross-channel ferry fare concessions, and employee loyalty. Whatever the cause of any distortion, the one fact we can rely on is that the quoted share price will never be totally accurate and is, at best, only ever a guide to the business valuation.

Price–earnings ratio valuation

The PE ratio approach has the advantage of generating a valuation figure derived from within a systematic calculation framework. It has the advantages of being inherently simple and uses historical and current data, both readily available, to say something about the future. It produces a figure which enables the current share price of one company to be compared with others.

The determination is simple enough:

$$\frac{\text{Current share price}}{\text{Earnings per share (EPS)}}$$

Thus a business with a current share price of, say, £3 per share and latest reported EPS or; say, 30p would have a PE ratio of:

$$\frac{£3}{30 \text{ pence}} = 10$$

This indicates that, at this moment in time, the share is valued at 10 times the earnings. The higher its PE ratio, the higher the quality of and the growth rate expected in earnings and, in theory, the higher the demand for that share. The lower the PE ratio, the riskier the likelihood of increasing quality and growth in earnings and thus the less the demand for the share. This enables one share to be compared with another.

At 31 March 1994 the PE ratio calculation for British Airways would have been:

$$\frac{\text{Share price at 31/3/94}}{\text{EPS for year to 31/3/94}} = \frac{495p}{31.3p} = 15.8 \text{ times}$$

This would then have been compared with the average PE ratio (taken from the *Financial Times* share indices table, published daily) for transportation companies to reflect a 'feel good' factor concerning BA. Of course, the PE ratio could then be compared with any other companies at all, anywhere.

PE ratios thus enable relative comparisons to be made across time, across companies, across industries and across countries. A company can thus be considered cheap or dear according to its relative PE ratio. To avoid distortions, however, account should be taken of a number of factors, including:

- the differing accounting methods and policies used by companies
- the timing of financial year ends in relation to cyclical trends
- typical variations in earnings records, particularly in light of creativity on the part of finance directions.

Stock market valuation in perspective

It is understandable that, for a quoted company, the best estimate of value is its share price. This is because investors and analysts will have devoted their best efforts to determine a company's value and to ensuring that the share price reflects the consensus view of that value. Of course, it can never be any more than an estimate. The PE ratio can enhance the quality of the quoted share price by relating the future to known details about the quality and level of earnings. Both together have traditionally formed a quick and ready guide to business valuation without having to commit a calculation to the uneasiness of a forecast. Unfortunately, however, forecasts can never be avoided completely and particularly so when it is the recognized duty of companies to produce future cash flows for shareholders.

Cash flow valuation

The forecasting ahead of cash returns to shareholders is a matter that cannot be ignored, no matter how desirable ignoring the difficulties associated with forecasting may be. There are two basic if contrasting approaches to cash flow valuation. These are:

- discounting expected forecast dividends by the required rate of return on the shares produces a value for *equity*
- discounting the expected future cash flows from the business by the weighted average cost of capital (WACC) of the firm to give a value for the *business*. (The value of any debt may then be subtracted if an *equity* valuation is required.) This is often termed the *free cash flow* approach.

Both of those approaches are more challenging to calculate than the previous approaches considered. Both, too, refer back to ideas met earlier in this text.

Discounting expected dividends

This approach refers back to the *dividend valuation* or *Gordon's Growth Model* which you met earlier in the book. To remind you, all future expected cash flows associated with a share are discounted by the required equity rate of return (i.e. equity cost of capital) to produce a present value for the share. Of course, the dividends may well grow at a constant rate of growth and this needs to be taken account of.

To remind you of Gordon's Growth Model, assume the following:

- last year's dividend was 10p
- required rate of return on share is 15%
- expected growth rate of dividends is 10%

In such circumstances the present value of the share would be:

10 (1 + 10)/(0.15 − 0.10) = 220p

In reality, the application of the growth model formula can be more complex, with only the immediate future growth being reasonably forecastable, say 2 years, and with any further forecasts requiring judgement.

A more immediate practical consideration must be that forecasting dividend growth rates makes those valuing not only consider the future profitability of the business – difficult enough to forecast at the best of times – but also the degree of discretion employed by a management team in determining dividend policy. Although the growth model suffers from this, the alternative, discounting future cash flows by WACC does not.

Discounting future cash flows by WACC – free cash flow

This approach values the business on the basis of discounted future cash flows, but disregarding whether it is financed by debt or equity or both. This has the advantage of allowing the business valuation to be separated from the type of financing. Thus if financing changes, perhaps by increased debt, all that happens is that the expected future cash flows are discounted by a new WACC. Similarly, any changes in dividend policy can be ignored. The approach has the further advantage of dealing in future cash flows which, while admittedly being only as sound as the assumptions employed, are less subject to the influence of judgement of accounting methods and policies as attributed to the *true and fair* determination of profit.

Defining free cash flow

Free cash flow is the cash which would be received each year by all categories of capital finance providers; that is to say, debt finance *and* equity finance. Thus the approach focuses on the *total* rewards to all, comprising:

- dividends to shareholders
- cash for share redemptions (buying back shares from shareholders)
- interest paid (less corporation tax as interest is a tax-deductible cost of capital, unlike dividends)
- cash for debt repayment.

The corresponding figures can readily be ascertained from a company's accounts, although the resulting figure is likely to represent the *gross* cash flow comprising the total of both the funds available for reinvestment in the business and the free cash flow (available as cash returns to financiers). Of course, some of the funds will be earmarked for reinvestment, as a normal cash holding is required to run current operations, whereas an excess balance may be available for investment in, say, marketable securities. In such a case, the excess should be included as part of free cash flow.

Free cash flow calculation

The free cash flow figure can be derived from the cash flow statement included in a quoted company's published accounts. A standard template may be used, incorporating an adjustment to take account of taxation timing distortions. Such a template is shown below.

The free cash flow figure calculated may then be incorporated in a forecasting calculation to produce a valuation. Such figures would normally be derived from a company's cash flow statement, such as that shown for British Airways in Figure 11.3.

Free cash flow calculation

(a) *Tax adjustment*   *£ million*

  Operating profit (taken as given from P and L Account)
  Less net interest paid/received (from cash flow statement)
  Net profit
  Tax paid

(b) Effective tax rate =

(c) Cash flow from operating activities after tax =

(d) Cash flow from returns on investment and
  servicing after tax =

(e) Free cash flow determination
  Gross cash flow (from operating activities)
  = Investment of xx + Free cash flow
  (from investment activities) (balancing figure)

GROUP CASH FLOW STATEMENTS

For the five years ended 31 March 1994

£ million	1990	1991	1992	1993	1994
NET CASH INFLOW FROM OPERATING ACTIVITIES	728	296	591	629	**736**
RETURNS ON INVESTMENTS AND SERVICING OF FINANCE					
Interest received	29	62	49	96	**62**
Interest paid on bank and other loans	(89)	(89)	(98)	(116)	**(133)**
Interest paid on finance leases and hire purchase arrangements	(22)	(33)	(53)	(80)	**(88)**
US Air preferred stock dividend received				3	**15**
Dividends received from trade investments	4	3	1	4	**2**
Dividends paid	(58)	(64)	(65)	(76)	**(86)**
Net cash outflow from returns on investments and servicing of finance	(136)	(121)	(166)	(169)	**(228)**
TAXATION					
UK corporation tax paid	(94)	(109)	(11)	(38)	**(21)**
INVESTING ACTIVITIES					
Tangible fixed assets purchased for cash	(619)	(813)	(539)	(577)	**(320)**
Refund of progress payments	268	189	158	32	**114**
Purchase of interests in associated undertakings	(10)	(10)	(6)	(532)	**(69)**
Loans made to associated undertakings	(1)	(3)		(42)	**(57)**
Purchase of interests in trade investments	(7)	(3)	(1)		
Net outflow of cash and cash equivalents in respect of the purchase of subsidiary undertakings	(1)	(5)		(10)	**(11)**
Sale of tangible fixed assets	157	268	90	103	**44**
Sale of investments				2	**1**
Sale of engine overhaul business			274		
	(213)	(377)	(24)	(1,024)	**(298)**

Net cash (outflow)/inflow before decrease/(increase) in short-term deposits and financing	285	(311)	390	(602)	**189**

(Increase)/decrease in short-term bank deposits with a maturity date at inception of more than three months			(334)	334	**(324)**
Net cash outflow from investing activities	(213)	(377)	(358)	(690)	**(622)**
Net cash (outflow)/inflow before financing	285	(311)	56	(268)	**(135)**
FINANCING					
Changes in borrowings					
Bank and other loans raised	714	546	390	735	**210**
Bank and other loans repaid	(966)	(395)	(215)	(301)	**(123)**
Capital elements of finance leases and hire purchase arrangements paid	(98)	(49)	(55)	(79)	**(116)**
	(350)	102	120	355	**(29)**
Changes in share capital					
Issue of ordinary share capital			2	3	**54**
Share premium received		1	9	20	**423**
		1	11	23	**477**
Convertible Capital Bonds issued	320				
Costs associated with Convertible Capital Bonds issue	(10)				
	310				
Net cash inflow/(outflow) from financing	(40)	103	131	378	**448**
Increase/(decrease) in cash and cash equivalents	245	(208)	187	110	**313**

Figure 11.3 The cash flow statement for the year to 31 March 1994 for British Airways

From free cash flow to valuation

Again, a number of basic steps may be followed here. These are:

- forecast the free cash flow
- take account of cost of capital
- estimate the continuing value
- assess the value of equity
- test and interpret the results.

Future free cash flow may be forecast by adjusting existing free cash flow by an assumed growth rate, taking account, of course, of likely internal and external strategic influences.

A series of estimated annual future cash flows over, say, a 5-year (or another appropriate) period may be forecast and discounted by a discount factor relating to the WACC. A discounted free cash flow value is obtained for the time period selected. Then a balance sheet value at the end of that time period can be estimated and also discounted, this is the continuing value and is, understandably, at best a good estimate. The total is of the discounted free cash flow value and the discounted continuing value, added together to produce the *value of operations*. From this is deducted outstanding debt finance to obtain a forecast value of equity – and thus the value of the business. An example is given in the next box.

A business has a current free cash flow of £ 10 million which is expected to grow as shown below. The cost of capital is 10% and the cyclical nature of the business is such that a 5-year period is appropriate for forecasting. At the end of Year 5, the continuing value shown in the balance sheet is likely to be £700 million. Outstanding debt is £200 million. The workings are:

Year	Free cash flow	Discount factor at 10%	Present value
	£m	£m	£m
1	10	0.909	9.09
2	11	0.826	9.086
3	12.1	0.751	9.087
4	13.21	0.621	8.203
5	14.321	0.564	8.077
Value of free cash	60.631		43.543
Continuing value	700.000	0.564	394.800
Value of operations			438.343
less debt			200.000
Value of equity/business			238.343

Testing and interpreting free cash flow based value

As ever, when forecasting ahead, the calculation is not the be all and end all. The resulting value needs to be checked against common sense and, if available, the market value of the company, with discrepancies identified and accounted for. Thereafter, the assumptions underpinning the cash flow forecasts will need to be subjected to sensitivity analysis, resulting in a range of suggested equity values rather than a single one.

Valuation in context

From your foregoing considerations of the range of differing approaches to business valuation, it is not unreasonable to wonder where and when a particular approach should be used, implicitly being preferred to others and presumably being better suited to a specific scenario. Next you will consider, in outline at least, the factors which influence the choice of valuation approach most appropriate in a variety of scenarios and associated circumstances. Specifically, you will consider the circumstances of acquisitions, management buyouts, flotations and liquidations.

Acquisitions

Here the final price paid may be very different, higher or lower, than the value generated by a particular calculation. Such a value usually, in the acquisition context, is the starting point for negotiations. The final, agreed price will reflect a combination of existing book value, market considerations, qualitative and emotional factors, and anticipated future earnings.

For the acquisition of a quoted company, the starting price is usually the stock market value. This, as highlighted earlier, is supposed to reflect an efficient market mechanism. However, a hostile bid may result in a higher price emerging. A higher or lower price may emerge if the acquirer owns part of the company and has additional information about the company, indicating that the current market price is too high or low.

A good example of additional information is illustrated in the 1995 bid for the UK health care group Scholl by rebel investors. On 7 October 1995 the market price was 232p, following a low of 125p in December 1994. The rebel investors felt however that, given their recent restructuring and future prospects, the share price should have been nearer to 300p.

> Rural bidders can also send share prices soaring as in the 1995 proposed takeover of Norweb, the UK regional electricity company. Rival bidders the UK North West Water and the US Texas Partners saw valuations soar from £9 through the £10 barrier to £11. These higher values were enhanced by the addition of extra cash and additional dividends and sweeteners to entice shareholders.

Market price

In taking over private companies, the market price is unavailable and thus market valuation is a non-starter. Traditionally, cash flow valuation has been applied to private companies. This ensures that the impacts of a particular preferred set of arrangements for debt and tax are minimized. This is important as a new private owner may have differing preferences. In the sensitivity analysis of a cash flow valuation, great emphasis will be placed upon potentially changing market scenarios, with the resulting implications for earnings and resulting cash flow.

PE ratios

On occasions, surrogate PE ratios – from similar but quoted companies – are used for private company valuation. To be of any real use, the range and profile of variable factors between the companies must be as common as possible – often difficult to achieve.

Book values

For both public and private companies, an acquisition may focus on asset stripping rather than acquiring a going concern. In such cases a contrast between book and market values of assets is essential.

Other approaches

On occasions, none of the conventional methods may suit the specific circumstances of a particular acquisition. Other approaches used include:

- percentage of funds under management (for investment management companies)

- percentage of sales per, for example, measure of area (for retailing concerns)
- Percentage of advertising revenues (for advertising companies).

Management buyouts

Such a buyout is the purchase of all or part of a business from the existing owners by one or more of the existing managers of a company. Valuations are often based on the expectation that performance will improve after the buyout. In light of this, earnings based and cash flow based valuations are appropriate. In both cases, however, there may be an increased level of risk to take account of, if debt finance has been used to finance the buyout. This will change the WACC, with a consequential impact upon expected rate of return and the discount factor applied in the valuation calculation. In such cases of increased gearing risk, the quality of earnings assumes an ever greater significance, and the in-house experience of managers may prove to be a vital ingredient in maintaining and improving earnings under difficult circumstances.

Flotations

These occur when companies come to the stock market for the first time or when public sector organizations are privatized. They are usually valued as going concerns, but with no market values as a guideline.

New issues

As stated above, no market price is available as a starting price or indeed as a guide. As a result, valuation approaches revolve around earnings based and cash flow forecasting techniques. The simple PE ratio is, however, often preferred to cash flow forecasting not least because of the latter's complexity but also because of the challenge of forecasting future earnings in the brave new world which a newly floated company enters into. In most private companies the EPS is readily available and this can be used within a PE ratio to compare with those of similar industry based quoted companies.

In such cases, one number that does attract attention is the EPS. As a consequence, focus is centred on the most recent earnings of the business, although it may be that management teams might be tempted to find excuses to artificially inflate the EPS figure through creativity and ingenuity.

> At the time of privatization of Rolls-Royce, it was a direct comparison of its EPS with British Aerospace which led to its valuation for share issue purposes.

Privatizations

The trend towards privatizations in Western Europe has led to a greater focus on valuation in such circumstances. At the time of the Rolls-Royce privatization referred to above, such occurrences were relatively rare. Now, particularly in the UK, they are almost common place.

Most public sector organizations are run without the specified intention of maximizing returns to government. In such cases the only appropriate valuation can be derived from cash flow. The standard approach detailed earlier may be applied, but there are considerations which must be paid attention to, given the nature of the organizations usually privatized. These include:

- the risk of subsequent compulsory renationalization
- contingent liabilities which may arise from the nature of the activity (e.g. nuclear accidents, river pollution) which are not applicable to government utilities
- future capital expenditures required to comply with legislation regarding the nature of the activity.

The cash flow valuation, taking account of the above, is often compared to the market price valuation of similar but already privatized concerns in, for example, the USA where utilities have been in private ownership for a long time.

The international perspective

The subject of valuation inevitably crosses borders. Takeovers of companies in other countries are now commonplace. Potential shareholder investment requires an understanding of how to value history and prospects in countries where accounting policies differ from, say, those in the UK. Indeed, many multi-nationals produce several sets of accounts for interested parties of different nationalities (although without reconciling any reported differences!).

The main problems with regard to international valuation centre on the book value and dividend or earnings based approaches.

Book value

In assessing the balance sheet of an organization based in another country, it is important to take account of:

- the accounting principles used to determine values
- the foreign exchange rates used to denote their value in the base currency of the accounts.

These are of particular significance when examining:

- consolidated or group accounts
- fixed asset valuations
- leases
- intangibles such as goodwill
- deferred taxation.

Consolidated accounts

In the UK and other countries with developed stock markets, the accounts for groups of companies are consolidated to produce an overall picture of the group. In some countries, however, only the accounts of the parent companies are produced. In such cases, subsidiaries are shown on the balance sheet as investments at cost; in profit terms, the dividends paid to the parent company are shown on the profit statement. Such moves can produce unusual balance sheet valuations and distort the profitability profile.

> Such distortion is well represented in the accounts of large international Japanese companies with many small investments in large numbers of foreign companies. In such cases, valuation measures such as PE ratios can appear substantially overstated. This is because the market price of the company in fact represents the group, whereas the earnings may only include very low dividends from minority interests.
>
> Other distortions occur with German companies which currently do not consolidate overseas subsidiaries. Moving further from reality, Spanish holding companies do not consolidate at all.

Fixed assets

Given that assets and investments tend not to be shown at revaluation value in the balance sheet, distortions again can occur. Referring to the

Japanese scenario in the box, this results in understatement of investment in minority companies. This is heightened by large rises in equity and in property, particularly in the 1980s.

Leases

The UK and USA are almost alone in the extent of disclosure of finance leases which presents interested parties with some additional perspective on the reality of part of the balance sheet. In many other countries, however, including France, The Netherlands and Germany, the possibilities for not revealing the true picture remain legion.

Intangibles

Goodwill treatment differs from country to country and the resulting approach to valuation and subsequent writing off (or not!) can influence both the balance sheet direct and the EPS calculated from a profit statement.

UK companies have an advantage here over, say, US companies, in that the latter have to write off goodwill through the profit statement, with an adverse effect on EPS. In the UK, such write-offs may be against Reserves.

Deferred taxes

The taxation system of any one country will invariably differ to a lesser or greater degree from that of any other country. This must therefore have an impact upon deferred taxation shown on a balance sheet. In addition, individual country taxation allowances and custom practice serve only to enhance such differences. This is well illustrated by the flexibility enjoyed by UK companies with regard to showing or not of deferred taxation, with it always being compulsory in the USA. Again, there are major implications for the balance sheet.

Market-based methods

In taking account of earnings, it is not surprising that values derived from PE ratios should be so popular. Unfortunately, in the international context, the quality of the earnings figure as a base for a value indicator varies tremendously from country to country. This is primarily a result of differing, sometimes greatly so, approaches to the production of financial statements.

Also, this the primary purpose of financial statements has an influence. For example, in the UK and USA financial statements do, for better or for worse, measure earnings with a degree of consistency, and thus a degree of reliance may be placed upon them in establishing PE ratios derived from the profit statement (particularly so in light of the tendency to maximize EPS as far as is possible).

In contrast, in many continental European, South American and Japanese companies, such statements are produced only to satisfy legal and taxation demands. This results in an emphasis on the balance sheet with liquidation values being of significance (to satisfy creditors' interests) and with little emphasis on the profit statement.

The challenge to finance directors in such companies is to minimize the tax bill rather than maximize EPS. As a consequence, everything and anything is charged as an operating expense in order to reduce operating profit.

Even between the UK and USA, substantial EPS differences can appear as a result of differing requirements. For example, a study of Jaguar's accounts for 1986–88 (taken from its Offer to Purchase document when being bought by Ford) shows:

	1986	1987	1988
	(all in £millions)		
UK net income	83.4	61.3	28.4
US net income	59.8	113.1	(30.4)

The impact on the relevant EPS figures is immense

Discounted cash flow

The advantage of dividend valuation models is that they can be applied to dividends irrespective of the currency. A drawback is that dividend yields and expected growth can vary considerably from country to country, thus causing difficulty in comparison.

In addition, other difficulties to be borne in mind when applying dividend valuation models include:

- the lack of available data, in light of legal requirements and culture
- tax and accounting differences as outlined earlier
- the determination of WACC.

Despite these difficulties, however, applying models such as Gordon's Growth Model remain popular.

Summary

In this chapter you have considered how to set about the valuation of companies. You have looked at valuation techniques and approaches, and identified the issues to be taken account of as you apply them.

By now you should:

- understand the issues of significance in valuation
- be conversant with a range of valuation techniques including book value, market value and cash flow based approaches
- be able to identify the advantages and shortcomings of each valuation technique
- be able to select and apply the most appropriate technique to a particular scenario demanding valuation
- recognize the complications caused by international considerations in assessing valuation.

Self-assessment questions

SAQ 11.1

Explain what is meant by the following approaches to business valuation:

- book value
- adjusted book value.

SAQ 11.2

Explain how the value of a firm may be determined using the PE ratio approach. Illustrate your answer appropriately.

SAQ 11.3

Explain the rationale of the free cash flow approach to business valuation.

Further reading

Copeland, T., Koller, T. and Murin, J., 1990. *Valuation: Measuring and Managing the Value of Companies*, John Wiley & Sons, Inc

Touche Ross, 1989. *Accounting for Europe – Success by 2000 AD?* Touche Ross

Coopers and Lybrand, 1993. *A review of the acquisitions experience of major UK companies*, Coopers and Lybrand

Wright, M., Thompson, S. and Robbie, K., 1990. Management buyouts: achievements, limitations and prospects, *National Westminster Bank Quarterly Review* (August)

Part V Managing through Information

12 Understanding information

Introduction

In this chapter you will look at the value of information and how it can help in managing the flow of finance and its associated aspects. The content provides a context for the ratio and budgetary considerations of the two chapters following. Setting the scene in this way will help you to understand better the advantages and problems of specific approaches to managing through financial information.

You will look specifically at:

- the value and role of information
- financial information systems
- the role of audit within the operation of financial information systems
- the behavioural effects, positive and negative, that information can have on managers.

By the end of this chapter you will:

- recognize the characteristics of useful management information
- understand how accounting information can help in managing the flow of finance from both the internal management and external stakeholder perspective
- be conversant with the nature and role of audit, particularly internal audit, in monitoring the efficiency and effectiveness of information systems
- have gained insight into the influence of information criteria upon the way managers behave in the workplace.

The value of information

Effective management of your considerations of the flow of finance thus far is dependent upon a corresponding flow of information. Information is required for the planning of financing and investment decisions and subsequent assessment of the efficiency of decisions.

For it to be of real use, managers need *timely, quality* and *relevant* information. A consideration of desirable attributes will help you to understand why these organizations operate management information systems and how.

What is information?

First it is important to understand that there is a distinction between the terms *data* and *information*. Organizations are awash with data, the data comprising all sorts of figures and statistics. In raw form, these data are unlikely to be of much use. To be of use the data need to be processed into some format which actually *means something to somebody*. Only then can it be classified as information. It then only becomes useful information when the relevant information is abstracted.

Of course, in meaning something to somebody, the information must therefore be relevant to a targeted individual or group of individuals, enabling some type of *action* to be taken. Thus, all the raw data available within the organization need to be channelled into a large database of information from which a number of appropriately designed information systems will carry relevant information to appropriately interested parties.

The desirable characteristics of information

One of the aspects emphasized above is that information needs to be relevant. There is little point in transmitting information to people if they are *not* going to use it. If information is ignored by managers, then, of course, it can play *no* useful role in their working lives.

In an attempt to enhance the possibility that managers will actually use the information supplied, it is important to ensure that the information reflects an appropriate blend of:

- relevance
- timeliness
- accuracy
- economic reality
- ease of comprehension
- detail.

Each of these desirable characteristics is considered in turn below.

Relevance

The information supplied should be *relevant* to the use to which the manager receiving it intends to put it. An extreme example is the supply of routine stock information to a marketing manager. The manager will clearly make no use of it. A counter-example is the supply of information on sales breakdown by area to that manager. This is obviously information that can be put to good use. Another example is the provision of debtor information enabling the monetary manager to judge whether or not it is worth selling further goods or services to a customer in light of a, say, poor payment record.

Timeliness

You saw in Chapter 2 that although the annual financial statements do report certain aspects, their use to management is limited by the fact that the information is reported at intervals of 1 year. If matters are not proceeding well, the supply of information will be too late for matters to be rectified. If it is to be used effectively, information must be supplied *in time* for its effective use. The UK retailer Marks & Spencer uses four weekly information, but in addition the Board of Directors meet on a weekly basis to consider the sales, stock and cash figures relating to the previous week. British Airways, too, monitors ongoing performance in addition to the formalized management accounts. Many management teams opt for 4-weekly or monthly reporting periods.

Accuracy

Perhaps what is required here is more an *appropriate* degree of accuracy. A manager, for example, might be more interested in an estimate than very accurate information provided some time later. If the appropriate degree of information is consistently achieved, then managers are more likely to make use of that information.

Economic reality

This is probably the most important characteristic. The information supplied should endeavour to reflect the underlying *economic* message. This may mean that the original format of information needs to be changed.

For example, returning to Chapter 3, an organization that is preparing conventional reporting statements using absorption costing might well restate the information on a contribution approach as an aid to decision-making.

Ease of comprehension

Although the information might be relevant, timely, accurate and economically valid, if it is presented in a form that managers cannot understand, then it will be used ineffectively or perhaps not at all. Good information should endeavour to avoid jargon, to highlight important matters and to use diagrammatic illustrations wherever possible.

Many spreadsheet packages used for internal management accounts now incorporate automatic charting facilities, including graphs, bar charts and pie charts. Published external accounts, too, often include diagrams to help readers understand key essentials of the information.

Detail

Managers exist at all levels of the organization and all will receive information. Thinking back to the pyramid of purpose in Chapter 1, it is predictable that the higher the level of management, the greater the need for *strategic-oriented* information. Thus, towards the top of the management hierarchy, information will be less detailed and more aggregated: the *lower* and more operational the level, the *more detail*. This is because operational managers will require more-detailed information to manage on a day-to-day basis.

Distorting and invalidating information

Within any information system, as the output for external or internal use, it is possible that no matter how hard management teams try to incorporate desirable characteristics into the information supplied, some other factors may still cause problems. At best the information may be distorted or, even worse, invalidated. Much research over many years has shown that typically, although there are others, there are three main factors that give rise to problems within information systems and therefore help to detract from the quality of the information supplied. These are:

- noise
- redundancy
- perception.

Noise

When the transmitter of information sends information to somebody, it is quite reasonable for the transmitter to assume that the information will arrive as intended. Unfortunately, this is not always so. Any factor which causes the information received to be different from the information sent is described as being **noise.** No information system is ever without a degree of noise. It can be minimized, however, and this is usually achieved by ensuring that appropriate attention is paid to the presentation of information. Good presentation will avoid jargon, will be well structured and will utilize good form design (a vital ingredient of effective communication of information). Anything which will help to minimize misinterpretation should be pursued.

Redundancy

This is the term applied to any embellishments which are not strictly necessary to a message. Some reports may be very verbose and/or full of interesting but unnecessary figures, filling two sides of paper when one side would be sufficient. This does not mean that all embellishments should be eliminated. Some redundant aspects feature as a matter of course in most information-transmission formats and can actually help in the interpretation of the information. What is important is to find an appropriate balance.

Perception

No matter how well presented the information received is, the aspect of perception by individuals must be taken into consideration. History is strewn with instances of the same message meaning different things to different people. This is usually the result of a number of factors, including especially the attitudes and experiences of the people serviced by an information system. It is important to note that any information transmitted is likely to have at least three meanings:

- the meaning the sender intended
- the meaning reflected in the contents of the message
- the meaning taken by the receiver.

It is important to recognize the implications of different perceptions, as appropriate recognition will help guard against misinterpretation.

A further problem: the design of the information system itself

In addition to the problems outlined above, it is important to note that all *design* of an organization's information system may also cause problems. This is because a specific system will have been designed in light of four major variables:

- technology
- environment
- *age* and size of the organization
- the hierarchical power distribution.

Any specific system will reflect both an individual and particular emphasis on each of the above, together with a resulting blend of them, which may be very appropriate or not so. There is a perception problem immediately, since somebody else designing a system may have interpreted the variables slightly differently. An additional problem is that the variables, being variables, will vary over a time period, whereas the information system will remain static unless changed by management. Thus the challenge is constantly dynamic, whereas the solution is relatively static.

Information and the uncertainties of life

A major problem facing management teams, particularly when planning for the future management of the flow of finance, is that nothing is ever certain. The best-researched, most accurate, well-presented and timely information can never foresee the unforeseeable. *Uncertainty* is present to some degree in all aspects of the planning, control and decision-making process introduced in Chapters 2 and 3. It is important that information reflects the degree of uncertainty associated with that information. This is particularly true where uncertainty may lead to a range of possible outcomes. The potential effects should therefore be incorporated into the information wherever possible. There are a number of approaches to this:

- presenting possible forecast results as ranges of values rather than just as individual point estimates – even if the indication is limited to descriptions such as highest or lowest, the value of the information will be enhanced
- attaching specific probabilities to likely results, even where such possibilities reflect a degree of subjectivity
- using confidence limits as markers to show the degree of confidence – say, for example, in sales forecasts
- using sensitivity analysis where the impact of changes is one of a number of variables traced and reported – this is used a great deal in project appraisal.

You may recognize that you have already considered this aspect when you assessed the impact of differing gearing levels in Part II and the probabilities of differing outcomes in Part III.

The value of information and value for money

Of course, everything mentioned above in relation to the provision of quality information has a cost. As with most other aspects of organizational life, it is important to try to ensure that the expenditure brings results and that the results reflect a positive cost-benefit relationship.

Anything which improves the decision-making process, thus increasing the chance of better results, should be looked at. Merely providing better information is not enough; the information itself must affect the quality of perceived results. Measuring this is a problem.

This is because the supply of information incurs cost – quantifiable in monetary terms – whereas it is actions following the use of information in the decision-making process which bring benefit. The two aspects are far apart and the situation is worsened by the fact that it is often difficult to quantify fully the benefits achieved and to place monetary values on them.

Vital here is information of *efficiency* and *effectiveness*. Efficiency is about how well we do what we do. Effectiveness is about how well we achieve our targets. Both are inextricably linked and demand a value judgement reflecting the degree of cost, often referred to as *economy*. The judgement reflects the blend of these 3 Es and results in a much sought after but eternally elusive value for money (VFM).

Information systems

Having looked at information in the broad sense, we now look a little more at information systems generally and at accounting information systems specifically, and their role in helping management teams to make appropriate decisions, and, subsequently, to stay in control.

Understanding systems

There are a number of definitions of what a system actually is. A simple definition might be:

> an assembly of components, be they mechanical or human, organized in such a way that specified objectives might be achieved.

This simple definition can be expanded by identifying and attaching characteristics which are shared between many types of information systems. Such characteristics include:

1 A system is holistic i.e. the whole is effectively greater than the sum of the parts.
2 Systems receive inputs and produce outputs.
3 Systems will have defined boundaries. Although a large system may comprise a series of subsystems, each individual system will have boundaries. The output of one system may well form the input into another system.
4 Systems will have inbuilt internal controls as an aid to efficiency and effectiveness.

Although many types of systems exist – lifecycle systems as in rain forest, motor combustion systems as with catalytic converters, etc. – what is being examined here is the organizational aspect of systems.

As such a system with an organizational emphasis could be defined as being one which: *collects, processes, stores, transmits and displays management information.*

The aspects considered above, leading from one definition to another, indicate that there are two sets of characteristics which are relevant. These are a set of **conceptual characteristics** and a set of **informational characteristics.** The latter set has already been considered (at the start of this chapter). The conceptual set is very much concerned with types of systems.

Types of system

There are three types of system commonly applied to the organizational context. These are:

- mechanistic
- probabilistic
- cybernetic.

Mechanistic or predictable

These are also known as *deterministic* systems. They are very simple systems which are completely predictable. This means that it is the inputs and outputs which are predictable. Typical machine and computer programs, particularly simple spreadsheets, are examples.

Probabilistic

In such systems the likely outcome can be predicted to a degree, but not completely. It is common for there to be an unpredictable margin of error. A typical probabilistic or *stochastic* system is that of stock control, where details are usually quoted in averages because of the impact of variables such as customer and production demands, price and quality.

Cybernetic

These are also known as *self-organizing* or *adaptive,* and are usually very complicated. Such systems adapt to their environment by altering their own systems structure. This type of system is well suited to long-term planning, although the problem of the variables which affect long-term planning can hamper a poorly designed system: just think of the number of organizations that have failed to respond to change!

A common feature shared by all types of system is that they may be *open* or *closed*. Open systems are those which interact and exchange information. Closed systems are usually fairly predictable, tending not to exchange information other than in the form of predictable inputs and outputs.

Designing the system

In designing an information system there are a number of factors which should be considered. These include:

- defining the boundaries of the system
- the objectives that the system is seeking to achieve
- the nature of the environment in which the system will operate, and the environmental effects upon that system
- the existing and potential resource demands of and constraints on the system
- the methods of evaluating the performance of the system
- any subsystems that are required, their natures and interrelationships
- the way in which the system will be managed.

Having set the scene, information systems may now be considered in a degree of detail. We now look at the role played by accounting information systems within the management control process.

Financial information systems

Any useful system will be dependent on the provision of timely and relevant information. This is just what information systems set out to do. They are designed to provide managers and/or external stakeholders, in a formalized way, with appropriate information for the planning and control activities for which they are responsible.

In a sense, financial information systems are really just one type of management information system, although in many organizations they form the basis of other systems. An appropriate definition might be that:

A financial information system processes financial transactions to provide scorekeeping, attention-directing and decision-making information to managers.

The **scorekeeping** aspect relates primarily to the financial account aspect where, in limited liability companies for example, accounting records must be kept by law and from those records annual accounts must be compiled and published for use by, for example, shareholders and loan providers.

From this information is derived more detailed information in the form of financial ratios for use by shareholders from providers and management teams.

Of much more significance to managers in the operational sense is the provision of attention-directing and decision-making information. (This is well represented by *budgetary control* and *ad hoc decision-making,* as you will see later.)

Types of financial information system

There are a larger number of financial information systems. In small organizations they will constitute all of the management information systems, whereas in larger concerns they will form only a portion. Most financial information systems are concerned with the processing of purely financial data.

Typically, financial information systems may be developed and applied to:

- production control
- stock control
- credit control
- cash control
- budgetary control
- fixed asset control.

Many organizations formalize the framework for accounting information systems by assigning the responsibility for control within key areas. Where applied, these are often taken to be:

- planning for control
- reporting and interpreting
- evaluating and consulting
- taxation
- protection of assets
- economic appraisal.

In light of the two listings given above, it is easy to see why a sound financial accounting system which has been developed to provide a sound management accounting system is important. It should be possible from these to develop further subsystems or to derive full systems to cope with all sorts of information that may be required by management.

Monitoring financial information systems

If financial information systems are to provide managers with the information for decision-making vital to the process of planning and control, and shareholders and loan providers with appraisal information, of course, it is important for there to be some way of checking the systems and the associated information to make sure that what should be happening actually is. This is achieved by the adoption of a major management support approach known as *audit,* comprising *external* and *internal* audits.

Here you will consider the nature of external and internal audits and their roles within organizations.

The nature of the internal audit

It would be sensible to start by attempting to define *internal audit.* Unfortunately, as with any aspect of organizational life, the definition which relates to the view of one management team may be slightly different to that of another team. Perhaps the definition offered by the Institute of Internal Auditors in the UK (IIA-UK) might be the most suitable:

> Internal audit is an independent appraisal activity established within an organization as a service to the organization. It is a control which functions by examining and evaluating the adequacy and effectiveness of other controls.

Originally, internal audit was concerned solely with accounting and financial controls, but evolution has brought about changes which have extended the scope to cover all aspects of organizational life.

Internal audit as a control function

Given that it is a key aspect of control, the key words of the second sentence of the definition above are important:

> It is a *control* which functions by *examining and evaluating* the *adequacy and effectiveness* of *other controls.*

The key terms in italic type are considered in turn below.

Control

The management process of planning and control may be viewed as a cyclical process. Planning will therefore initially precede control, but subsequently control will be fed into future plans, both aspects taking place within a time period, be it a month, a quarter or a year. It is in this light that internal audit must be forward-looking, with a positive influence attached to it. Checking the controls installed by management within systems is therefore very important and, given that internal audit is a control mechanism, it too should be afforded appropriate consideration.

Examining and evaluating

This aspect places a requirement upon internal auditors to support the results of their auditing with evidence. To function effectively as a control function, the auditors cannot be allowed to adopt a slapdash approach, but must be professional in collecting and analysing data. It is now commonplace for internal audit sections to develop and apply standards in relation to this.

Adequacy and effectiveness

It is important for management teams to be satisfied that systems are working well. If internal auditors can confirm this, the systems will be producing the outputs required by managers. They will be, at least, adequate and appropriately effective.

Other controls

In a sense, internal audit is located within the control loop of an organization, but it will influence the other aspects of the control cycle, be they associated with stock control, credit control or asset authorization, or whatever else.

Organizing for internal audit

The following are important:

- independence
- staff, as opposed to line, responsibility
- freedom of access to information.

Independence

To be effective, any approach to the monitoring of systems controls must be independent. This is certainly the case with internal audit. Usually, internal auditors are prevented from taking part in the day-to-day operations of organizational life. It is also usual for the head of internal audit to report to the chair, or equivalent, of the organization.

Staff function

Internal auditors, being independent of operations, should have no responsibility for the design, implementation, establishment or modifications of control systems. Internal audit thus fulfils a staff, rather than a line, function – an important reinforcement of the independence aspect

Freedom of access

If internal audit as a function is to achieve what it is required to achieve, then it is important for the auditors to have the right to examine unhindered, at all levels of the organization. If it were hindered, its independence would be questioned and its standing within the organization would fall.

Assessing internal checks and controls

It is important for systems that are economic, efficient and effective to be established. In order for this to be facilitated systems must include *internal checks* and *internal controls*. Internal audit will monitor the efficiency of these checks and controls, and hence will appraise the performance of systems when operating. In a sense, therefore, internal audit serves as an unusual but nevertheless valid technique of management performance and control.

There is an important difference between internal checks and internal controls, and the relevant aspects are iterated below.

Internal controls

These are controls which have been set by management in pursuit of organizational objectives. Examples of internal controls include:

● delegation of authority via the implementation of appropriate spans of control

- the formation of subcommittees for the monitoring of tenders, personnel applications, etc.
- ensuring that the organization's assets, including staff, are adequately insured.

Internal checks

Internal checks are mechanisms that are built into systems, and which are designed to prevent error and maintain a certain quality and quantity of work. Rather than being always monitored by the independent internal auditor, as internal controls usually are, internal checks usually involve one employee's work being monitored periodically by another – usually superior – member of staff. At longer periodic intervals, internal auditors would seek to ensure that the internal check approach is actually being operated and operated effectively.

Typical examples of internal check are:

- checking of cash book against bank statements
- checking cheque issuances and applications of required signature(s).

The balance of external with internal auditors

The processes employed by management in arriving at the published financial statements are monitored externally in limited liability companies and some public bodies by external auditors. The *Concise Oxford Dictionary* defines the word 'audit' as 'official examination of accounts; searching examination'. Herein lies a link that exists between external and internal audit: the *searching examination* aspect.

Both sets of auditors undertake searching examinations, but with different primary objectives. The external auditors conduct a searching examination of the organization's accounts with a view to confirming the accounts' *true and fair* view to the owners of the organization. Of course although the internal auditors will examine only certain aspects of the accounting system, they will examine all other systems. This is because they need to have a degree of confidence in the organization's system of internal control, in order to be able to comment realistically on their financial audit.

There is therefore often a degree of overlap between the two and, in a cost-reduction exercise, it is not unusual for the external auditors to place reliance on audits undertaken in these other areas by the internal auditors. Of course, external auditors will only do this if they are happy with the standard of internal auditing and the depth of auditing. Increasingly, as internal audit has improved its standards and professionalism, external auditors have been happy to place such reliance.

When a policy of cooperation is embarked upon, regular meetings and exchanges of information take place.

Information and its impact on managers

Any information system, but particularly so a financial one, will interact with managers using the system, be it at the input, output or processing stages. This is because managers realize that other managers, particularly more senior ones, tend to judge their performance by the results, financial and otherwise, conveyed by information systems. This is particularly the case with budgeting, as you will discover in the next chapter.

This book does not have the aim of turning you into a behavioural scientist. An understanding and appreciation of the links between *accounting, decision-making* and *human behaviour* will, however, enable you to understand more fully the implications of the material contained within the book.

Why bother with behaviour?

Traditionally, accountants within organizations tended to look upon organizations from a technical viewpoint and virtually to ignore what has been termed **human asset accounting.** In more recent times, accountants and other managers have become increasingly aware of the fact that accounting reports, in all their forms, shapes and sizes, play a major role in influencing the actions that humans take. Accounting therefore influences behaviour, and if behaviour is influenced for the better, then improved actions may result, bringing greater rewards for the organization. It is with this aspect to the fore that the American Accounting Association stated quite categorically in 1971 that 'In short, by its very nature, accounting is a behavioural process'. It is no surprise therefore to discover that (some) managers will manipulate information systems to present themselves in a better light.

Given that financial information systems are commonly used

- to assess how effectively managers have carried out their responsibilities
- to identify those areas which require corrective action
- to motivate managers towards goals
- to assess individual and comparative sector-based contribution towards organizational goals,

it is not surprising that the whole of this process will be influenced by the behaviour and actions of managers. In light of this, you will next consider some of the behaviour aspects which are most influential. They are grouped under four broad headings:

- organizational influences
- leadership and control
- people and planning
- management by objectives.

Organizational influences

All organizations have structures: some good, some bad, some appropriate, some inappropriate. The structure of an organization is influenced by the same variables that we identified earlier as influencing information systems. The more traditional approach to organizational structure is termed the *classical* approach. This is very concerned with the identification of tasks that need to be carried out in order to attain organizational objectives. A contrasting approach is the *human relations* approach. This moves away from the idea of identifying tasks towards the behaviour of people and how such behaviour can be used in achieving goals. It asserts the theory that, since individuals are the important focal point of organizations, structures should be designed with individuals to the fore. In the classical approach the individual has been very much a secondary consideration.

Of course, whichever approach is adopted you can guarantee that the organizational structure eventually adopted will be ideal. In recognition of this, a third approach – the *contingency* approach – has been developed in quite recent times. In an effort to design the best structure possible, even if not perfect, attention must be paid to four particular factors or **forces.** These are:

- forces in the *manager*
- forces in the *environment*
- forces in the *task*
- forces in the *subordinates*.

Each is considered in turn below.

Forces in the manager

Managers all possess unique, individual characteristics in relation to their managerial qualities. What links all managers is that their own specific managerial qualities will have resulted from a blend of experience, background and values. This blend will influence their own actions, particularly in relation to their perception of strategies and objectives. Given that organizations comprise managers, attention must be paid to their characteristic and individual forces, as it is the managers who will shape and define strategies and objectives, not the organization. Taken further, appropriate attention should be paid to the changes in forces that occur when people change, for whatever reason.

Forces in the environment

The environment In which an organization exists and functions will play a major role In determining information systems, in that they help to shape organizational structure. A problem is that the environment is dynamic and constantly changing, and organizations are often slow to change in response. Research has shown that more formal and bureaucratic structures – those closely aligned to the classical approach – are less capable of adjusting to environmental changes. On the other hand, less bureaucratic structures are able to respond more easily to new environmental conditions.

Forces in the task

As with environmental forces, there has been a great deal of research into this area. Evidence supports two main influential factors. The first is the influence of new technology. This is borne out by the impact that information technology has had, but this example is not the only one. Think about the impact of robotics and automation in, for example, car manufacturing and telephone equipment assembly. The second is that the nature of an individual's task influences the inherent personal forces. Thus, those concerned with skilled or managerial tasks usually wish to be more involved in decision making processes, whereas unskilled individuals often have lower expectations.

Forces in the subordinates

As we have just seen, to a greater or lesser degree, employees will have a desire to be involved in the decision-making process. It follows that the greater the concentration of skilled and/or managerial employees, the greater is the likelihood of demand for a more democratic and participative structure.

Leadership and control

If an organization recognizes the fact that managers are the fulcrum for the decision-making process, it is important for the organization to have leaders who fully appreciate and support that approach. Leadership styles may be typified by the identification of three particular styles, **Theory X**, **Theory Y** and **Theory** Z.

Theory X

This theory, developed by Douglas Macgregor, supports an authoritarian style of leadership involving a bureaucratic and hierarchical structure. It advocates that management is responsible for all aspects of an organization and that individuals are very much secondary in relation to the needs of the organization. It asserts that management knows best and that all else is effectively subsumed.

Theory Y

This theory, also a Macgregor philosophy, is at the opposite end of the spectrum to Theory X. It supports the idea that organizations will benefit from recognizing, developing and satisfying the personal demand of employees. It follows that such recognition, supported by appropriate action, is an important feature of effective control.

Theory Z

This theory, as developed by W.G. Ouchi, promotes the idea of consensus and trust as being essential prerequisites to the operation of complex enterprises operating particularly in competitive current global markets. Research by the author is indicating that this theory is particularly applicable within high-technology companies.

People and planning

As with each of the other areas considered above, much research effort has been concentrated into the effect of budgets on people. You will look at budgetary control in the next chapter, but it is worth noting the following now.

There are a number of weaknesses associated with traditional budgetary control systems and, even if they cannot be rectified, at least an awareness of them will help. The major areas of weakness and/or concern include:

- the standard-setting process
- the short-term perspective
- top-management's viewpoints
- poor communication
- lack of goal congruence
- bias in budgeting
- restraining of initiative.

The significance of each is highlighted below.

The standard-setting process

Senior management tend to talk rather glibly about standards, but it is important not to lose sight of the fact that the actual standard-setting process is in itself not an easy task. Indeed, it is fraught with difficulties. To be effective the process requires:

- clear goal definition
- clear assignment of responsibilities
- flows of delegation of authority and accountability
- effective communication
- attention being paid to motivation.

If individuals feel that the standards by which they are being judged are in some way invalid, it is not to be unexpected for problems to occur.

The short-term perspective

A common trap that organizations fall into is to concentrate on short-term profitability at the expense of long-term optimization. Typically, cuts in areas such as research and development or maintenance and safety or training could have important long-term consequences.

Top-management's viewpoints

Traditionally, budgetary systems have tended to concentrate on cost-restraint and profitability measures. Top management has therefore often concentrated on the significance of the attainment (or otherwise) of planned profit levels. The problem is that the degree of attainment of profit depends on so many variables, the majority of which are probably outside the control of the individual managers being evaluated. Top management may receive the wrong message and act accordingly; in other words, mistakenly.

Poor communication

Research has shown that where organizations display traditional Theory X style of management characteristics, managers tend to produce inappropriate budgetary information in the pursuit of self-survival. In such circumstances, top management tends to react by imposing tighter controls on managers. This activates a vicious circle which leads to a diminution in the quality and transmission speed of information, which in turn affects planning and control.

Lack of goal congruence

Given that budgetary control tends to be closely concerned with managerial responsibilities, it is understandable that individual managers will focus their attention on their departments. For this reason, not only do departmental direct interrelationships suffer, but goal congruence suffers, with consequential suboptimal performances at organizational level.

Bias in budgeting

Where managers are unhappy, it is natural to expect budgets to suffer from an enhanced degree of bias. Even when they are quite happy, managers can still manipulate budgets to their own advantage to suit particular prevailing circumstances. The natural reaction is for top management to balance this bias via counter-bias, and thus what has been termed **budgetary games** begins.

Restraint of initiative

Budgetary control systems tend to have the effect of constraining managers, in that opportunities for the use of initiative are lessened. Managers can become like robots and not use their initiative, even where it is needed and the opportunity exists.

Management by objectives

The behavioural aspect considered above should have indicated to you that there is a framework for planning and control systems which takes account of such aspects and can be incorporated within information systems. Such a framework is provided by the process of **management by objectives (MBO)**.

MBO translates the objectives of the organization in such a way that they become the personal objectives of individual managers. If this is successful, goal congruence is enhanced. Remember that some managers may feel detached from the overall organizational goals and would not act in the most effective manner in their pursuit. What MBO does by translating overall goals into personal goals is to implement effectively a system of *self-control* for managers, rather than imposed control from above.

The process

Ensuring that MBO works requires the implementation of a number of aspects contributing to the overall process. These are:

- reviewing both long- and short-term organizational objectives
- reviewing and, where appropriate, revising the structure of the organization
- establishing a clear picture of the hierarchy of delegation
- obtaining a consensus between top management and managers, regarding the standard-setting process
- stressing that budgetary control systems should not be seen as constraints, but rather as guidelines and resource providers which will help managers to achieve recognized goals
- implementing a participative measurement process which involves joint discussion with managers
- undertaking regular periodic reviews of the factors affecting the organization and its structure and, hence, its management systems
- incorporating the above in financial information systems.

Summary

In this chapter you have considered the nature of information and the role it plays in managing the finances of an organization. In particular you have looked at the relationship of information to the process of management and at its use in planning, budgeting and control. In addition, you have been introduced to the idea of internal audit as a management tool in monitoring the appropriateness of an organization's information systems.

What you have considered is relevant in its own right but assumes a greater significance in light of what lies ahead in the next two chapters. An appreciation of the nature and role of information is vital if you are to take on board the key role of budgeting and thereafter understand how performance can be measured. Of course, in light of this it is important that the relevant information systems generate reliable, accurate and timely information, and should be seen to do so.

By now you should:

- recognize the characteristics of useful management information
- understand how useful accounting information can be to internal and external stakeholders
- appreciate the roles of both internal and external audit in verifying the accuracy and reliability of information
- be able to link information with the actions of managers.

Self-assessment questions

To assess your own progress, attempt the self-assessment questions below.

SAQ 12.1

Detail the desirable characteristics of information.

SAQ 12.2

(a) Draw up a list of typical financial information systems.
(b) Select any two systems from your list in (a) above and highlight their utility.

SAQ 12.3

Distinguish between external and internal audit and in so doing examine their respective natures and roles.

SAQ 12.4

Explain and illustrate how information can motivate and/or demotivate a manager and thus influence managerial decisions and actions.

Further reading

Beaver, W.H., 1989. *Financial Reporting: An Accounting Revolution*, Prentice-Hall

13 Managing through budgetary information

Introduction

For the majority of managers, in all types and sizes of organizations, it is information relating to the preparation and operation of budgeting systems which represents their reality of the theory of information.

In this chapter you will look at how managers can use information to plan ahead (in the context, of course, of the pyramid of purpose), and then monitor and control progress towards achieving objectives. Finally, you will see that information is used by them to assess performance, not least through efficiency, effectiveness and value for money.

By the end of this chapter you will:

- understand the nature and purpose of a budget
- be able to construct and manage a budget
- understand the nature and utility of standard costs
- be able to produce and interpret simple measures of efficiency and effectiveness.

The context of budgeting

The pyramid of purpose you met in Figure 1.1 showed how visions and missions are translated into day-to-day activities. Planning ahead to achieve a mission requires the development and implementation of a strategy to accompany the business plan. Budgeting as an information system reflects the immediate, normally put to a year, planning to enable managers to set their day-to-day targets and negotiate for required resources.

In the next chapter you will meet the idea of ratios being used to analyse past performance. These, however, are invariably applied at the corporate level and look back over a year.

An effective budgeting system looks both forwards and backwards. It represents the overall plan for making the best possible use of the resources of an organization. Budgets will typically be concerned with aspects such as anticipated income and cash flows, costs and expenditure, and the capital that needs to be used to achieve the stated objectives of the particular period.

Figure 13.1 shows the main functions of a budget.

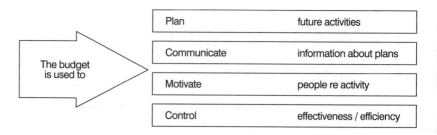

Plan	future activities
Communicate	information about plans
Motivate	people re activity
Control	effectiveness / efficiency

The budget is used to

Figure 13.1 Functions of a budget

The functions

One of the functions of a budget is to help managers to *plan* future activities. Another is to *communicate* information about these activities to the people who will be involved in carrying them out. An important part is the way in which a budget will serve to *motivate* – or frustrate – those people, by setting out what is expected of individuals. The planning, communication and motivational aspects of the budget are clearly predominantly concerned with setting out future levels of activity. However, it is, of course, important for people to know whether the actual levels of activity or performance measure up to planned levels. This is where the fourth function comes in: the *control* function.

Planning and objectives

A budget is defined by the Chartered Institute of Management Accountants as:

> A plan quantified in monetary terms, prepared and approved prior to a defined period of time, usually showing planned income to be generated and/or expenditure to be incurred during that period and the capital to be employed to attain a given objective.

This definition is important as it emphasizes the relationship between objectives and resources. A survey of practising managers, started in 1989 and revised each year since then, showed that up to 65% of managers held, through the behaviour impact of budgeting as a financial information system, the view that budgeting is purely and simply concerned with a pot of money. That is only part of the process. Budgeting is essentially a planning tool, embracing resources, but also providing managers with a control facility by supplying regular feedback on performance.

Detailed budgets are often prepared to cover a limited future period, usually a maximum of 1 year, subdivided into shorter periods. These shorter periods are often 13 monthly periods or 13 4-weekly periods. The plan for the short term must be consistent with the organization's longer term objectives, and outline budgets for longer periods are often prepared. The feedback is then supplied monthly or 4-weekly.

Control

Of course, no matter how good a plan is, it is useless if there is no effective control to ensure it is put into effect. The budget represents a set of yardsticks or guidelines for use in controlling the internal operations of an organization. By continuous comparison of the actual figures with the budget, management can appraise the performance of every level of the organization. Using the principles of **management by exception,** deviations from budgeted performance will be highlighted and corrective action can be taken. If this is not possible, it will be necessary for management to revise its plan (and hence its budgets) to recognize this. Management by exception is a technique applied by management to *control* systems. If the system does not indicate that something is amiss, management will assume that the system is operating well and nothing needs checking or investigating.

A control scenario

Imagine, for example, the following scenario. The sales team are falling short of their budgeted targets. They say that under current market conditions they just cannot achieve the original estimates. Well, perhaps conditions have changed dramatically – perhaps the forecasts and targets were unrealistic in the first place; or maybe they just are not pulling their weight, in which case it might be time for a bit of plain talking with the head of the sales team. Certainly, only if it is absolutely impossible for targets to be met should the plan be scrapped or revised. Whatever action was decided upon, the control mechanism would be maintained by continued observation and appraisal of performance in the light of any new benchmarks.

The budgeting process

There are three main elements in the budgeting process, these being **objectives, planning** and **control.** First, the *objectives* of the organization are defined, then these objectives are translated into *plans* which are consistent with the policies and guidelines laid down by management. Performance is then *monitored* against these plans, once they have been expressed in monetary terms to form the budgets. These elements are not independent and should not operate in isolation. At each stage *important feedback* effects take place, and interactions will occur between objectives and planning and between planning and control, as shown in Figure 13.2.

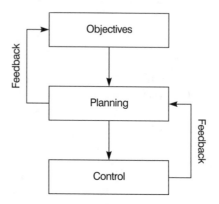

Figure 13.2 The interaction in budgets

One must always keep in mind that budgeting is not just a mechanistic process. The plan of action which the budget represents, and the control mechanisms related to it, involve every member of the organization, and that involvement can provide a singular motivating force throughout the company.

With this behavioural aspect in mind, some building on the behavioural dimension you considered in the last chapter is valuable.

Participation in budget preparation

Budgets are not made in heaven or carved on tablets of stone to be handed down from on high: at least, they should not be. Budgetary preparation means a lot of to-ing and fro-ing, from the humblest management level to the board room, securing the involvement of everyone in setting realistic but challenging targets and coordinating different plans of action for every level of the company, so as to plan for the best possible result for the company as a whole. A blend, in light of whether the organization opts for Theory X, Y or Z style management, with top down and/or bottom up planning, is the reality of this to-ing and fro-ing. This is shown in Figure 13.3.

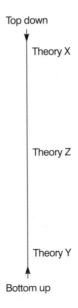

Top down

Theory X

Theory Z

Theory Y

Bottom up

Figure 13.3 Top down and bottom up planning

The advantages
There are many advantages to be gained from involving all levels of management in the budgetary process. Here are some of the more obvious ones; you can probably think of several others:

- advantage is taken of each individual manager's knowledge, initiative and experience
- A manager' s morale is boosted by the sense of being part of the planning process
- every manager is made aware of how his or her particular functions fit into the overall operational picture of the enterprise
- inter-departmental cooperation is fostered
- low-level managers become familiar with the policies and objectives of the business and are made aware of its problems and difficulties
- the targets implied by the budget are more likely to be accepted by all those whose task it will be to achieve them.

The budget should serve as a **communication channel** – from top management, all the way down the organizational hierarchy to the lowest level of management, and vice versa. Managers at all levels are more likely to understand the justification for any changes in operations and are more likely to be prepared to offer constructive criticism if they are fully aware of the context that gives rise to the need for such changes.

The organizational framework

It is important to be able to trace costs, revenues, assets and liabilities to the individual managers who are primarily responsible for making decisions about these issues. Thus, the usefulness of a budget for control purposes is dependent upon the existence of a sound organizational structure. The authority and responsibilities of each individual manager must be clearly defined. In a proper organizational structure, managers at any level must be aware of their *responsibilities* for the performance of their departments within the framework of the organization's objectives, and must possess the authority which is needed. Monitoring the actual accomplishments of each manager, in terms of responsibilities, necessitates clear-cut divisions of responsibility and authority. Thus budgeting is integrally related to the delegation of authority and responsibility.

Authority, responsibility and accountability

Although the statement of the principles of **responsibility accounting** may appear to be straightforward, the implementation of these principles is varied, and often difficult in practice. Normally, it is suggested that managers should only be held responsible for those costs and revenues over which they are able to exercise significant influence. In turn, managers would expect to have a strong influence in budgeting for those items for which they are to be held accountable.

If the system of allocating responsibility is to be real, it requires that sufficient authority should be delegated to managers, both to take the decisions and to exercise the controls which are necessary. The extent to which top management delegates this authority is an important factor in determining the responsibility of individual managers.

The ideas of responsibility accounting are normally implemented through what are termed *responsibility centres*. For the purpose of responsibility accounting, performance reports should be limited to those items which have been identified as *controllable* by the managers in question. Apportionments of items such as head office costs, over which managers in other functions have little direct influence, should therefore, perhaps, be excluded from their periodic statements of actual and budgeted performance.

Dual responsibility

Problems also arise where some measure of **dual responsibility** exists. For example, in respect of material costs, it may be that both the buyer and the manager of the department in which the materials are used have significant influence over the total material costs. To identify price as the responsibility of the buyer and usage as that of the pro-duction department does not provide for the situation in which infe-rior quality material is purchased, with consequent adverse effects on usage.

A budget implicitly establishes a procedure for teamwork, geared towards accomplishment of the ultimate objectives of the enterprise. Ideally, a budget should create what is sometimes described as **goal congruence.**

There should, understandably, be consistency between the aims of individual managers and departments and the aims of the organiza-tion as a whole. This means creating a situation where each individual, in attempting to satisfy personal interests, will be making the greatest contribution to achieving the objectives of the enterprise. Otherwise, individual managers may be more likely to try to satisfy their own needs, regardless of the objectives of the organization.

In budgeting, the operations of different individuals and depart-ments must be coordinated in the context of the objectives of the enter-prise as a whole. The procedures used in formulating the budget must therefore provide mechanisms to resolve conflicts of interest between departments which may have mutually contradictory plans.

> Take, for example, a typical situation that can arise in a manufac-turing concern. One of the major problems of managing such a business is that the interests of various departments often conflict with one another. In our example, the sales department may want a wider range of products, or ask for minor changes to the prod-ucts or their packaging. On the other hand, the production depart-ment may favour a more limited range of products and wish to avoid modifications.

Performance evaluation

A great deal of care must go into setting the level of performance that each department will be expected to reach. A budget must represent a goal that is capable of achievement – if it does not, no matter how great the rewards on offer, people are not even going to try to meet the target.

Budgets must therefore be realistic and individual managers must be convinced of the attainability of their targets. Conversely, however, performance standards should be tight enough to motivate individu-als to work to their targets. *Realistic but challenging* would seem to be the winning formula.

The actual performance of any segment of the enterprise, compared to the target figures, provides **feedback** on the efficiency of the management of that segment. Failure of the enterprise, or parts of it, to achieve the objectives set in the budgetary plan may mean failure of the enterprise as a whole. On the other hand, the ability of a manager to better the planned estimate is a measure of better performance. There should therefore be guidelines, yardsticks and procedures which have been agreed by managers for evaluating the performance of their departments. However, evaluation of the performance of managers should obviously not be entirely dependent on how closely they have conformed to their budgets. There may have been changes in the technical, economic or industrial environments which it is important to take into account.

Building a budget

Reading about the theory of budgeting is one matter; understanding the reality of how it is put into action is another. Next, you will consider common approaches to planning and ways in which progress is monitored.

The time aspect

A budget relates to a particular time period. The period chosen may depend on a number of factors, such as the nature of the concern and the length of any manufacturing and/or trading cycles. Just as important, of course, are the feasibility and dependability of forecasting in the market sector concerned. However, 1 year is the most usual maximum budgeting period for control purposes. Increasingly, organizations are also engaging in longer term planning, preparing a financial plan which may stretch over several years. An annual budget (which differs from a financial plan in that the budget has a control function) will then, of course, be set in the context of the longer range planning.

For control purposes, the period of the budget is usually broken down in shorter periods, often called **control periods.** At the end of each control period the actual figures are compared against those of the budget. (Control periods of 4 weeks, rather than a month, are quite usual, to avoid the difference in the number of days in each month which may make comparisons difficult.)

Many businesses prepare an annual budget at one point in the year – say, for January to December or for April to March. Others have 'continuous' or 'rolling' budgets – as each month (or quarter) is completed, the budget for another month (or quarter) is added to the end of the budget so that a budget for a full year ahead is always available. This is, in general, a desirable policy, since it encourages managers to look ahead continuously. But whether budgets are prepared for a fixed period ahead or on a continuous basis, a carefully thought out timetable for all budget activities is essential.

It is worth noting that although the budget process should be carefully thought out in relation to the goal congruence aspects looked at above, some managers still ignore that factor. Many managers are guilty of building *slack* into budgets. Indeed, empirical research indicates that this practice is quite widespread. The problem facing top management here is not just the unwelcome effects of slack being built into budgets and the associated knock-on effects on performance, evaluation and control. There is also the problem of top management not always having the requisite information to challenge effectively the estimates of lower management.

Preparing the budget

Budgeting is a **management function** not simply an *accounting function*. Ideally, all levels of management should have a good understanding of the nature and objectives of the organization's budget and should participate in its preparation. Furthermore, all members of the management teams should have the conviction that budgeting is a means for creating an atmosphere of teamwork and cooperation. The actual responsibility for the supervision and coordination of the preparation of the budget is normally delegated by top management to a member of the chief accountant's staff called the **budget officer.** In some organizations, the budget officer is directly responsible to top management in order to ensure independence. The budget officer should not prepare the budget. Rather the function of the post is to provide technical assistance to management at all levels and to organize the collation of the various budgets prepared by the managers of each department. A good example is where departmental managers need information regarding past performance, or analysis of this information in relation to future prospects and objectives They would seek this information or analysis from the budget officer.

The budget committee

In larger organizations, a group of executives serve in a budget committee. This may consist of the heads of the main functions of the business – the sales manager, the production manager, etc. – together with the senior management accountant. The budget committee, which is often a very powerful committee within the organization, is charged with the tasks of preparation and administration of the organization's budget. The budget officer then usually acts as secretary to the budget committee.

The bottom up approach

Most of the costs of a business are incurred at the operational level, which is also where the results are accomplished. Lower level supervisors and managers, like foremen on the shop floor or local sales managers, often have the most realistic view of what operational results can be accomplished and at what cost. This is a sound reason for the budgeting procedure to be started on a **bottom up** basis. However, as the preparation of budgets is part of the long-term planning process, which will have been based on top management's policy decisions, details of these policies and any necessary guidelines must be communicated to the managers responsible for the budget's preparation – a top down aspect. Where a bottom up approach is adopted and responsibility and authority are widely delegated, managers prepare the budget for the operation of their subareas of responsibility and submit these to their superior managers for consideration and incorporation into the larger units' budgets.

The review procedure

Before each budget is incorporated, it will be reviewed critically by the superior manager to ensure that it is realistic and reflects the standards of performance expected. The review procedure will be repeated at each stage of consolidation, including the final presentations to the budget committee. Managers who are held accountable for the budgets of their reporting subordinates will seek to be thoroughly convinced before accepting these budgets as part of their own responsibility area.

Coordination

The next step is coordination of the draft departmental budgets. Since departments within an organization are necessarily interrelated, any decision in one department regarding the budget is bound to affect other departments' projected operations and budgets. Indeed, in many cases data from one budget will form the input to another. Ideally, one would like to examine the effect of every decision on all the segments of the business simultaneously, and computer modelling is increasingly making this possible. However, it is often not possible. Frequently, therefore, a trial-and-error process is necessary. The communication and exchange of information between departments are features of the budgeting process and the budget officer has an important role here.

Coordination, communication and conflict

At the first meeting of senior departmental managers with the budget committee to consider the first rough drafts, it is not surprising to come across contradictions. After a few such meetings each budget's implications on the others will have been studied and mutual inconsistencies resolved – both between the various departmental budgets and between these budgets and the board of directors' guidelines and objectives. Once agreement is reached and inconsistencies have been resolved, each department can embark on the detailed design of its own budget.

The final stage is reached when each department has come up with a detailed budget which is mutually consistent with every other department's budget and with the organization's objectives. These budgets will then be reviewed by the board of directors or their equivalent. If the results are judged to be unsatisfactory, more guidelines will be issued and the interactive process continues. When finally, the budget is approved by the board, the budget figures are no longer forecasts – they have become targets and the budget has become the operational plan for guidance of managers at every level.

Setting the budget

Traditional budgeting: the incremental approach

In preparing budgets for ongoing activities, an approach which is frequently adopted is to determine the past outcomes in respect of both revenues and costs and to use these as the base for preparing the budgets for the forthcoming period. Adjustments are made to this base in order to allow for expected price changes and changes in either the volume or nature of activities to be undertaken. The budgets are prepared on a basis which is *incremental* to the costs and revenues from existing activities. This is known as **incremental budgeting.**

The incremental approach has the advantage of being relatively simple and cheap to implement. This is useful in organizations where activity and resourcing tools remain fairly constant. Where they do not, past inefficiencies are reflected in the existing base, and are likely to be perpetuated in the plans and budgets of the future period.

Playing games

The incremental approach can lead to managers adding, say, 10% to a budget, knowing that inflation is, say, 4% and that they are likely to be cut down. If they are cut down by, say, 6%, they and other managers have gained more money than they really need and the organization's scarce resources are not put to best use.

Another consequence of this approach is captured in Figure 13.4. This shows what happens at the year end. Surplus (i.e. not required) is spent on the promise that if it is not spent it will not be in the budget next year! Alternatively, expenditure and activities may need to be curtailed.

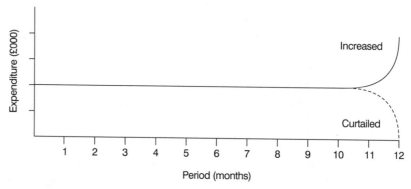

Figure 13.4 Hockey games

Limiting factors

All plans have to start somewhere, and budgets are no exception. It is one matter to talk about achieving mission, another to realize it. The reality of the world is such that those events which managers would like to happen do not automatically take place. There are constraints which need to be taken into account before planning can start. These are usually referred to as *limiting factors* and must be identified before the process can start at all.

> For many commercial concerns, perhaps like British Airways, a common limiting factor is the level of sales which can realistically be achieved over the next year. For others it may be the limitation of scarce resources such as skilled labour or materials or space. For yet others, particularly voluntary and public sector concerns, the scarce resource may be funding!

Zero-base budgeting

An alternative approach to budgeting is that of *zero-base budgeting*. Managers are required to justify their entire budget requests in detail, with the onus of proof placed firmly on the managers to justify the expenditure which their proposals will incur.

An essential characteristic of the approach is for managers to prepare budgets for the cost of operating their activities at a minimum level of service, and then to identify in separate decision packages the costs and benefits of additional increments to the activity for which they are responsible. Top management is then better informed to determine priorities. This may result in the transfer of resources from existing activities which are considered to have low priority to new activities with higher priority ratings.

As a practical illustration, consider the ways in which government could budget for the provision of services to deal with the problems of drug or alcohol abuse. Basic medical care costs might be budgeted to deal with survival and crisis situations. As additions to this, as separate packages and at various levels of supply, the costs of continuing supervised therapy could be prepared. The provision of general counselling services and programmes of general education would be represented by further decision packages. On the basis of information supported by research, on the costs and benefits of the various services, government would decide which combination of decision packages to offer.

The use of ranked packages provides top management with detailed information on which to base its decisions to achieve objectives. It is also claimed that the use of zero-base budgeting will improve the performance of middle and lower levels of management. Managements will be required continuously to evaluate their own efficiency and effectiveness in providing value for money and achieving objectives.

Incremental versus zero-base budgeting

Do not be misled from what has gone before into thinking that zero-base budgeting is always superior to incremental budgeting. Incremental budgeting does have the advantage of being relatively simple to operate. In addition, the drawbacks associated with inbuilt budget slack and inefficiencies can partly be negated where management teams are experienced and very aware of such problems.

Zero-based budgeting, on the other hand, although theoretically sound, may prove difficult to implement. If it were applied to all budgets the process would be very time consuming. In addition, it could give rise to considerable friction and bring departmental managers into conflict with each other and the organization. Recent history has indicated that zero-base budgeting is very susceptible to political influence and pressures.

Whichever approach is adopted, it is vital for:

- identifying variances *in good time* to effect remedial action
- determining *why* variances have recurred
- ensuring that *appropriate action* is taken.

Activity-based budgeting

This approach builds upon the philosophy of ZBB. Its rationale is that in order to achieve targets, managers must undertake activities, and it is activities which generate cost. Thus, it is argued, an analysis of activities as the generator, or driver, of cost should lead to a more realistic assessment of required resource.

Monitoring the budget

The essence of monitoring on, say, a 4-weekly or monthly basis is usually based upon fixed or flexible budgeting, both of which are looked at next. The flexible approach is important as it relates revenue/expenditure to activity levels which the fixed approach does not.

Fixed budgeting

A budget which is designed to remain unchanged regardless of the volume of output or other level of activity attained is known as a **fixed budget.** Fixed budgets are suitable either for enterprises whose level of business is predictable and stable or, conversely, where changes in the levels of activity in the business do not change its revenues or costs. Examples of the latter are difficult to find and may be a consequence of a policy to restrict expenditure to a predetermined amount.

Fixed budgets are relatively simple to prepare and need no revision for activity changes. Nevertheless, even in this type of budget there should be room to allow at least some minor adjustments if necessary. It would be tiresome, to say the least, if sales staff were all stuck behind their desks at head office, simply because their fixed petrol budget allowance was exhausted!

Flexible budgeting

Flexible budgets (or **variable budgets** as they are sometimes known) are designed to be changed with fluctuations in output, sales or other measures of activity affecting an organization's level of revenues or costs.

During the control period, fixed cost items such as rent and rates will normally be unaffected by increases or decreases in activity. Other costs will vary in proportion to the level of output or sales. Clearly, it would be unrealistic to expect the direct material cost of 1,000 units to be the same as that for 500 units in any manufacturing concern.

In flexible budgeting, the cost behaviour pattern of each item is recognized by revising the budget allowance in light of the actual level of activity attained. For the purposes of cost control, this provides a meaningful comparison between the actual cost and the budget allowance, which are now both based on the same level of activity.

Flexible budgeting in practice

In practice, the system can be operated by preparing a series of budgets for revenues and costs for discrete levels of activity, say 500, 1,000 and 1,500 units. Alternatively the budget allowances can be reworked at the end of the control period when the activity level is known.

As an example, look at the details shown in Table 13.1. This shows the original budget for Period 1 of a manufacturing concern's production activities. You will note that this anticipates a budgeted output of 1,000 units. The actual figures and the resultant variances are shown alongside. Of course, the problem here is that the actual figures relate to an output of 1,500 units during the period. Because the activity levels differ, the variances are not very meaningful at all. If you refer to Table 13.2 you will see that the budget has been flexed to an activity level of 1,500 units. It is now possible to compare like with like. Consequently, the variances are more meaningful.

Table 13.1 Performance statement – Period 1

Detail	Budget	Actual	Variance
Output	1,000 units	1,500 units	
	£	£	£
Direct materials	1,000	1,250	250 (adverse)
Direct labour	1,000	1,750	750 (adverse)
Variable overheads	2,000	1,500	500 (favourable)
Fixed overheads	4,000	4,000	–

The term 'flexible budgeting' is used by accountants to denote the adjustment of budgets to reflect changes in activity level. Other changes affecting an organization's operations, such as unanticipated price changes or the effect of technological change, may justify the revision of budgets. However, revisions of this type should not be confused with the flexing of budget allowances for activity reasons. In economists' terms, flexible budgets are movements along a cost curve, whereas changes of the other type alter the curve's position.

In reality, many computerized information systems show the fixed and flexed budget columns, ensuring that the totality of the situation is revealed to managers. After all, the variance on the flexed budget statement in Table 13.2 relates resources to activity but does not show how much the resources have been over- or under-spent. It may justify extra spending but, of course, if there is no extra money left to spend, problems will not be far away!

Table 13.2 Performance statement – Period I*

Detail	Budget	Actual	Variance
Output	1,000 units	1,500 units	
	£	£	£
Direct materials	1,500	1,250	250 (favourable)
Direct labour	1,500	1,750	250 (adverse)
Variable overheads	3,000	1,500	1,500 (favourable)
Fixed overheads	4,000	4,000	–

*The flexible process, in this case, assumes a linear relationship. Of course, this will not always be the case in practice.

An extension of the fixed and flexible joint approach is contained within the technique of standard costing which is considered below.

What preparation order?

In many commercial organizations, preparation of the sales budget comes first, because expenditure cannot be planned until the source and amount of income have been estimated. However, there are important exceptions to this. For example, in parts of the construction and engineering industries, where production capacity is the key limiting factor of the business, the production budget must be the starting point. Even in sales-driven organizations, the sales managers are wise to take account of supply and manufacturing capacity potential. In non-profit-making concerns, the limiting factor may often be the level of anticipated funding.

Sales budget

The first part of the sales budget, based on forecast sales volume, is the **projected sales income** which reflects the sales manager's estimate of several factors. These factors include:

- the size of markets for products and services
- the forecast growth of these markets
- the selling prices of the products
- competition from other firms
- the effect of advertising and incentive schemes for salesmen based on market share.

It is from the limiting factor that the rest of the budget is derived.

In many organizations, the budgets are meaningfully used in strict performance measurement and control terms via a technique termed **standard costing.**

Standard costing

Standard costing is a technique which:

- sets standards and establishes standard costs
- monitors performance via feedback
- determines differences – called variances – between what should have happened and what actually happened
- analyses the variances by cause.

It is, in essence, an extension of the budgetary control technique, but it progresses the technique a stage further by *analysing any variances by cause.*

Standard costing is particularly used in manufacturing industries wherever there is an aspect of standardization. It is particularly suited to repetitive assembly-type work and mass production. Increasingly, however, many service and non-profit-making concerns are using standard costs for units of activity.

What is a standard cost?

A **standard cost** is a carefully predetermined cost that management establishes and uses as a basis for a comparison with actual costs. Remember that the standard cost is likely to have been established in relation to specified working conditions. If these change, so could costs. For most manufactured products, whether they are finished goods or component parts, it is often possible to determine in advance the amounts, and hence costs, of materials and labour that should be necessary to make each product. It is also possible to extend the application of standard costing to manufacturing overheads.

Standard costs may be based on marginal costs, in which case they do not include an element for fixed overhead absorption. However, it is not essential to develop standard marginal costs when considering budgetary control in production or operation departments of a company. In practice, many companies develop standard full costs in order to compare total actual costs with total budgeted costs, both based on absorption costing.

Types of standard

As with many other aspects of life, the same term can mean different things to different people. The same is certainly true of the term 'standard' . There are four main interpretations:

- basic
- ideal
- attainable
- current.

Basic standards are those which could remain unchanged over a long period, perhaps even years. Management teams have traditionally tended to ignore basic standards within reporting systems, as they tend to comprise an almost unquantifiable mixture of controllable and non-controllable costs and factors.

Ideal standards are those which take no account of wastage, breakdowns, natural breaks or idle time. They are based on optimal operating conditions, and should be treated as long-term targets rather than for use in current control systems.

Attainable standards are those which are usually used within standard costing systems. The standard should be attainable in that it is realistic, but it should also be challenging and stimulating. It is attainable standards that we will be referring to here.

Current standards will often equate with attainable standards, in that they are those currently being used. Where something unexpected happens, say a problem with material quality, a new and temporary standard might be determined and applied. It might need to be applied (i.e. be current) until the material quality problem disappears.

The standard cost card

Management will endeavour to set standards for each cost element of a product. These standards, along with standard specifications, will be recorded and displayed on a **standard cost card**. It is these details that will play an essential role in the standard costing process.

A typical (blank) standard cost card is shown in Figure 13.5.

Determining the standard cost card details

Cost element	Detail
Direct materials	100,000 kg costing £100,000
Direct labour	25,000 hours costing £150,000
Variable production overhead	£100,000
Fixed production overhead	£75,000

Cost element	Detail	£
Direct materials		
Direct labour		
Production overheads:		
Variable		
Fixed	Total standard production cost	

Figure 13. 5 Typical standard cost card layout

The standard costs and specifications will be derived from the budgeted details for the year. Consider the details shown in the box relating to Standard Ltd.

The direct *materials* are budgeted as being 100,000 kg costing £100,000. If the budgeting process has been carried out correctly, we can set a standard cost thus:

$$\frac{\text{Budgeted usage}}{\text{Budgeted production}} = \frac{100,000 \text{ kg}}{100,000 \text{ units}} = 1 \text{ kg per unit}$$

and

$$\frac{\text{Budgeted costs}}{\text{Budgeted usage}} = \frac{£100,000}{100,000 \text{ kg}} = £1 \text{ per kg}$$

These results mean that the details to be entered in on the standard cost card should be

Direct material   1kg at £1 per kg   £1 cost per unit

The *direct labour* element is budgeted as costing £150,000 for 25,000 hours. The standard cost will be set as follows:

$$\frac{\text{Budgeted hours}}{\text{Budgeted production}} = \frac{25,000 \text{ hours}}{100,000 \text{ units}} = 0.25 \text{ h or 15 min}$$

and

$$\frac{\text{Budgeted cost}}{\text{Budgeted hours}} = \frac{£150,000}{25,000 \text{ hours}} = £6 \text{ per hour}$$

The details to be entered on the standard cost card are thus:

Direct labour   15 min at £6 per hour   £1.50 cost per unit

The *production overheads* will need to be absorbed into the total cost per unit. To do this, an overhead absorption basis will need to be adopted.

Assuming that the organization uses a direct labour-hour absorption rate and segregates the production overheads into variable and fixed categories. If this is the case, our calculations are:

$$\text{Variable overheads} = \frac{\text{Budgeted overheads}}{\text{Budgeted hours}} = \frac{£100,000}{25,000 \text{ hour}}$$

$$= \text{Rate of £4 per direct labour-hour}$$

$$\text{Fixed overheads} = \frac{\text{Budgeted overheads}}{\text{Budgeted hours}} = \frac{£75,000}{25,000 \text{ hours}}$$

$$= \text{Rate of £3 per direct labour-hour}$$

The details to be entered are:

Variable overheads 15 min at £4 per hour £1 cost per unit
Fixed overheads   15 min at £3 per hour £0.75 cost per unit

The completed standard cost card is shown in Figure 13.6.

Cost element	Detail	Cost per unit
Direct materials	1kg @ £1 per kg	£1.00
Direct labour	15 min. @ £6 per hour	1.50
Production overheads:		
Variable	15 min. @ £4 per hour	1.00
Fixed	15 min. @ £3 per hour	0.75
Total cost per unit		4.25

Figure 13.6 Standard Ltd: standard cost card for 1 unit

Applying the standard costs

The standard costs detailed in the standard cost card are used in a process which compares the actual with the standard costs.

Updating the information shown earlier and adding the actual activity details for the first month of the year, the details shown in Table 13.3 are obtained. You are now faced with an extreme example of the need to flex the fixed budget. In this case it needs to be flexed from

100,000 units down to 8,000 units. Only then will we be able to compare like with like and obtain meaningful variances.

Table 13.3 Annual budget and actuals for month 1

Detail	Annual budget	Actual for month 1
Production	100,000 units	8,000 units
Direct materials	100,000 kg costing £100,000	9,000 kg costing £8,100
Direct labour	25,000 hours costing £150,000	1,800 hours costing £13,600
Variable production overheads	£100,000	£9,600
Fixed production overheads	£75 ,000	£6, 500

Flexing the fixed budget

If the fixed budget is flexed, the figures shown in Figure 13.7 are obtained. These flexed figures are obtained by multiplying 8,000 units by the individual cost per unit figures shown on the standard cost card.

Detail	Flexed budget	Actual	Variance
Direct materials	£8,000	£8,100	£100 (adverse)
Direct labour	13,000	13,600	600 (adverse)
Variable production overheads	8,000	9,600	1,600 (adverse)
Fixed production overheads	6,000	6,500	500 (adverse)

Figure 13.7 Standard Ltd: flexed budget/actual details, month 1

The variances shown in Figure 13.7 have been derived from the inclusion of standard costs within the budgetary control process. That the variances are adverse will alert management to the fact that matters have gone wrong and need correction. This leads us to the next aspect of standard costing: analysing variances by cause.

Analysing variances by cause

Each of the variances shown in Figure 13.7 will be the direct result of either one of, or a combination of, two causes. A variance will arise for the reasons shown in Table 13.4. You will see that for all of the variances, the causes may be divided into two groups:

- causes associated with spending
- causes associated with efficiency.

Table 13.4 Causes of variance

Variance	Possible causes
Direct materials	Paying a higher or lower price per kg or metre, etc. Using a different quantity of material in relation the standard amount allowed
Direct labour	Paying higher or lower rates per hour or per units
Production overheads Variable	Spending more or less than anticipated. Where production overheads are linked to direct-labour hours, achieving greater or lower efficiency in production.
Fixed	Per variable production overheads.

By applying software commands, the cause of the variances may quickly and easily be identified and analysed. With regard to the variances shown in analysis tree in Figure 13.8, the analysis is shown in Figure 13.9 after taking account of comparisons relevant between actual and standard spending and efficiency details.

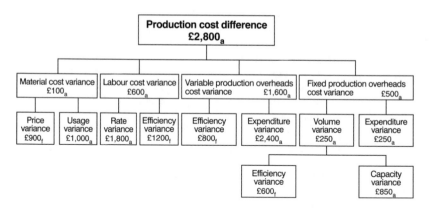

Figure 13.8 Standard Ltd: analysis tree, $_a$ = adverse; $_f$ = favourable

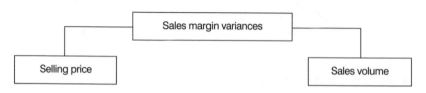

Figure 13.9 Standard Ltd: the analysis derived from Figure 13.8

The analysis tree

The 8,000 units produced in month 1 in Standard Ltd should have cost:

8,000 units × standard cost per unit of £4.25 = £34,000

The actual cost was:

Materials	£8, 100
Labour	£13,600
Variable overheads	£9,600
Fixed overheads	£6,500
	£36,800

The difference between the two is obviously £2,800, and the causes of this difference can be depicted diagramatically, as in Figure 13.8.

In addition to establishing the size and cause of production cost variances, management would also want to know why the actual profit differs from the budgeted profit. Obviously the cost variances you have just calculated would account for some of the difference, but not for all of it. The rest of any difference will be accounted for by a **sales variance.** As with the cost variances, there are two possible reasons why a sales margin variance might have arisen. These are shown diagrammatically in Figure 13.9.

We will return to the Standard Ltd example that you considered in relation to cost variance analysis and update Table 13.3, the revised version being detailed in Table 13.5. This will produce a revised standard cost card as shown in Figure 13.10. Again by using preprogrammed software, comparing appropriate actual into standard details, 'analysis by course' variances may be obtained.

Table 13.5 Annual budget and actuals for month 1, expanded to include sales

Detail	Annual budget	Actual for month 1
Production	100,000 units	8,000 units
Direct materials	100,000 kg costing £100,000	9,000 kg costing £8,100
Direct labour	25,000 hours costing £150,000	1,800 hours costing £13,600
Variable production overheads	£100,000	£9,600
Fixed production overheads	£75,000	£6,500
Sales	100,000 units @ £6	8,000 units @ £7

Reconciling actual budgeted profits

Taking Standard Ltd as an example again, and including all variances calculated, an operating statement may be obtained (Figure 13.11).

This details all the relevant information which managers need to stay in control.

Cost element	Detail	Cost per unit
Direct materials	1kg @ £1 per kg	£1.00
Direct labour	15 min. @ £6 per hour	1.50
Production overheads		
Variable	15 min. @ £4 per hour	1.00
Fixed	15 min. (@ £3 per hour	0.75
Total cost per unit		4.25
Standard profit margin		1.75
Standard selling cost per unit		6.00

Figure 13.10 Standard Ltd: updated cost card for 1 unit

Detail	Favourable variances £	Adverse variances £	£
Budgeted profit for 8,333 units			14,583
Profit variances			
Sales volume		583	
Sales price	8,000		
Direct material price	900		
Direct material usage		1,000	
Direct labour rate		1,800	
Direct labour efficiency	1,200		
Production overheads			
Fixed expenditure		250	
Fixed volume		250	
Variable expenditure		2,400	
Variable efficiency	800		
	10,900	6,283	4,617
Actual profit for 8,000 units			19,200

Figure 13.11 Standard Ltd: operating statement for month

The statement in Figure 13.10 shows that the original budgeted sales of 8,383 units would have produced a standard profit of £1.75 each, i.e. £14,583. Because of the events that subsequently transpired, the 8,000 units actually sold produced a profit of £19,200. The variances obviously account for the difference.

Interdependence of variances

While always wishing to be able to reconcile budgeted and actual profits, management **will also want** to know why the individual variances arose. Often, there will be interrelated reasons for the causes.

For example, the £900 favourable variance is, of course, welcome. This may be the result of unexpected bulk purchase discounts. On the other hand, it may represent the purchase – at a lower price – of lower quality material. The use of such material has **resulted in** an adverse material usage variance of £1,000, wiping out the gains.

Again, the direct labour efficiency variance of £1,200 favourable is welcome, and perhaps the staff have been working very hard and conscientiously. On the other hand, perhaps they responded to a bonus or incentive system and the £1,800 adverse rate variance shows that, this time, the policy did not pay off.

An advantage of standard costing is that it can help to pinpoint areas of efficiency and effectiveness, as indeed can all budgetary control systems. Of course, however, to measure efficiency and effectiveness we first need to understand what such terms mean.

Efficiency, effectiveness and economy

It is common to hear many managers talk about the need for the three Es. However, it is often the case that the terms are used within a group without a good understanding of what is captured within the term. As mentioned earlier in the book, the term 'three Es' stands for efficiency, effectiveness and economy and is usually used as a measure of value for money.

Efficiency is about how well we do what we do – how we set about achieving our targets, whereas effectiveness is about the degree to which we hit our targets. As ever, the realities of life demand that all should be achieved within an acceptable financial expenditure and thus the economy is added. Of course, an appropriate balance needs to be struck, which may vary from organization to organization and from management team to management team. An example of the three Es is given in the box.

The three Es – an illustration

Take a student grant administration department of a local authority. Assume that last year it was limited to a total resource allocation of £100,000 and used the resources to process 5,000 applications. This year it anticipates that its resources will rise by 10%, but that applications will also increase by 20% to 6,000. The management team is concerned about the criteria that might be set in judging the department's performance.

Well might the team be concerned. Along the spectrum of balance, those judging could adopt a number of positions. In terms of effectiveness the department could be judged very favourably if all 6,000 applications were processed and without mistakes. Of course, there would be criticism if the resources consumed in so doing were in excess of £110,000. On the other hand, if the money were all spent but only 5,000 or even 4,000 applications processed, there would be harsh judgement. The judgement criteria would be based on: the best output for a given level of cost, or the least cost for a given level of output.

Each management team and those judging should agree the criteria in advance and, of course, agree acceptable quality standards.

In finding an appropriate blend, attention must be given to so many other factors. In the box above, all 6,000 applications may be dealt with, but if a hidden cost occurs in, say, telephone and postal charges for correcting mistakes, the original favourable judgement will be invalidated whatever any **performance indicators** might show.

Performance indicators
Before any attempt can be made at blending the three Es, the priorities of senior management would need to be established and account taken preferably of the intrinsic needs of the staff.

Whatever the outcome of the blend process, it is common to express the three Es by way of performance indicators. You may wish to look at Appendix A for performance indicators relating to British Airways.

Summary

In this chapter you have looked in some detail at the nature, purpose and operation of a budgetary system. In particular you have examined how a budget is prepared, developed and implemented and then how it may be managed once operations are under way.

You have also looked at how the idea of budgeted costs may be developed into fixed and flexible budgeting and thereafter into a full standard costing system. Both approaches, of course, then demand appropriate variance analysis and investigation.

The chapter concluded with a consideration of simple performance indicators as a supplement to the more normal financial figures included in a budgetary system.

By now you should:

- understand the nature and purpose of a budget
- be able to construct and manage a budget
- understand the nature and utility of standard costs
- be able to produce and interpret simple measures of efficiency and effectiveness.

Self-assessment question

SAQ 13.1

Think about your own organization or one you are familiar with. How familiar are you with the procedures by which the budget is prepared? If you are not, find out exactly how things are done. It could be helpful to draw up a chart to show the different stages which are gone through and what the relationships are between these stages. You might then wish to take your analysis a little further. What do you consider are the good and the bad features of your organization's procedures?

Further reading

Drury, C., 1992. *Management and Cost Accounting*, Van Nostrand Reinhold (International)

14 Using information to measure financial performance

Introduction

In the previous chapter you considered and examined how budgets may be used as information tools for managers. In this chapter the focus is more on information which is of use to external parties, such as shareholders, current and prospective, and loan providers; indeed anyone with a legitimate interest in the organization's affairs. You will consider why and how such information may be extracted from profit statements and balance sheets.

By the end of this chapter you will:

- understand how to make more sense of corporate financial statements
- be able to identify, calculate and interpret key measures of how well the flow of finance has been managed
- be able to identify, calculate and interpret key measures in response to the interests of shareholders, loan providers and other interested external parties.

The figures and details contained within a set of financial statements provide enough information for interested parties to gain a deeper insight into the affairs of an organization when certain ratios are calculated. The ratios calculated usually require comparison with other ratios. For example, it would prove beneficial for internal comparison purposes for the ratios relating to this year to be compared with the same ratios relating to previous years. For external comparison purposes the ratios for one organization could be compared with those of other similar concerns. Both sets of ratios will be of interest to internal and external parties.

In competitive markets particularly, it is desirable to find some way of comparing one company's performance with that of another – especially one operating in the same field. If you wished to compare the size and worth of a company with its previous position or with that of another company, you might use the total assets or the net assets from the balance sheet. However, this would be a misleading measure if, say, a heavy engineering company were being compared to a financial institution. The latter could be a very substantial concern, but this would not be reflected by counting how many machines it owned. So, other measures (e.g. turnover, staff employed) should be used as well to obtain a broader picture.

If more complicated comparisons (e.g. profitability, liquidity) are to be made, straightforward comparison of single figures is totally inadequate. For example, a very large company may have a bad year and make only £50,000 profit. This may be the same profit as a small company employing just a few people. It would clearly be misleading to suggest that they are similarly probable.

It is for this reason that figures for profit and assets are best examined in the form of ratios. Ratios are the primary means of analysing accounts for both 'internal' and 'external' purposes – they are useful tools both for management and as a guide to investors, creditors, etc. They provide a means of interpreting and comparing financial results, as well as of establishing performance objectives or yardsticks.

Analysing ratio analysis

From your considerations so far, you are aware of the limitations of published financial reporting statements. Such reports are aimed at presenting a true and fair view to interested parties, but what the true and fair view is of one party will not necessarily be that of others.

The reports will have been influenced by the application of a mix of:

- account and financial reporting standards
- traditional concepts and conventions
- methods of valuation
- legislation
- personal judgements
- facts – the events that have taken place and their impact.

Unfortunately, no prescription for a standard mix exists, and therein lies the problem. The particular mix applied by one specific management team will display the acknowledged implicit limitations of accounting information. Where management teams have changed over a period of time – if you stop and think about this you might agree that they obviously do so to a greater or lesser degree – the particular mix applied by any one management team will serve to make internal comparisons more difficult. Equally, external comparisons will be distorted by the mix strategy – even when informal and subconsciously arrived at – applied by the management teams of other organizations.

The collection and application of a series of ratios on a systematic basis will enhance the understanding of interested parties. This is particularly so in gaining a perspective on results and recognizing the impact of different operational areas of the organization upon those results. Whether comparisons are internally or externally oriented, the aggregate figures detailed in financial statements will be of differing orders of magnitude. Ratio analysis is one widely used technique which overcomes such problems and aids the interpretation and comparison of financial reports.

The interested parties

Those who are interested in wanting to establish and evaluate the performance of organizations may be divided into two main groups: **management** and **investors**. These two groups can, in turn be subdivided, as shown in Figure 14.1.

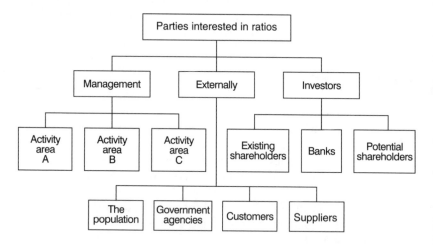

Figure 14.1 Parties interested in ratios

The role of the financial analysts is interesting in that busy investors, existing and potential, will look to them for advice. Internally, management attention will be very much focused on two particular aspects:

- profitability as a measure of operating performance
- liquidity and solvency as a measure of financial condition.

Of course, given management's obligatory concern with the *efficiency of financial performance* and the *ability of the organization to survive,* it is natural that they should apply ratio analysis techniques in the areas of operating performance and financial condition.

Externally, existing/potential investors and financial analysts will expect management to be concerned with these aspects anyway. This is because they see part of management's role as being to facilitate efficiency and survival, thus ensuring that two of the major objectives of investors are met. These two major objectives of investors are:

- at least the maintenance of but hopefully an increase in the value of investment
- the achievements of an appropriate and/or expected level of income from the investment.

Just as management's objectives are interrelated and interdependent, so are the objectives of investors. Indeed, it is true to say that management and investors are essentially concerned with the same objectives but from different perspectives.

Management and operating performance

Management's initial concern will be with the ability to generate profit. As such, ratios measuring the degree of financial efficiency will focus on the relationships between profit and assets employed, and profit and sales.

Perhaps the most important measure of operating performance is the return on capital employed (ROCE), also termed the primary ratio. In practice, there are a number of ways of expressing this ratio but perhaps the most commonly applied is:

$$\text{Return on capital employed (ROCE)} = \frac{\text{Net profit before interest}}{\text{Total capital employed}}$$

This ratio relates profit to all the capital sums invested in the organization, such capital sums comprising both owner's equities (i.e. capital and reserves) and long-term liability loans (i.e. creditors due after 1 year).

The investment-return process

A detailed description of what is meant by *capital employed* is important in that it has implications for what is meant by *return*. Referring to the information in the balance sheet of Public Plc (Figure 14.2) shows that capital sums have been obtained from two distinct sources.

If you were an investor of capital sums in Public Plc – either a shareholder or bank loan provider – you would, quite reasonably, expect to receive a reward for providing the company with the funds that management invests in various assets. If you had provided bank loans, you would expect to receive an appropriate amount of interest as a reward. If you were a shareholder, and although as an ordinary shareholder you would not be guaranteed a dividend, nevertheless you would usually expect to receive a dividend amount of some description. This is particularly the case in times of prosperity. In addition you would, short or long term, be looking for capital appreciation in the value of your shares.

	Last year			This year
	£	£	£	£
Fixed assets				
Land and buildings		750		900
Plant and machinery		750		800
Fixtures and fittings		100		200
		1,600		1,900
Current assets				
Stocks	500		600	
Debtors	450		600	
Cash	350		400	
	1,300		1,600	
Creditors (falling due in less than 1 year)				
Trade creditors	430		500	
	430		500	
Net current assets		870		1,100
Total assets		2,470		3,000
Less creditors falling due in more than 1 year				
Net assets representing		770		1,000
investment of				
		1,700		2,000
Capital and reserves				
Issued ordinary				
share capital (per value per	800		830	
share £0.50)				
Reserves	900		1,170	
Shareholders' funds/net		1,700		2,000
worth		1,700		2,000

Figure 14.2 Public Plc: abbreviated balance sheet at 31 December (£000)

The ROCE ratio attempts to measure the overall return generated by day-to-day activities and thus available to pay for exceptional times, to pay for tax, to reward investors and to reinvest profits in the organization. The challenge is, however, measuring that return.

Whatever the return is that we are attempting to measure, we do know that in Public Plc it is a direct result of part of the flow of finance process you met in Part I of this book (see Figure 1.3). If we use the net profit figure as our return in the role calculation, the reward to one class of capital provider – the loan interest – will have been taken into consideration. No account will have been taken, however, of the other reward item – dividends to shareholders. Given that ROCE is an attempt to measure a return which is a direct result of the process of the investment of funds from two distinct sources, it is appropriate either to include both rewards in profit/reward determination or to exclude them both. This is depicted in Figure 14.3, which reproduces the flow of finance you met in Part I. As you can see, the terms ROCE, ATO (asset turnover) and ROS (return on sales) have now been added. It is these which are to be determined to measure the overall performance of the management team, starting with ROCE.

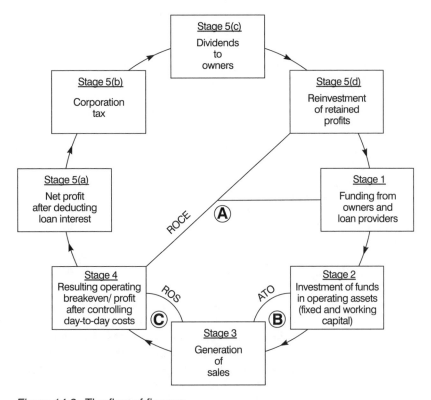

Figure 14.3 The flow of finance

Probability and capital: the circular flow

Referring back to Part I, you will see that the flow of finance requires a set of management decisions to ensure that the most appropriate return on capital employed is obtained.

The ROCE ratio expresses the relationship between the operating profit – the return – and the capital employed. In other words, Section A of the flow shown in Figure 14.3 . The rest of the flow – Sections B and C – may be analysed by the calculation of two further ratios. These further ratios are often termed **secondary ratios,** looked at next.

ROCE- a practical illustration

Return to the balance sheet in Figure 14.2 and, taking account of the profit statements below, follow through the determination of ROCE as shown below the profit statements.

Profit statement for Public Plc – year ended 31 December (£'000s)

	Last year £		This year £	
Sales turnover		3 ,800		5,000
Cost of sales		2,300		3,260
Gross profit		1,500		1,740
Less				
Distribution expenses	100		105	
Administration expenses	500	600	505	610
Operating profit		900		1,140
Loan interest		90		110
Net profit before tax		810		1,020
Tax		400		500
Profit after tax		410		520
Dividends		200		250
Transfer to retained earnings		210		270

This means that in Public plc the return in ROCE is not the net profit figure, but either a profit figure which has had both the loan interest and dividends deducted or one which has not deducted them at all. In reality there is no choice. Dividends cannot be included in the calculation of profit as they are an appropriation of profit and not an expense. Therefore, both rewards must be excluded. In Public plc this means that the debenture interest must be added back to the net profit figure and thus the *operating profit* rather than net profit is used. Where feasible it is normal practice to place the operating profit figure over the **average capital employed** for the year and thus using the figures for Public Plc for last year this latest calculation is:

$$\text{ROCE} = \frac{\text{Operating profit}}{\text{Average capital employed}}$$

$$= \frac{\text{£1,020 add back £110}}{\frac{1}{2}\,(2,470 + \text{£3,000})}$$

$$= \frac{\text{£1,130}}{\text{£2,735}} = 41.32\%$$

This averaging reflects more appropriately the spread of investment over a year, a spread which has led to the generation of
profits throughout the same 12-month period.

This ROCE figure is very important in that it measures the
earning power of the total long-term investment from all sources in
the organization. Management will be able to use this **primary**
ratio as the starting point in the calculation of a series of ratios
which will pinpoint efficiencies and inefficiencies within different
functional and operational areas. Remember that the resulting
ratio needs interpretation, an aspect visited shortly. For the time
being, we will not attempt to interpret our ratios.

The secondary ratios

Following on from the steps and flows depicted in Figure 14.3, it is
possible to focus in on two main areas which are particularly concerned with the level of organizational operating performances as
revealed by the ROCE ratio. These two areas are:

- managerial efficiency in the utilization of the assets in which the
  capital obtained from capital providers has been invested
- managerial performance in relation to profit levels once sales have
  been generated, related particularly to cost control.

The performance of each area is measured by the **asset turnover ratio**
or (asset utilization ratio as it is sometimes called) and the **return on
sales ratio.**

The asset utilization (AUR) ratio or asset turnover (ATO) ratio
This reflects the level of intensity with which assets are employed.
A low ratio will indicate to management that here is an area which
needs attention in order to improve performance. It provides information about Section B of Figure 14.3.

Using the figures in Figure 14.3, the ATO for this latest year will
be:

$$AUR/ATO = \frac{Sales}{Average\ operating\ assets}$$

$$= \frac{£5,000}{£2,735}$$

$$= 1.83 \text{ times (or 183\%)}$$

The £2,735 represents the average of the opening and closing asset involvements. The average is used for the same reasons as the average was used in the ROCE earlier.

The actual average operating assets figure used comprises:

Detail	Opening £	Closing £
Fixed assets	1,600	1,900
Net current assets/working capital	870	1,100
	2,470	3,000

Having indicated the relative efficiency of this area to management, a further asset analysis could be undertaken. For example, the overall asset utilization efficiency level will be the result of high or low levels of utilization of the fixed assets portion and the working capital portion. Such an analysis would, for this latest year, comprise:

$$\frac{\text{Sales}}{\text{Average fixed assets}} \qquad \frac{\text{Sales}}{\text{Average working capital}}$$

$$= \frac{\pounds5,000}{\pounds1,750} \qquad\qquad = \frac{\pounds5,000}{\pounds985}$$

$$= 2.86 \text{ times} \qquad\qquad = 5.08 \text{ times}$$

These can be subdivided further, as you will see when you consider the **pyramid of ratios** shortly.

Again, remember that at this stage you are not attempting to interpret the results. Apart from not having been shown how to interpret the results, you do not have enough information to do so anyway. For an internal assessment you would require the previous year's ratios. For an external assessment, ratios from other organizations or from a firm supplying industry overseas are required.

It is important to note here that experience has taught many management teams of the value of historical asset utilization ratio trends in predicting future profit plans. Of course, unless there are comparative figures it is difficult at this stage to interpret and assess the significance of this particular percentage.

As with the asset utilization ratio considered earlier, the return on sales ratio may also be subdivided and further aspects analysed. This is depicted in the forthcoming section on the pyramid of ratios.

> ### The return on sales (ROS) ratio
>
> This ratio seeks to assess the process of the generation of sales, which necessitates certain levels of expenditure. Both aspects are critical in the generation of profit and should be assessed. The ratio analyses Section C of Figure 14.3.
>
> Using the figures in the profit statement, the return on sales ratio for this latest year will be:
>
> $$\text{ROSR} = \frac{\text{Operating profit}}{\text{Sales}}$$
> $$= \frac{£1,130}{£5,000}$$
> $$= 22.6\%$$

The circular flow analysis in perspective

You perhaps will have noticed that we have not analysed one particular section of Figure 14.3. This is the section linking capital obtained and its investment in operating assets. There is no need to analyse this, as the answer will always be 100%. This has to be the case because the capital sums invested will always balance with the operating assets.

Another feature of the analysis you may have noted is that as the primary ratio can be subdivided into the two secondary ratios, so the two secondary ratios should together equal the primary ratio. Let us take the results of our primary and secondary ratios:

$$\text{AUR } \frac{£5,000}{£2,735} = \text{ROSR } \frac{£1,130}{£5,000}$$

In mathematical terms, the sales figures of £5,000 on each cancel each other out, leaving:

$$\frac{£1,130}{£2,735}$$

Which, of course, equals the primary ratio. Thus:

$$\frac{\text{Sales}}{\text{Operating assets}} \times \frac{\text{Operating profit}}{\text{Sales}} = \frac{\text{Operating profit}}{\text{Capital employed}}$$

The pyramid of ratios

In analysing business performance, management subdivides ratios further. This will facilitate an evaluation of each area of the business and its degree of contribution towards the organization's overall financial results.

There is much to be said for all managers having a good 'feel' for all aspects of the business in order to enhance their contribution to the business as a whole, foster cooperation with the other middle managers, and prepare themselves for possible future promotion.

The biggest single failing which is often met at middle management level is the attitude that 'It's *somebody else's concern*, not *mine'*. To try to prevent insularity and the possibility of managers budgeting and working towards incompatible or conflicting goals, many businesses now adopt integrated schemes of ratios, commonly referred to as **pyramids of ratios.**

There are four main advantages of businesses adopting integrated schemes of ratios:

- to ensure that different managers are not working towards incompatible or conflicting goals
- to focus the attention of all managers upon the business as a whole and to ensure that they see their contributions in that context and in relation to those of their colleagues
- to provide a means whereby unsatisfactory budgeted (or actual) performance can be investigated systematically
- to make direct comparisons with similar businesses, if standardized definitions of ratios are used.

Return to the idea that the principal ratio of business performance is ROCE – the primary ratio. This is, of course:

$$\frac{\text{Operating profit}}{\text{Capital employed}}$$

You will recall that this can be broken down into:

Return on sales $\times$ Asset turnover

in other words

$$\frac{\text{Operating profit}}{\text{Sales}} \times \frac{\text{Sales}}{\text{Operating assets}}$$

This shows that if ROCE is evaluated as being unsatisfactory, there are only two *overall* strategies possible in order to improve performance:

- improve return on sales, or
- improve turnover of capital via improved turnover of assets.

You then have the start of a pyramid scheme of related ratios as shown in Figure 14.4. These three ratios represent the top or apex of the pyramid. The full pyramid is shown in Figure 14.5. As you can see, each area is progressively broken down, analysing by cause why matters have gone well or not so well.

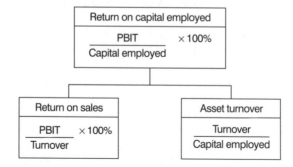

Figure 14.4 The apex of the pyramid of ratios

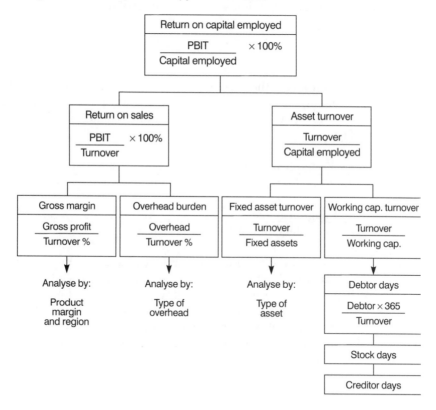

Figure 14.5 The full pyramid of ratios

An analysis of each of these areas will provide a measure of past managerial efficiency and, as such, may be used as a basis for forecasting future efficiency. This aspect is often overlooked by the uninformed manager. The tendency is to use ratio analysis to look backwards rather than forward.

Further ratios

The long-term solvency of an organization will be related to the ability to pay both current and long-term liabilities. The relevant ratios for assessment are directly related to the **capital gearing** structure of the organization you met when considering the financing decision in Part II of the book.

As you already know, capital sums may be obtained from more than one source. In Public plc in Figure 14.2 they have been obtained from shareholders and a bank. In addition to the gearing ratio, shareholders in particular will be interested in the **interest coverage ratio.** The short-term implications of the resulting profile of the origin of capital has already been seen in the form of the interest coverage ratio. Another relevant ratio, but more concerned with the long term, is the **shareholders' equity ratio.** This in itself is a variation of the measurement of gearing.

Gearing

As you know, there are two common ways of measuring the gearing structure and thus expressing the relationship between the groups of capital providers. These are, using the balance sheet for Last year in Figure 14.2:

$$\frac{\text{Long-term loans}}{\text{Total capital employed}} \times = \frac{£1,000}{£3,000} \times 100 = 33.3\%$$

$$\frac{\text{Long-term loans}}{\text{Shareholders' interest}} \times 100 = \frac{£1,000}{£2,000} \times 100 = 50\%$$

High capital gearing may have the disadvantage of leading to dangerously high interest payments. However, this need not be a problem if profits are secure or expanding. On the other hand, there is a substantial advantage to be gained by the shareholders in a highly geared company. That is, as profits rise, the lenders continue to receive the same interest payments. This leaves more profits, and an *increased proportion* of profits, for the shareholders; the 'earnings' are *geared-up*, compared to the net profit before interest and tax.

As ever, for comparisons over time or with organizations, consistency in the destination of the ratio is more important than the exact ratio selected.

Interest coverage ratio

Moving away from working capital, there is another aspect which should be considered. This is the extent to which an organization's profit (usually before interest and tax) is pre-empted by the need to pay interest on long-term loans. This is important because if the organization is legally obliged to pay interest, certain profit levels must be earned. If profit levels are low, management will feel continually pressurized. In addition, low profit levels mean that little is left for shareholders after deduction of the interest. This aspect may be measured via the **interest coverage ratio.**

Shareholders' equity ratio

This ratio is considered to be very important by financial analysts. The figures for Public Plc for 19x4 show:

$$\frac{\text{Shareholders' equity}}{\text{Total assets (fixed assets + current assets)}} \times 100 =$$

$$\frac{£2,000}{£1,900 + £1,600} \times 100 = \times 100 = 57.\,1$$

It is usually acknowledged that the higher the proportion, the stronger the financial position of the organization. The lower the proportion, the more possibility of the organization becoming over-dependent on outside providers of capital sums.

Price/earnings ratio

This shows roughly how long it would take to recover the share price out of the earnings, at current levels, of the company. If we assume that the market price on the last day of this year was £2.01 per share and EPS 31.3 pence, it is determined thus:

$$\frac{\text{Market price per ordinary share}}{\text{Earnings per share}} = \frac{£2.01}{31.3 \text{ pence}} = 6.42 \text{ times}$$

This means that if £2.01 is paid for a share, then 6.42 years of current levels of earnings are effectively being purchased. The theory here is that investors are concerned about future levels of returns and the market price reflects the market's anticipation and estimation of those future returns.

Dividend yield

This ratio targets on the return in hard cash to the investor upon the investment in shares. It is determined thus:

$$\frac{\text{Dividend per ordinary share}}{\text{Market price per ordinary share}} = \frac{15 \text{ p}^*}{£2.01} = 7.5\%$$

*(£250,000 divided by 1,660,000 shares).

This, of course, will be affected in the future by changes in both the rate of dividend and the market price per share.

Dividend cover

This is also known as the **payout ratio.** It provides a guideline to the company's ability to maintain the dividend payment. It also measures the proportion of earnings retained by the company and the probability of the company being able to maintain current levels of dividend payments should earnings decline in future years. It is determined thus:

$$\frac{\text{EATOS}}{\text{Ordinary dividends}} = \frac{£520}{£250} = 2.08 \text{ times}$$

Making comparisons

You will have gathered by now that ratios can be particularly useful as indicators of company performance in relation to:

- the organization's own past performance
- the recent performances of other similar concerns
- the aspirations of investors.

For the purposes of evaluating performance, the use of a ratio in absolute terms is extremely limited. There are cases where an established and agreed norm exists, thus providing a useful yardstick or objective. However, this tends to apply only in the case of major ratios of profitability and capital structure and use. More detailed ratios, such as those contained towards the base of the ratio pyramid, require more specific comparisons to be of any real use.

Although there are considerable advantages to be gained from internal comparisons, there are also disadvantages that must be warned against. For example, when carrying out internal comparison, there is no need to stick rigidly to an externally determined set of ratios – you can design your own to fit your needs. In addition, if developed at all levels of management, the whole management team can be involved and motivated in a cohesive way.

On the other hand, there are certain significant disadvantages of internal comparisons. For example, they can lead to insular and narrow-minded thinking. Take the example of an organization where the ratios show clear, even considerable improvement in performance.

How does management know whether the improvement is sufficient and/or fast enough? Managers can also be presented with ratio data and be unable to interpret adequately and/or correctly, leading to false conclusions being drawn. Of course, most organizations will want to know how their performance measures up against that of competitors.

There are several advantages to be gained from making external comparisons:

- they guard against complacency as far as performance is concerned
- they can help to motivate performance
- they provide a foundation for the development of yardsticks
- they are a reminder that the organization does not exist in isolation.

Using inter-firm comparison is not without its problems, however. Unless the data is standardized in both the terminology and ratios used, comparisons can be meaningless or even dangerously misleading. Some of the difficulties of ensuring that like is concerned with like arise because different organizations adopt different accounting policies – for depreciation or for stock valuation, for example – and this affects the reported profit figures.

Another difficulty in making comparisons arises where organizations report in consolidated accounting report format. This problem will only be accentuated if the group is active in many fields.

In addition to these disadvantages there is another of major proportions in that, without care, it is very easy to lose absolute objectivity about your own organization's performance and to adopt a totally relative view. It is important to decide what is your overriding objective – to generate satisfactory returns for your business or to be equal to or better than your competitors. If, for example, all your competitors are going to the wall, is it any real comfort to know that, although you are also going to the wall, you will be the last one there?

Many organizations subscribe to organizations such as the Centre for Inter-Firm Comparison (CIFC), investment houses and trade associations, where ratios are calculated for particular groupings of organizations. By taking part in such inter-firm comparisons, most organizations find out about those areas where they can improve and, no less important, areas where they have strengths which must be maintained. You have an opportunity to revisit Public Plc in the self-assessment questions below and to calculate the relevant ratios for last year and compare them with this year.

Ratios and predicting failure

We have stressed that although ratios look backwards, in that they analyse historical figures, they are usually employed as **predictors.** This is particularly the case as far as financial analysts are concerned regarding survival – or should we say *failure.*

Over the years a number of research studies have indicated that ratios may indeed highlight those organizations which are prime candidates as far as failure is concerned. In the 1960s, a pioneer in this field was W. Beaver who suggested that an appropriate mix of ratios could be used to predict failure anything up to five years in advance. Others followed Beaver's example. The results of empirical studies by people such as Altman, Tafler and Tisshaw, and Dev, confirmed the view that the weakness of a series of certain ratios would often pre-empt collapse. Of course, the ratios themselves have inherent limitations as we saw earlier. As such, they should never be considered in isolation. You should always remember this as you consider the value and importance of ratios to you as a manager.

Summary

In this chapter you have considered the role of ratios in understanding financial statements and their determination.

By now you should be able to:

- understand how to make more sense of corporate financial statements, calculate and interpret key measures of how well the flow of finance has been managed by a management team
- identify, calculate and interpret key measures in response to the interests of shareholders, loan providers and other interested external parties.

Self-assessment questions

SAQ 14.1

At this stage, return to the Public Plc details in Figure 14.2 and the profit statement in the box below that figure and calculate the ratios indicated below for last year, and offer your interpretation of the results in comparison to the ratios for this latest year. The ratios to be calculated are:

(i) ROCE
(ii) asset turnover
(iii) return on sales
(iv) capital gearing
(v) shareholders' equity
(vi) EPS
(vii) price/earnings (assume 3 1/12/x3 market price of £1.75 per share)
(viii) dividend yield
(ix) dividend cover.

SAQ 14.2

Below are the financial statements relating to the latest financial years
of Dreamboat Limited and Nightmare Ltd.

Profit statement for the year	Dreamboat £000s	Nightmare £000s
Sales	800	800
Operating expenses	−600	−600
Loan interest	−25	−40
Net reported profit	175	160
Taxation	−70	−64
Dividends	−35	−26
Balance of retained profits	70	70

Summaried balance sheets at end of year		
Fixed assets	500	750
Net current assets	500	250
	1,000	1,000
Share capital	500	500
Retained profits	250	100
10% Bank loan (long-term)	250	400
	1,000	1,000

Using the statements calculate and, as far as is able, comment compar-
itively upon three for both companies:

   (i) ROCE
   (ii) asset turnover
   (iii) return on sales
   (iv) capital gearing
   (v) return on shareholders' equity
   (vi) EPS (assuming that both companies have 500,000 shares each)
   (vii) PE ratio (assuming Dreamboat's shares have a market value of
      £1.40 each and Nightmare's of £0.70 each)
   (viii) dividend yield
   (ix) dividend cover.

Further reading

Jarvis, R., Kitching, J. Curran, J. and Lightfoot, G., 1966. Performance measures and
   small firms, *Certified Accountant* (November)

Taffler, R.J., 1982. Forecasting company failure in the UK using discriminant analysis and
   financial ratio data, *Journal of the Royal Statistical Society*.

Taffler, R.J., 1991. Z-scores: an approach to the recession, *Accountancy* (July)

Appendix Glossary of accounting terms

This glossary brings together some of the more important and relevant technical accounting and financial terms included in the text. Terms picked out in bold within definitions are themselves defined elsewhere in the glossary.

The scope of this Glossary extends beyond inclusion of terms in the text to include other terms you may come across in your dealings with matters financial.

Acknowledgements

The author is indebted to the Chartered Institute of Management Accountants (CIMA) and the International Stock Exchange of the United Kingdom and the Republic of Ireland Limited for permission to reproduce definitions from their official terminology.

Absorption costing – The procedure that charges fixed as well as variable overheads to cost units (CIMA definition). The term may be applied where production costs only, or all functions, are so allotted. *See also* **overheads, fixed costs** and **variable costs**.

Account – A structured record of monetary transactions, kept as part of an accounting system. This may be kept in a ledger or on a computer file, relating **assets**, **liabilities**, **revenues** and/or **expenses**.

Accounting rate of return – Ratio sometimes used in **investment appraisal**, based on **profits** as opposed to **cash flows**. Not a recommended measure (*based on CIMA definition*).

Accruals concept/convention – The concept that **revenues** and costs are matched one with the other and dealt with in the **profit and loss account** of the period to which they relate, irrespective of the period of receipt or payment (*CIMA definition*). To accrue an amount is to enter it in the accounts in accordance with the accruals concept. Also known as the **matching concept/convention**.

Accrued expenses – Costs relating to a period which have not yet been taken into account because they have not yet been invoiced by the supplier or paid. These will include such items as electricity and telephone calls, which are generally invoiced in arrears.

Acid test – *See quick ratio* and *liquidity ratio*.

Activity-based costing – **Cost attribution** to **cost units** on the basis of benefit received from indirect activities (*CIMA definition*).

Added value – The increase in realizable value resulting from an alteration in form, location or availability of a product or service, excluding the cost of purchased materials and services. *Note:* Unlike **conversion cost**, added value includes profit. Also known as **value added**.

Apportioning – The dividing up of overhead costs.

Apportionment – *See* **apportioning**.

Assets – Resources of value owned by entity. *See also* **fixed assets** and **current assets**.

Avoidable costs – The specific costs of an activity or sector of an organization which would be avoided if that activity or sector did not exist. *See also* **relevant costs**.

Bad debt – A debt that is known, assumed or expected not to be settled. This is normally written off as a charge to the **profit and loss account**.

Balance sheet – A statement of the financial position of an entity at a given date, disclosing the value of the assets, liabilities and accumulated funds such as shareholders' contributions and **reserves**, which is prepared to give a true and fair view of the state of the entity at that date (*based on CIMA definition*).

Break even – The level of activity (e.g. level of sales in a period) at which the organization makes neither a profit nor a loss, as its total costs exactly equal its total income. This is often referred to as **break-even point**.

Break-even analysis – The analysis of points at which sales equal total cost for various levels of output, prices, etc.

Break-even chart – A chart that indicates **profit** or loss arising at different levels of sales volumes within a limited range.

Break-even point – *See* **break even**.

Budgeting – The preparation of financial plans, based upon the organization's objectives, for a future period (usually a year). The constituent budgets may relate to costs, **revenues**, **working capital** movements, **capital expenditure** and **cash flow(s)**.

Capital allowances – Deductions from **profit** allowed by the Inland Revenue in respect of the cost of recent **capital expenditure** on **fixed assets**; these replace an organization's **depreciation** charge in the calculation of taxable profit.

Capital and reserves – As a composite term, the investments made by shareholders comprising direct capital investment and retained profits, belonging to shareholders, not distributed but invested on their behalf by management.

Capital employed – The funds used by an entity for its operations (*CIMA definition*). **Net capital employed** is often used to describe the long-term and semi-permanent funds in the organization (i.e. **issued share capital**, **reserves** and long-term **loans**, but excluding **current liabilities**).

Capital expenditure – Expenditure on **fixed assets** (in contrast to **revenue** expenditure) intended to benefit future accounting periods or expenditure that increases the capacity, efficiency, lifespan or economy of an existing fixed asset (*based on CIMA definition*).

Cash budget – A budget showing the pattern, from period to period, of: **cash flow** into the organization (receipts); **cash flow** out from the organization (payments); the resultant effect upon bank balances or **overdrafts**.

Cash flow – The difference between cash generated and cash spent in a period. Cash flows differ from **profit** flows not least because of the application of the **accruals** or **matching concept/convention**.

Cash flow statement – A statement listing the inflows and outflows of cash. It normally details such flows in relation to day-to-day items and capital items. It may be a projection (cash flow forecast) or historical.

Committed costs – Those fixed costs, planned on a relatively long time-span, that cannot be eliminated or even cut back without having a major effect on **profits** or the organization's objectives.

Common fixed costs – Those **fixed costs** that are related to all or several of the organization's segments (products, product groups, markets, services, etc). and cannot therefore be identified uniquely with any particular segment.

Conservatism concept/convention – *See* **prudence concept/convention**.

Consistency concept/convention – The principle that there is a consistency of treatment of like items (e.g. accounting bases and policies) within each accounting period and from one period to the next (*based on CIMA definition*).

Consolidation – The aggregation of the constituent financial statements of group companies as if they were the accounts of a single organization.

Continuous budget – *See* **rolling budget**.

Contribution – The difference between sales value and the **variable cost** of those sales, expressed either in absolute terms or as a contribution per unit or a percentage of sales (*based on CIMA definition*).

Contribution ratio – *See* **contribution to sales ratio**.

Contribution to sales ratio – The relationship between **revenue** and the **contribution** that it generates. For example, if a product sells for £10 and generates £3 contribution, its contribution to sales ratio is 30 per cent. Also known as the **contribution ratio** and the **profit/volume ratio**.

Controllable costs – A cost, chargeable to a budget or **cost centre**, that can be influenced by the actions of the person in whom control of the centre is vested (*based on CIMA definition*). Also known as **managed costs**.

Control period – A period (commonly four weeks or one month) during which actual performance is compared against budget for control purposes.

Conversion cost – Cost of converting material into finished products, i.e. **direct labour** costs, direct material costs and **production overhead costs** (*CIMA definition*).

Cost allocation – That part of **cost attribution** that charges a specific cost to a **cost centre** or **cost unit** (*CIMA definition*).

Cost apportionment – That part of **cost attribution** that shares costs among two or more **cost centres** or **cost units** in proportion to the estimated benefit received, using a proxy such as square metres (*CIMA definition*).

Cost attribution – The process of relating costs to **cost centres** or **cost units** using cost allocation or **cost apportionment**.

Cost centre – A location, function or items of equipment in respect of which costs may be ascertained and related to **cost units** for control purposes.

Cost driver – An activity that generates cost. Particularly related to **activity-based costing**.

Cost of goods sold (COGS) – *See* **cost of sales**.

Cost of sales (COS) – The sum of **direct costs** or **variable costs** of sales plus factory **overheads** attributable to the **turnover**. In management accounts this may be referred to as production cost of sales or **cost of goods sold** (*based on CIMA definition*).

Cost-plus pricing – A method of pricing in which the cost of one unit is computed (using **absorption costing** or **marginal costing**) and then a percentage mark-up is added.

Cost unit – A unit of product or service in relation to which costs are ascertained (*CIMA definition*).

Cost-volume profit (CVP) analysis – Study of the relationship between **variable costs** per unit, **total fixed costs**, level of output, and price and mix of products sold, and the effect of changes in these upon **profit**.

Credit – An entry in the accounts of an organization. A decrease in the organization's assets or an increase in its **liabilities**.

Creditor – A person or an entity to whom money is owed (*CIMA definition*). Generally the term is applied to those whose invoices will be paid within a short period of time, such as suppliers (trade creditors). Those to whom longer-term debts (such as **long-term loans**) are owed are often described as *creditors – over one year*.

Creditors' turnover – A ratio that relates the total money owed to creditors (generally suppliers) at a particular date to the current rate of purchase of the goods and services supplied. This is normally expressed in calendar days, indicating the average time taken to pay for goods and services bought on **credit**.

Current assets – Cash or other **assets** (e.g. **stocks**, **debtors**, short-term investments) that are likely to be converted into cash in the normal course of trading (*based on CIMA definition*).

Current cost accounting (CCA) – A system of accounting based upon a concept of capital represented by the net operating assets of an organization. These net operating assets (**fixed assets, stocks** and monetary **working capital**) are the same as those included under **historic cost accounting,** but in the current cost accounts the fixed assets and stocks are normally expressed at current price levels. The objective of current cost accounts is to provide guidance for management, shareholders and others on such matters as the financial viability of the organization and distribution decisions.

Current liabilities – **Liabilities** that all organizations would normally expect to settle within a relatively short period (normally one year), e.g. **creditors, dividends** and tax due for payment; also that part of a **long-term loan** due for repayment within one year.

Current ratio – One of two common working capital solvency ratios (the other being the **quick ratio** or **acid test** or **liquidity ratio**). This one is an overall test of **liquidity**, measuring whether or not current assets will remain after **current liabilities** have been paid off.

Debenture – A particular form of **long-term loan**.

Debit – An entry in the accounts of an organization. An increase in the organization's **assets** or a decrease in its **liabilities**.

Debtor – A person or an entity who owes money to the organization. Primarily, customers who have yet to pay for goods or services provided.

Debtors' turnover – A ratio that relates the total money owed by **debtors** (generally customers) at a particular date to the current rate of sale of the goods or services purchased. This is normally expressed in calendar days, indicating the average time taken to pay for goods and services bought on account.

Declining balance depreciation – A method of depreciation, applying a constant percentage (determined by management) to the period-end net book value of a fixed asset over its useful life. Also known as reducing balance.

Depreciable base – The cost of an asset less any anticipated resale or residual value. The resulting figure is then depreciated over the useful life of the asset.

Depreciation – The internal charge made by an organization against its **revenue**, to provide for the use and/or progressive deterioration/obsolescence of its **fixed assets** within operations. This is an example of the **matching concept/convention**.

Direct costs – Costs that can be traced directly to units of production (or other activity of the organization). Typically these may include materials used, production labour and certain production expenses.

Direct fixed costs – Those **fixed costs** that are uniquely incurred in respect of an identifiable segment (product, product group, service, market, etc). of the organization's activities.

Direct labour – That part of an organization's workforce directly concerned with the manufacture of goods or provision of services.

Direct labour cost percentage rate – A method of charging **overheads** to **cost centres**. Calculated by dividing the budgeted or estimated overhead costs attributable to a cost centre by the amount of **direct labour** cost expected to be incurred (or which would relate to working at normal capacity) and expressing the result as a percentage.

Direct labour hour rate – A method of charging **overheads** to **cost centres**. Calculated by dividing the budgeted or estimated overhead costs attributable to a cost centre by the number of **direct labour** hours expected to be worked (or which would relate to working at normal capacity).

Direct material price variance – The difference between the standard direct material cost of the actual production volume and the actual cost of direct material.

Direct material usage variance – The difference between the standard quantity specified for the actual production and the actual quantity used, at standard purchase price. Also known as the **direct material quantity variance**.

Discounted cash flow (DCF) – An evaluation of the future **net cash flows** generated by a capital investment project, by discounting them to their present-day value (*based on CIMA definition*).

Dividend – A distribution made to shareholders in proportion to the number of shares that they hold, generally from post-tax profits. An 'interim' dividend is paid half yearly, the 'final' dividend at the year end.

Double entry accounting – The principle of ensuring that the monetary value of any transaction is recorded in such a way as to ensure that the balance sheet remains in balance.

Double entry bookkeeping – The recording of the monetary value of transactions and their impact within the accounting records of an organization. The recording system reflects the need for at least two entries for the balance sheet to remain in balance.

Earnings – Generally the post-tax profits of an entity which, in effect, belong to the shareholders either to take out (**dividends**) or to leave in (**reserves**).

Earnings per share (EPS) – An investors' ratio calculated as:

$$\frac{\text{Earnings for the year}}{\text{Number of shares in issue}}$$

Expenses – Any expenditure that is chargeable to the trading activities of an accounting period.

Financial accounting – Reporting how the organization has performed in the recent past, principally for the benefit of 'outsiders' through the organization's financial statements. The work of financial accountants.

Fixed assets – Those assets that would normally remain in the organization to enable it to carry on its business (e.g. plant and machinery, vehicles, property).

Fixed budget – A budget that is designed to remain unchanged irrespective of the level of output or **turnover** attained.

Fixed costs – Costs that do not vary as the level of activity varies (e.g. if sales doubled many administrative costs would be unaffected and thus would be regarded as fixed).

Flexible budget – A budget that, by recognizing the differences in behaviour between **fixed costs** and **variable costs** in relation to fluctuations in output, **turnover** or other variable factors such as number of employees, is designed to change appropriately with such fluctuations (*based on CIMA definition*). Also known as the **variable budget**.

Funds flow statement – One of an organization's financial statements which shows the way in which funds have been generated and used by the organization and how any resulting surplus of **liquid assets** has been applied or any deficiency financed. It provides a link between the **balance sheet** at the beginning of the period, the **profit and loss account** for the period, and the balance sheet at the end of the period, and forms part of the audited accounts of the company. Also known as the **source and application of funds statement**.

Gearing – The relationship between the different sources of capital (in monetary terms) comprising the total **capital employed** of an organization. Also known as **leverage**.

Goal congruence – The situation in which each individual, in attempting to satisfy his or her own interests, is also making the greatest contribution to the objectives of the enterprise.

Going concern concept/convention – The assumption, in producing the financial statements, that the organization will continue for the foreseeable future.

Goodwill – An **intangible asset** that appears on some **balance sheets** under **fixed assets**. Generally the difference between the price paid for the purchase of a subsidiary company and the book value of the subsidiary. May be expressed (*CIMA definition*) as the difference between the value of an organization as a whole and the aggregate of the fair value of its separable identifiable **assets**.

Gross margin – *See* **gross profit margin**.

Gross profit – Sales **revenue** less **cost of sales**, but before deduction of **overheads** such as selling costs, administration costs and financial costs. Also known as the **gross margin**.

Gross profit margin – The difference between sales and the cost of goods or services sold. Also known as the **gross margin**.

Historic cost of accounting – A method of accounting that does not make allowance for the effects of inflation. A system of accounting in which all values (in **revenue** and capital accounts) are based on the costs actually incurred or as revalued from time to time.

Holding costs – The cost of holding **stocks**, which may include the costs of interest paid or lost, deterioration costs, pilferage costs, storage costs, insurance costs and obsolescence costs.

Indirect costs – Costs that cannot be directly traced to units of production (or other activity of the organization). Typically these may include property costs, administration costs and selling costs. Also known as **overheads**.

Intangible asset – An asset that does not have a physical identity, e.g. trademark, patent, goodwill.

Internal rate of return (IRR) – The rate of return at which the cost of a capital investment project and its future **cash flows** balance out.

Investment – Expenditure by an organization in anticipation of obtaining a return at some future time.

Investment appraisal – The use of accounting and mathematical techniques to establish the likely returns from particular investment projects; particularly applied to **cash flows**.

Irrelevant costs – Costs that are irrelevant to a decision because they will be unaffected by that decision. Also known as **unavoidable costs**.

Issued share capital – Shares actually issued and held by shareholders. Normally, in the UK, the face value (par value, nominal value) of the shares of an entity that have been issued are recorded at face value, regardless of what price they realized when sold or what price (for public companies) they are currently attracting.

Labour efficiency variance – The difference between the standard hours for the actual production achieved and the hours actually worked, valued at the standard labour rate.

Labour rate variance – The difference between the standard and the actual direct labour rate per hour for the total hours worked.

Least-square method – A mathematical technique for finding the straight line that best fits a series of points on a graph.

Leverage – *See* **gearing**.

Liabilities – The financial obligations of an organization, both internal (e.g. to shareholders) and external (e.g. to **creditors**, **debenture** holders and, in the case of a bank **loan** or overdraft, to a bank) (*based on CIMA definition*).

Limited company – An organization which in the eyes of the law is a separate entity, apart from its shareholders. The shareholders' liability to third parties in the event of company failure is limited to their capital contributions and any reserves owed to them.

Linear programming – A series of mathematical calculations used to find the optimum combination of a number of factors via the construction of a model. Often used in examining the most profitable use of scarce resources within an organization.

Linearity – The assumption by accountants and managers that revenues and costs are not affected by the level of activity.

Liquid assets – **Assets** that are in the form of cash, or that can rapidly be converted into cash. Generally, **stocks** are not regarded as liquid assets.

Liquidity – The level of cash and **assets** readily convertible to cash, relative to the expected calls to be made on them (i.e. relative to **current liabilities**). This may be expressed as the liquidity ratio (or **quick ratio** or **acid test**)

Loans – *See* **overdrafts** and **loans**.

Long-lived assets – Assets which when purchased are expected to have a useful life of more than one year. Also known as **fixed assets**.

Long-term loan(s) – *See* **overdrafts** and **loans**.

Long-term liability – A liability which does not have to be met within one year.

Machine hour rate – A method of charging **overheads** to **cost centres**. Calculated by dividing the budgeted or estimated overhead costs attributed to a machine or group of similar machines by the appropriate number of machine hours (the number of hours for which the machine or group of machines is expected to be operated, the number of hours that would relate to normal working for the factory or full capacity) (*based on CIMA definition*).

Managed costs – *See* **controllable costs**.

Management accounting – The provision of financial information to the various levels of management within the organization for the purposes of planning, decision making, and monitoring and controlling performance.

Management by exception – Control and management of costs and **revenues** by concentrating on those instances where significant **variances** occur and are highlighted by an operational control system.

Marginal costing – *See* **variable costing**.

Marginal costs – *See* **variable costs**.

Margin of safety – The excess (if any) of budgeted (or capacity) level of activity over the level of activity required to **break even**, sometimes expressed as a percentage of budgeted or capacity level of activity. For example, if break even is 8000 units and budgeted sales are 10 000 units, the budget could be said to embrace a 20% margin of safety.

Master budgets – The overall budgets of an organization, built up from a range of individual budgets and comprising the **cash budget**, the forecast **profit and loss account**, and the **forecast balance sheet**.

Matching concept/convention – *See* **accruals concept/convention**.

Materiality concept/convention – Acceptance that there are some transactions or events that are not significant enough for accountants to disclose, while also accepting that those that are significant enough should be disclosed separately.

Material price variance – *See* **direct material price variance**.

Material quantity variance – *See* **direct material usage variance**.

Minority interest – Shares held in a subsidiary company other than those held by the parent company, plus the appropriate portion of accumulated reserves.

Money measurement concept/convention – The convention that financial accounting information relates only to those activities that can be expressed in money terms

Net book value – The cost of an **asset** less its accumulated depreciation to date. Also known as the **written down cost**.

Net capital employed – *See* **capital employed**.

Net cash flow – The net inflow or outflow of cash (i.e. total cash in *less* total cash out) resulting from proceeding with an investment project.

Net current assets – *See* **working capital**.

Net present value (NPV) – The value obtained by discounting by a chosen percentage all cash outflows and inflows attributable to a capital investment project (*based on CIMA definition*).

Net realizable value – The price at which assets are estimated to be saleable less any further costs that would be incurred in selling them.

Net reported profit – The profit remaining after deducting all expenses from sales. Also known as net profit.

Net working capital – *See* **working capital**.

Net worth – The book value of an organization as reflected by the value of shareholders' funds shown on the balance sheet.

Objectivity convention – The convention of using reliable facts relating to one way of valuing an asset rather than estimates relating to some other way, even if the latter is more realistic.

Operational gearing – *See* **operating leverage**.

Operating leaverage – The relationship between fixed and variable costs. Also known as **operational gearing**.

Operating profit – The profit remaining after deducting all operating expenses (not cost of capital expenses) from sales. Can also be arrived at by adding back the cost of capital interest to net reported profit.

Operating statement – An internal management control document generally produced at frequent regular intervals, which reports actual costs and/or **revenues**, and which usually compares these with budget and shows **variances**.

Opportunity cost – The value of a benefit sacrificed in favour of an alternative course of action (*CIMA definition*).

Overdrafts and loans – An overdraft is money borrowed, nominally for a short period, the amount of which may fluctuate from day to day. Loans are finite amounts of money borrowed for finite periods;

some are short term, i.e. for less than one year, others are long term, i.e. for more than one year.

Overhead absorption rate – The basis on which **indirect costs** are charged to individual products or services. Common methods are **direct labour cost percentage rate, direct labour hour rate** and **machine hour rate**.

Overhead efficiency variance – The difference between the standard **overhead** cost for the production achieved and the standard overhead cost for the actual hours taken (*based on CIMA definition*).

Overhead expenditure variance – The difference between budgeted and actual **overhead** expenditure (*based on CIMA definition*).

Overheads – *See* **indirect costs**.

Overhead volume variance – The difference between the standard **overhead** cost of the actual hours taken and the **flexible budget** allowance for the actual hours taken (*based on CIMA definition*).

Payback period – The number of years that will elapse before the cash outlays on a capital investment project are recovered.

Position statement – Another name for the balance sheet.

Preference shares – These are normally fixed-**dividend** payment shares, whose holders receive dividends in preference to ordinary shareholders but after **debenture** and loan stock holders. Holders may also have a prior claim to the repayment of capital in the event of liquidation.

Prepayments – Expenditure on goods or services for future benefit which is to be charged to future operations, e.g. rentals paid in advance (*CIMA definition*).

Price/earnings ratio – An investors' ratio calculated as:

Current stock – market price of one share

Most recent available earnings per share

Prime costs – The **direct costs** of production, generally comprising direct material costs, **direct labour** costs and other direct production expenses.

Production overheads – The **indirect costs** of production generally comprising any labour and materials not unique to one product or service, and indirect expenses of running the plant and production premises.

Profit – The figure representing the amount by which **revenues** exceed **expenses**.

Profitability index – A statistic used in **investment appraisal** to supplement **internal rate of return** and/or **net present value**, calculated as:

 Present value of cash inflows from project

Present value of cash outflows from project

(i.e. the **net present value** of each monetary unit value, e.g. £1, $1, invested in a project).

Profit and loss account – A summary of an enterprise's transactions over a stated period (usually one year), which shows **revenue(s)** generated, the related costs and thus the **profit** or loss for the period. It may also show the appropriation of **profit before tax** into taxation, **dividends** and **reserves**.

Profit before tax or pre-tax profit – The profit of the organization after all its costs have been set against its **revenues**, but prior to the appropriation of corporation tax, **dividends** and **reserves**. Sometimes referred to as net profit, although this latter term can be ambiguous.

Profit variance – The difference between the standard profit on the budgeted sales volume and the actual profit for a specific period (*based on CIMA definition*).

Profit/volume (P/V) ratio – *See* **contribution to sales ratio**.

Prudence concept/convention – The convention of using the lowest of all reasonable values for an **asset** and of not anticipating **revenue** or **profits**. Also known as the **conservatism concept/convention**.

Quick ratio – A prime measure of an organization's liquidity, defined as:

$$\frac{\text{Liquid assets}}{\text{Current liabilities}}$$

Also known as the **acid test** or the **liquidity rati**o.

Rate of return pricing – A more sophisticated version of **cost-plus pricing,** in which the mark-up on unit cost is calculated with regard to the organization's required rate of **return on capital employed**.

Realization convention – The concept that profit is only accounted for when it is realized and not when it can be recognized.

Relevant costs – Costs that will be incurred only if a course of action being considered is taken, and which are therefore relevant to making specific management decisions. *See also* **avoidable costs**.

Relevant range – The range of activity level with which **fixed costs** and **variable costs** behave in a linear fashion according to their definitions (i.e. fixed costs remain unchanged and variable costs vary in direct proportion to the activity level).

Reserves – The value of **shareholders' funds** in excess of the par value of their shares. Reserves can comprise: the cumulative value of reinvested **profits** (also known as **retentions** or *retained earnings* or *retained profits*); appreciation in value of **fixed assets**; and share premium.

Responsibility accounting – A system of accounting that segregates revenues and costs into areas of personal responsibility in order to assess the performance attained by persons to whom authority has been assigned.

Responsibility centre – A part of the organization for which a nominated manager has direct responsibility for performance.

Retained profits – Profits which have not been distributed as dividends to shareholders but retained within the organization and reinvested in assets.

Return on capital employed (ROCE) – A ratio, usually calculated as:

$$\frac{\text{Profit before tax and interest paid}}{\text{Capital employed}} \times 100$$

Return on net assets (RONA) – *See* **return on capital employed**.

Return on sales – A ratio usually calculated as:

$$\frac{\text{Profit before tax}}{\text{Sales}} \times 100$$

or

$$\frac{\text{Profit before tax and interest paid}}{\text{Sales}} \times 100$$

Revenue – *See* **turnover**.

Revenue centre – A **responsibility centre** where the manager is responsible for generating **revenue**.

Revision variance – The difference between an original and a revised **standard cost**.

Rolling budget – A continuously updated budget in which, as one period passes, another is added (e.g. a one-year budget would have a new month or quarter added as each month or quarter passed). It is beneficial where future costs and/or activities cannot be forecast reliably (*based on CIMA definition*). Also known as the **continuous budget**.

Sales volume-profit variance – The difference between the standard quantity of units sold and the actual units sold, priced at the standard **profit** per unit (*based on CIMA definition*).

Segment margin – The **contribution** made by an individual segment (e.g. product, product group, service, market, etc). of an organization's activities less any direct **fixed costs** attributable to that segment.

Segment reporting – The use of **marginal costing** (techniques to examine the profitability of individual segments, e.g. product, product group, service, market, etc. of an organization's activities).

Selling price variance – The difference between the actual selling price per unit and the standard selling price per unit, multiplied by the actual number of units sold (*based on CIMA definition*).

Semi-variable costs – Costs that include both **fixed cost** and **variable cost** components, i.e. costs that vary as the level of activity varies but not in strict proportion. For example, a telephone bill will be larger in a quarter when more calls have been made, but will not double if the number of calls doubles, owing to the rental element remaining unchanged.

Set-up costs – The costs involved in setting up a venture or activity, e.g. a company or machinery, etc. to produce a batch of goods.

Share capital – *See* **issued share capital**.

Shareholders' funds or shareholders' interest – **Issued share capital**

plus **reserves**, i.e. that part of the capital in the organization that is owned by the shareholders.

Short-term investment – An investment which is intended to last less than one year.

Short-term loan (s) – *See* **overdrafts and loans**.

Solvency – A state in which an organization is able to pay its debts as they fall due.

Source and application of funds statement – *See* **funds flow statement**.

Stability convention – The assumption that money does not change in value when, for example, consolidating the values of two identical **assets** purchased some years apart at different prices.

Standard cost – A carefully predetermined cost that management establishes and uses as a basis for comparison with actual costs.

Step costs – Those **fixed costs** that within certain limits of activity level are unchanged, but which step up or down to a new level when these limits are exceeded.

Stock(s) – That portion of an organization's **assets** held for further production and / or sale.

Stock turnover – A ratio that measures the speed at which raw materials or **stocks** for resale are being consumed or sold.

Straight line depreciation – A method of depreciation which divides the **depreciable base** relating to a fixed asset by the number of years of anticipated useful life, the resulting figure being the annual depreciation charge over the useful life of the asset.

Sunk costs – Those **irrelevant costs** that have already been incurred and thus play no part in a particular decision.

Surplus(es) – The difference between income and expenditure in some public and voluntary sector concerns, equating to the term profit(s) in commercial concerns.

Total assets – The total **net book value** of all the **assets** in the organization.

Total liabilities – The total money owed by the organization to 'outsiders' and to its shareholders.

Turnover – The total sales of the organization for a period, regardless of whether or not customers have yet paid. Also known as the **revenue**.

Unavoidable costs – *See* **irrelevant costs**.

Value added – *See* **added value**.

Variable budget – *See* **flexible budget**.

Variable costing – The approach to costing in which only the **variable costs** are charged to **cost units**. The fixed costs attributable to the relevant period are not apportioned to individual units or activities, but are met out of the total contribution generated.

Variable costs – Costs that vary in proportion to the level of activity (sales level or production level). For example, raw material costs would generally double if production or sales doubled and thus would be regarded as variable. Also known as **marginal costs**.

Variance – The difference between planned, budgeted or **standard cost** and actual cost (and similarly in respect of **revenues**) (*CIMA definition*). Variances are generally referred to as favourable or adverse, depending upon whether they increase or decrease **profit**.

Variance analysis – The analysis of variances arising in a standard costing system into their constituent parts (*based on CIMA definition*).

Working capital – The capital available for conducting the day-to-day operations of the organization. Usually defined as **current assets** less **current liabilities** (*based on CIMA definition*). Also known as **net working capital** and **net current assets**.

Working capital cycle – The cycle associated with the flow of cash through the purchase of stocks, receipt of money owed and payments of money owing.

Written-down cost – *See* **net book value**.

Index